BIRDS OF THE OCEAN

Birds of the Ocean

New and Revised Edition

CONTAINING DESCRIPTIONS OF ALL THE SEA-BIRDS
OF THE WORLD, WITH NOTES ON THEIR HABITS
AND GUIDES TO THEIR IDENTIFICATION

By W. B. ALEXANDER, M.A. (Camb).

Fellow, Royal Australasian Ornithologists' Union
Corresponding Fellow, American Ornithologists' Union

WITH 140 ILLUSTRATIONS

G. P. PUTNAM'S SONS   NEW YORK

PUBLISHER'S NOTE

This standard work—long out of print—has been reissued to meet a steady demand for the only book of its kind available at this time.

MANUFACTURED IN THE UNITED STATES OF AMERICA

Van Rees Press • New York

Preface to the Second Edition

~~~~~~

DURING the years from 1920 to 1926 the writer made a number of long sea voyages and, with a view to the identification of the sea-birds he might meet with, filled a notebook with descriptions of birds and outlines of their distribution. These were taken from various books, especially the appropriate catalogues of the birds in the British Museum. During the voyages he made sketches of the appearance in the air or in the water of the more striking birds encountered.

It seemed likely that a small handbook on these lines would prove useful to other voyagers and during the winter 1926-1927 the text of this book was prepared by a more complete search of the literature and by the examination of specimens in various museums, especially the American Museum of Natural History, where the writer received valuable help from Dr. R. C. Murphy. Ornithologists in various countries, who were known to have taken photographs of sea-birds, were asked to provide prints for reproduction and without exception agreed to do so. A complete list of the names of these and other helpers appears in the preface to the first edition, published in 1928.

During the twenty-five years which have since elapsed the author has received numerous letters from seamen and travellers in many parts of the world, mostly acknowledging the help that the book has given them in identifying sea-birds and frequently suggesting additional points which would aid in the identification of particular species. He is most grateful for all such friendly criticisms. The past quarter century has also seen a very great increase in our knowledge of the distribution and habits of sea-birds and in the literature on the subject. Dr. Murphy's monumental work *The Oceanic Birds of South America* (1936) is by far the most complete book on the sea-birds of any large region; Mr. James Fisher's book *The Fulmar* (1952) is one of the most complete monographs devoted to a single species of bird; while the series of papers by Dr. L. E. Richdale on the life-histories and behaviour of Albatrosses, Petrels and Penguins breeding in New Zealand embody the results of studies as prolonged and detailed as any devoted to land birds. During the last decade meteorological stations have been established and maintained throughout the year on many of the subantarctic islands and on the Antarctic continent and members of their staffs have added greatly to our knowledge of the sea-birds breeding in regions formerly uninhabited and only occasionally visited.

In the present edition of this book an attempt has been made to correct errors, and to add information bringing it up to date, without any essential alteration of its style and arrangement. The writer hopes that it will still prove useful to students of birds on board ships and in other localities where they are unable to consult libraries.

W. B. ALEXANDER

Oxford

Contents

CONTENTS

Illustrations

(All following page 82)

〰〰〰〰〰〰〰〰〰〰〰〰〰〰〰〰〰〰

PLATE

1. Brown Pelicans Feeding. Panama Bay
2. Fig. 1. Wandering Albatrosses. South Georgia
   Fig. 2. Wandering Albatross on Nest. South Georgia
3. Fig. 1. Wandering Albatross. South Pacific Ocean
   Fig. 2. Shy Albatrosses. Stewart I., New Zealand
4. Albatrosses
5. Albatrosses
6. Black-browed Albatross. South Atlantic Ocean
7. Black-browed Albatross and Young in Nest. Falkland Is.
8. Black-footed Albatrosses Nesting. Laysan, Hawaiian Is.
9. Black-footed Albatross and Young. Laysan, Hawaiian Is.
10. Fig. 1. Light-mantled Sooty Albatross. South Atlantic Ocean
    Fig. 2. Light-mantled Sooty Albatross and Young. South Georgia
11. Petrels
12. Giant Petrels Nesting. Falkland Is.
13. Fig. 1. Pintado Petrel or Cape Pigeon. South Atlantic Ocean
    Fig. 2. Giant Petrel (White Phase) on Nest. South Georgia

ix

ILLUSTRATIONS

ILLUSTRATIONS

ILLUSTRATIONS

CHAPTER I

Albatrosses

(Order *Procellariiformes*: Family *Diomedeidae*)

THE LARGE SEA-BIRDS which constitute this family have stout bodies, rather large heads and somewhat elongated necks. Their tails are short in the majority of the species, rather long and wedge-shaped in the Sooty Albatrosses. Their wings are exceptionally long and narrow. Their legs are short and placed rather far back and in flight the webbed feet are carried open on each side of the tail.

Apart from various characters of the skeleton and internal parts the most distinctive feature of an Albatross is its bill. This is stout, with the upper mandible hooked, and is covered with a number of distinct horny plates, instead of having a single sheath on each mandible as in most birds. The nostril-openings form short tubes on each side of the middle plate of the upper mandible.

The plumage of an Albatross may be brown, black and white, or almost entirely white; their bills may be yellow, grey or black, or black with yellow or blue lines; and their legs and feet may be yellowish or pinkish white, grey or black.

A dead specimen found on the beach or one captured on board ship may always be recognised by the features of its bill mentioned above. At sea their large size, very long slender wings and characteristic gliding flight are distinctive. The only bird of another family which may be mistaken for an Albatross is the Giant Petrel described on p. 22.

Ornithologists commonly refer to all members of the family *Diomedeidae* as Albatrosses, but *the* Albatross *par excellence* is the Wandering Albatross (*D. exulans*). This species when adult is mainly white with black tips to the wings, but in younger specimens the greater part of the wing is black, and immature birds are dirty brown with a white patch on the face. Sailors not infrequently call these brown birds Mollymawks, Molly-hawks or Mollymokes, names which they also sometimes apply to other large brownish sea-birds such as the Giant Petrel, Skuas or immature Gulls. What are more usually called Mollymawks are the smaller species of Albatross, distinguished from the Wandering Albatross by having the back black as well as the wings. Gony or Goony is another name frequently applied to birds of this family by seamen.

The name Albatross is a corruption of the Spanish (originally Moorish) word "Alcatraz" (= a Pelican) and has nothing to do with the whiteness of the bird as is sometimes supposed. Mollymawk is a corruption of the Dutch "Mallemuck," derived from "mal" (foolish) and "mok" (gull); whilst Gony is an English dialect word for a simpleton or booby.

A great part of the life of an Albatross is spent in the air, gliding over the waves with its narrow pointed wings held almost motionless. The birds usually rise in a slanting direction against the wind, then make a turn in a large circle during which one wing points downwards, the other upwards, and finally make a rapid descent down wind. Only when the wind is fairly fresh can the Albatrosses continue their sailing flight for any length of time; when the wind drops they begin to flap their wings much more frequently, and are often left behind by a steamer. Like gulls some species have learnt to take advantage of the currents of air produced by a steamer in motion and will hang in the air over the stern intently scanning the scene below with their large eyes. Even in such favourable circumstances their great size is not very obvious and passengers are generally astonished to learn that the Wandering Albatross has a span of wing of from ten to twelve feet.

Albatrosses feed chiefly on cuttlefish, also eating fish and other marine animals and galley refuse from ships. It is probable that much of their food is obtained during the night when cuttlefish and other creatures come near the surface. To obtain their food the birds settle down gently on the water, usually with the wings raised, sometimes submerging the body to obtain food a little below the surface. When settled on the water with the wings closed they float very high. In order to start off again in flight they commence by running along the surface with outstretched wings in order to obtain sufficient impetus to carry them up into the air, usually flapping the wings a good deal until clear of the waves. They rarely approach land, except their breeding grounds, sufficiently close to be seen by observers on shore.

The distribution of the Albatross family is somewhat remarkable. Of the thirteen known species nine are found in the southern oceans, chiefly between latitudes 30° S. and 60° S., ranging south to the Antarctic ice and sometimes north to the tropic of Capricorn. On the west coast of South America several of the southern species follow the cool waters of the Humboldt current well into the tropics. One species is found only in the tropics, ranging from the Galápagos Islands to the coasts of Ecuador and northern Peru. The other three species are confined to the North Pacific Ocean. Very occasionally individuals of southern species have been met with on the coasts of Europe and North America, but whether they got there unaided may be doubted. From sailing ships these birds are not infrequently captured, and it is

3

noteworthy that the records of southern Albatrosses in the northern hemisphere mostly date from the period when sailing ships had not yet been largely displaced by steamers on the ocean routes. Very possibly some at least of these individuals had been brought across the tropics by ships and liberated north of the line.

From a becalmed ship, or one travelling slowly, Albatrosses can often be captured without injury by hook and line, salt pork being used as bait. The hook lodges in the bill without penetrating it, but, as the bird when hooked pulls backwards, by keeping the line taut it may often be landed on deck. The bulwarks prevent captured specimens from flying as they cannot rise upwards from a level surface but need a slope or cliff from which to launch themselves into the air. On deck Albatrosses show symptoms of sea-sickness and usually soon vomit the contents of their stomachs. Old-fashioned sailors sometimes captured them in order to make feather-rugs or other articles of their skins, and this is presumably why they were sometimes called "Cape Sheep." The webs of the feet were made into purses or tobacco-pouches and some of the long hollow bones into pipe-stems.

The number destroyed in this way was only small, but in more recent times the breeding grounds of some species in the North Pacific have been raided by plume-hunters and thousands of nesting birds slaughtered for their feathers, whilst their young were left to starve. Now that most civilised nations have prohibited the import of these feathers it may be hoped that such barbarities will not occur again, but meanwhile the number of Albatrosses in the North Pacific has been greatly diminished and the Short-tailed Albatross appears to have been exterminated.

It is a common belief that Albatrosses (and other sea-birds) follow ships day after day for thousands of miles. Writing of the Cape Pigeon or Pintado Petrel Mr. J. T. Nichols states: "I have seen nothing to lead me to suppose that the same individuals of this or other species stayed with the ship for many days in succession. My observations rather foster the belief that the personnel is constantly changing. The number of birds varies from day to day, and on several occasions when birds with some peculiar marks, which would not be readily duplicated, have been noted, they have not been seen again. Furthermore I have so frequently had intelligent persons (obviously in error, or quite unjustified in their conclusions) point out sea-birds as having followed a ship for long periods, that I have become very sceptical of such assertions." The writer's observations have led him to the same conclusion. In regions where Albatrosses are numerous it has almost invariably been noted that the numbers following the ship were smallest early in the morning and steadily increased during the day, till by evening there might be thirty or forty astern. Next morning there would usually again only be a few, perhaps half a dozen, and by evening once more they would be plentiful. In the case of the Wandering Albatross there is so much variation in plumage due to age that it is possible to note the numbers in various plumages, especially in lower latitudes where the numbers are smaller. One day those seen may be two immature brown birds, three young birds with much black on the wings and one adult with the wings almost white; next day there will perhaps be one immature, five young and no adult; on the third day three immature, two young and two adults; and so on.

On the other hand Professor Hutton was "informed by Lieutenant Weld, R.N., that a Cape Pigeon, with a piece of red ribbon round its neck, once followed the ship he was in for 1,500 miles." An Albatross which was found dying on the beach at Fremantle, Western Australia, in the year 1887 had round its neck a tin on which some French sailors had scratched a message stating that they had been shipwrecked on the Crozet Islands over 3,500 miles away. Enquiries elicited the fact that the bird had followed a sailing ship to Fremantle from the neighborhood of those islands. It is possible in both these instances that the ring round its neck prevented the bird from swallowing its ordinary food and induced it to follow the ship for the sake of scraps, and the fact that the Albatross was choked in attempting to swallow a fish supports this suggestion. The question is one of considerable interest and might be settled by placing coloured rings on the legs of captured birds so as to enable them to be recognized without interfering with their powers of feeding.

An adult Albatross marked with a French ring at Kerguelen in 1914 was captured three years later near Cape Horn, some 6,000 miles away, proving conclusively that these birds do range over great distances in the southern oceans. But in this case there was no evidence that it had followed a ship. Black-footed Albatrosses marked as young birds at Midway have been recovered on the coasts of Oregon and Alaska and at sea north-east of Japan. The latter had travelled at least 2,200 miles within 6 months of being marked. Young Giant Petrels ringed in the nest in the South Orkneys have been recovered in Western Australia within 6 weeks, and in New Zealand within 5 months, distances of over 10,000 miles.

Albatrosses are generally silent birds but some species are said to make grunting noises when captured on a line and probably all of them have calls which are uttered when they are on their breeding grounds. Some species are also noisy when assembled and disputing for food. They breed in colonies on remote oceanic islands, some species resorting to low coral islands and others to steep, rocky and almost inaccessible islets. Some species perform very curious antics when courting, bowing to one another, rubbing their bills together or standing with the bill raised vertically while they utter their strange cries. These performances are by no means confined to the nuptial period. Albatrosses walk with a waddling gait.

The nest is sometimes a depression in the ground, but more often a hollow on the top of a mound of grass, moss and trampled earth or of feathers and excrement. Only a single large egg is laid. It is white with a chalky surface, somewhat pear-shaped and usually marked with some reddish spots or blotches at the larger end. The breeding season of all the species, including those which nest in the North Pacific, is in the later months of the year, chiefly from September to December. The young are fed by their parents, on food regurgitated from the stomach, for many weeks, and become extremely fat. They remain in the nest for a further period while their down is being replaced by feathers, living at the expense of the accumulated fat. It is known that in some cases the adults only breed in alternate years.

In some species the first plumage is decidedly different from that of the adult, which may not be attained for several years.

Except in the Wandering Albatross the sexes are alike. Further information as to the breeding habits and plumage changes of most species is very desirable.

The determination of the species of Albatrosses seen at sea is usually possible if a good view is obtained, since the colour pattern of most of them is distinctive, though the most essential characters are found in the form of the bill. In colouration the species fall into four groups, according to their adult plumage:—

I. With the whole body, including the back, white. (Species 1–3.)
II. With the body mostly white, but the middle of the back dark like the upper surface of the wings. (Species 4–9.)
III. With head and neck white, but rest of plumage mainly dark. (Species 10.)
IV. With plumage mainly brown. (Species 11–13.)

7

I. ALBATROSSES WITH THE WHOLE BODY, INCLUDING THE BACK, WHITE

1. **Royal Albatross** (*Diomedea epomophora* = *D. regia* = *D. sanfordi*)

Adult.—Entirely white, except the primaries, which are black, and some of the scapulars and wing-coverts, which are mottled with grey; bill whitish; feet bluish-white; length 48 ins.; wing 25.5; tail 8.2; bill 6.8; tarsus 4.8; span of wings 9 to 10 feet. *Young.*—Similar.

Range.—Seas of South America, north to central Chile and Uruguay, New Zealand and southeastern Australia. Breeds at the Chatham Is., Auckland Is., Campbell I. and Taiaroa Head, south New Zealand, and probably in Tierra del Fuego. *Egg-dates:* Nov.–March.

Notes.—Resembles old male specimens of the Wandering Albatross, from which it may be distinguished by the size and structure of its more slender bill.

2. **Wandering Albatross** (*Diomedea exulans*). (*Plates 2, 3 and 4*)

Adult Male.—Mainly white; primaries black; tail and upper wing-coverts mottled with black and white, whitest on the portion nearest the body, the amount of white increasing with age; some feathers on back and sides usually freckled with narrow zigzag dark cross-bars; a pink or orange patch frequently present on the sides of the head; bill yellow or pinkish-white; feet pale flesh-colour; length 44–53 ins.; wing 27; tail 9.5; bill 7–8; tarsus 4.5–4.8; span of wings from 10 feet to 11 feet 6 ins., said occasionally to reach 14 feet. *Adult Female.*—Resembles male but is smaller and has a dark cap on the crown. *Young.*—Mainly brown; wings almost black above, white below except at the tips; face and throat white; abdomen often mottled whitish; bill fleshy white; feet brownish.

Range.—Southern oceans, chiefly between 60° S. and 30° S., occasionally north to the tropic of Capricorn. Breeds at Tristan da Cunha and Gough I. (*D. e. dabbenena*), South Georgia, Marion I., Prince Edward I., the Crozet Is., Kerguelen, the Auckland Is. and Antipodes I. (*D. e. exulans*). *Egg-dates:* Dec.–April.

Notes.—The largest ocean bird cannot easily be mistaken, though old males can only be distinguished from the Royal Albatross by the size and shape of the stouter bill. Younger birds and females always show some vermiculated feathers on the head, back or wings. Young birds in brown plumage are easily distinguished from Sooty Albatrosses by the white under surface of their wings.

3. **Short-tailed Albatross** (*Diomedea albatrus = D. brachyura*)

Adult.—Mostly white, washed with buff on the head and neck; primaries and tip of tail dark brown; bill pinkish flesh-colour; feet bluish white; length 37 ins.; wing 22; tail 6.3; bill 6.2; tarsus 3.9. *Young.*—Chocolate brown; chin somewhat paler; bill pinkish; feet flesh-colour.

Range.—North Pacific from the China Sea to the west coast of America and from the Sea of Okhotsk and Bering Straits south into the tropics. Now almost extinct; formerly bred in the Izu, Liu Kiu and Bonin Is. *Egg-dates:* Aug.–Dec.

Notes.—The adult is the only white Albatross in the North Pacific. The young resembles the Black-footed Albatross but is larger and darker and has pale bill and feet. It is a shy bird and rarely follows ships.

II. ALBATROSSES WITH THE BODY MOSTLY WHITE, BUT THE MIDDLE OF THE BACK DARK LIKE THE UPPER SURFACE OF THE WINGS

4. **Shy Albatross** (*Diomedea cauta = Thalassogeron layardi*). (Plates 3 and 5)

Adult.—Whole under-surface including the under wing-coverts and axillaries white; head, neck and upper back white, more or less suffused with grey especially on the cheeks and nape; line over the eye greyish-black; back, wings and tail greyish-brown; bill yellow or grey with a yellowish streak down the centre of the upper mandible, usually with a narrow band of black at the base of the upper mandible and a belt of orange at the base of the lower mandible; feet bluish flesh-colour; length 35–39 ins.; wing 22–22.5; tail 8.5–9; bill 5–6; tarsus 3.3–3.7. *Young.*– Similar to adult but the bill dark grey.

Range.–Southern Oceans in temperate latitudes. Breeds at Albatross I., Bass Strait (*D. c. cauta*), Pyramid Rock, Chatham Is. (*D. c. eremita*), Snares I. and the Bounty Is. (*D. c. salvini*). *Egg-dates:* Aug.–Oct.

Notes.–It resembles Buller's Albatross, and differs from the other species with dark backs, in having the under-surface of the wings white except at the tips. From Buller's Albatross it differs chiefly in the form of the culminicorn (superior plate of the bill), which is not expanded at the base, and its larger size.

5. Buller's Albatross (*Diomedea bulleri = D. platei*)

Adult.–Head and neck pale grey; a dark patch in front of the eye; back, wings and anterior edge of their lower surface sooty brown; rump, upper tail-coverts and under-parts, including under wing-coverts, white; bill grey, with a yellow stripe along the middle of the upper mandible broadening at the base; feet bluish-white; length 34 ins.; wing 20.8; tail 7.7; bill 5.1; tarsus 3.3. *Young.*–Head, neck and back brownish-grey; bill horn grey.

Range.–South Pacific from New Zealand to Peru and Chile. Breeds at Snares I. and the Chatham Is. *Egg-dates:* Jan.–Feb.

Notes.–This species is distinguished from the preceding by its smaller size and the form of the culminicorn (upper plate of bill), which widens at the base and is not separated from the latericorns (side plates) by skin. It is the rarest and least known member of the Albatross family.

6. **Black-browed Albatross** (*Diomedea melanophris*). (*Plates 5, 6 and 7*)

Adult.—Head, neck, rump, upper tail-coverts and under-parts, including under wing-coverts, except those at the edge of the wing, white; through the eye a slaty streak; back and tail slaty-black; wings above dark brownish black; bill yellow, rosy pink at the tip, with a narrow black line round the base; feet yellowish or pinkish white, the webs and joints washed with pale blue; length 32–34 ins.; wing 19.3–21.2; tail 7.3–8.2; bill 4.1–5; tarsus 2.9–3.7. *Young.*—Resembles the adult but the crown and back of the neck are suffused with slaty, the under surface of the wings is mainly dark, and the bill is greyish-black. Later the head becomes white and the bill yellowish-brown.

Range.—Southern Oceans between 60° S. and the tropic of Capricorn. Breeds on islets off Cape Horn, Staten I., South Georgia, the Falkland Is., Kerguelen, the Auckland Is., Macquarie I., Campbell I., Antipodes I., and Ildefonso I., Chile. *Egg-dates:* Sept.–Jan.

Notes.—The yellow bill distinguishes adults of this species from the Yellow-nosed, Grey-headed and Buller's Albatrosses, and the white head from the Shy Albatross. The immature bird with its dark bill and dark grey crown and neck is unlike any of the grey-faced species.

7. **Yellow-nosed Albatross** (*Diomedea chlororhynchos =*
    Thalassogeron eximius = T. carteri). (*Plate 5*)

Adult.—Head and neck white, sides and back of head sometimes suffused with grey, usually with a dark grey patch above and behind the eye; rump, upper tail-coverts and underparts white; under wing-coverts white, except at the edge of the wing; back slaty-brown; wings above brownish-black; tail ashy-brown; bill black with a yellow line down the centre of the upper mandible which is orange at the tip, usually a little yellow at the base and tip of the lower mandible; feet pinkish or bluish flesh-colour; length 29.5–34 ins.; wing 18.5–19; tail 7.7; bill 4.5–5.2; tarsus 3. *Young.*—Similar but bill uniformly black.

11

Range.—Southern Atlantic and Indian Oceans and Australian seas, chiefly between 50° S. and 30° S. lat., especially in temperate regions, frequently wanders further north. Breeds at Tristan da Cunha, Gough I. and St. Paul I. *Egg-dates:* Sept.–Oct.

Notes.—This species closely resembles the Grey-headed Albatross from which it can only be distinguished with certainty by the shape of the culminicorn (superior plate of the bill), which is pointed posteriorly. The upper-parts are sooty rather than grey, the head usually white and the bill very black (with yellow markings). Its range is more northern than that of its congeners, so that it is the dark-backed Albatross with dark bill most frequently met with on the routes of passenger steamers in the southern hemisphere.

8. Grey-headed Albatross (*Diomedea chrysostoma = D. culminata*)

Adult.—Head and neck slaty-grey (becoming white in old birds); back and tail dark grey; wings above blackish-brown; a dark patch above and in front of the eye; rump, upper tail-coverts, breast, abdomen, under tail-coverts and under wing-coverts, except at the edge of the wing, white; bill blackish, with a yellow stripe down the middle of the upper mandible which is red at the tip, and a yellow band at the base of the lower mandible; feet pinkish-grey; length 28–32 ins.; wing 18.5–20; tail 7; bill 4.2–5.2; tarsus 3. *Young.*—Resembles the adult but is browner; the head is leaden grey; the under surface of the wings is mainly dark, and the bill uniform brownish-black.

Range.—Southern Oceans, from the Antarctic ice north to about 40° S., occasionally ranging further north. Breeds at Diego Ramirez Is., C. Horn, South Georgia, the Falkland Is., Kerguelen, Prince Edward I., The Crozet Is. and Campbell I. *Egg-dates:* Oct.–Feb.

Notes.—This species can only be distinguished with certainty from the Yellow-nosed Albatross by the form of the culminicorn (superior plate of the bill), which is rounded posteriorly. Its head is usually grey, and the bill dark-grey with a yellow line along the lower mandible. Its range is more southerly than that of the Yellow-nosed Albatross so that it is rarely seen on the routes of passenger steamers.

9. Laysan Albatross (*Diomedea immutabilis*)

Adult.—Head, neck, rump, upper tail-coverts and underparts white; a spot before the eye sooty black; back, wings and end of tail dark sooty brown; under wing-coverts blackish-brown and white, irregularly mingled; bill grey, darker at base and tip, base of mandible pale yellow; feet fleshy pink; length 32 ins.; wing 18.5; tail 5.8; bill 4.6; tarsus 3.3. *Young.*—Similar.

Range.—Central North Pacific, east to coast of Lower California, north to about 40° N., west to the Bonin Is. Breeds on northwestern islands of Hawaiian group. *Egg-dates:* Nov.–Dec.

Notes.—The only dark-backed Albatross in the North Pacific with white head and underparts.

III. ALBATROSSES WITH HEAD AND NECK WHITE, REST OF PLUMAGE MAINLY DARK

10. Waved Albatross (*Diomedea irrorata*). (*Plate 5*)

Adult.—Head and neck white, nape tinged with buff; back, wings and tail greyish, sooty brown; upper back and rump variegated with dusky and white; abdomen dusky, minutely freckled with white; bill yellow; feet bluish white; length 35 ins.; wing 21; tail 5.5; bill 6.2; tarsus 3.8. *Young.*—Said to be uniformly brown.

Range.—Seas of Peru and Ecuador and the Galápagos Is. Breeds at Hood I. in the Galápagos group. *Egg-dates:* April–July.

Notes.—The only Albatross confined to the tropics.

13

IV. ALBATROSSES WITH PLUMAGE
MAINLY BROWN

11. Black-footed Albatross (*Diomedea nigripes*). (*Plates 8 and 9*)

Adult.—Sooty brown, paler on the forehead, cheeks, neck and abdomen; area round the bill and behind and below the eyes white; bill dark reddish-brown; feet black; length 28 ins.; wing 18; tail 5.5; bill 4.6; tarsus 4.4. *Young.*—Similar to adult but crown and sides of head whiter; rump and upper tail-coverts white, or white mottled with brown.

Range.—North Pacific from the Kurile Is., Japan and the Formosa Channel to Alaska and Lower California, and from the Aleutian Is. and southern Bering Sea almost or quite to the equator. Breeds at the Hawaiian Is., Marshall Is., Volcano Is., and Bonin Is. *Egg-dates:* June, Sept.–Dec.

Notes.—The common Albatross of the North Pacific distinguished from the young of the Short-tailed Albatross by its black feet and dark bill.

12. Sooty Albatross (*Phoebetria fusca = P. fuliginosa*). (*Plate 4*)

Adult.—Sooty brown, paler below and in the middle of the back, darker on the wings and face; quill-feathers with white shafts; a ring of short, white feathers, broken in front, round the eye; tail long and wedge-shaped; bill black, the lower mandible with a yellow or orange groove along the side; feet pale flesh-colour or hazel; length 33 ins.; wing 20.5; tail 9.5; bill 5; tarsus 2.8 *Young.*—Resembles the adult but the nape is white and the neck whitish all round.

Range.—Southern Atlantic and Indian Oceans between 50° and 30° S. lat. Breeds at Tristan da Cunha, Gough I., St. Paul and Amsterdam Is. *Egg-dates:* Sept.

Notes.—Differs from the young Wandering Albatross in its smaller size, wedge-shaped tail and dark under surface

14

of the wings. From the Light-mantled Sooty Albatross it is distinguished by its darker back and the yellow groove on the lower mandible.

13. **Light-mantled Sooty Albatross** (*Phoebetria palpebrata* = *P. cornicoides*). (*Plates 4 and 10*)

Adult.—Head dark greyish-brown, nearly black on lores; back and under surface ashy-grey; wings dark brownish-grey; primaries and long, wedge-shaped tail greyish black; shafts of quills whitish; a white ring round the eye broken in front; bill black, with a groove along the side of the lower mandible pale blue or pearl-grey; feet pale flesh-colour; length 28 ins.; wing 19–22.7; tail 8.8–11.5; bill 3.7–4.6; tarsus 3–3.4. *Young.*—Similar but more uniformly brown and somewhat mottled.

Range.—Southern Oceans from the Antarctic ice north to about 33° S. lat. Breeds at South Georgia, Kerguelen, Crozet Is., Heard I., Antipodes, Auckland, Campbell and Macquarie Is. *Egg-dates:* Oct.–Jan.

Notes.—In form this species resembles the Sooty Albatross but the grey back and underparts give it quite a different appearance and the groove on the lower mandible is purplish. It has a more southern range than the Sooty Albatross and is less often seen on the routes of passenger steamers.

CHAPTER II

Petrels, Shearwaters and Fulmars

(Order *Procellariiformes:* Family *Procellariidae*
= *Puffinidae*)

THE SEA-BIRDS which constitute this large family exhibit great diversity of size and colouring, though comparatively uniform in their habits. Apart from various internal and skeletal characters almost the only distinguishing feature of the family is the bill, which is hooked at the tip, somewhat compressed at the base and with the two nostrils opening together at the end of a double tube on the upper mandible.

In size the members of this family vary from the Giant Petrel, which is as large as a small Albatross or a Goose, to the little Whale-birds or Prions about the size of Starlings. The Storm-Petrels, which are even smaller, are dealt with in the next chapter. In colouring petrels are black, brown, grey or white or some combination of these colours and even their bills and feet are usually not very brightly coloured, though sometimes bluish or pink. In spite of this diversity the members of the family may generally be recognised at a distance by their rapid gliding flight, which resembles that of Albatrosses, though less perfect and more often interrupted by flapping of the wings. They usually skim low over the waves, a habit which has earned for some of them the name of Shearwater, whilst the term Petrel, applied by ornithologists to members of this family, may be a diminutive of Peter, alluding to St. Peter's attempt to walk on the water. Seamen have no general name for these birds, and usually apply the term petrel only to the Storm-Petrels. Individual species well enough known to be discriminated by sailors are the Giant Petrel known as the Nelly, the Cape Hen, Cape Pigeon, Cape Dove and Fulmar. The Prions are commonly known as Icebirds or Whale-birds and Shearwaters sometimes as Mutton-birds or Hags.

Except when breeding Petrels spend all their time at sea, some of them confining themselves to a larger or smaller area in the neighbourhood of their breeding grounds, others migrating right across the equator into the other hemisphere. The migratory flights, though not yet properly investigated, appear to be as definite as those of land-birds, and there is little ground for believing that any of the species wander over the oceans indiscriminately, though by what means the birds recognize particular areas of the ocean and find their way to them from their breeding-grounds or how they find their way back to their island homes is a complete mystery.

Their food consists of small fish and squids, crustacea and other floating or surface-living animals supplemented by scraps from ships. The Giant Petrel is a scavenger and also kills and devours small sea-birds. The majority of the species glean their living from the surface waters as they skim over the waves, but where food is concentrated they often settle and swim about to feed and many of the species will dive for food a short distance below the surface. At sea they are usually silent but at night during the breeding season utter loud, mournful wails and calls.

The species are more or less sociable when at sea and often congregate in vast numbers to breed. For this purpose they resort to islands, or in a few instances to fairly inaccessible cliffs on the mainland. Most petrels nest in holes, either burrows excavated

17

by themselves in soft ground, or beneath roots or trailing vegetation or rocks. The same species may make burrows in one locality and resort to crevices among fallen rocks elsewhere. The Fulmar, Silvergrey Petrel, Antarctic Petrel, Pintado Petrel and Snow Petrels nest on ledges of cliffs, and the Giant Petrel and Kermadec Petrel on the ground in the open. Most of these species are able to stand normally, but the legs of the burrowing species are not strong enough to support them and when on land they shuffle along on their breasts with the help of their wings. The nest is merely a hollow at the end of the burrow or a natural cavity lined with a few bits of grass or feathers. Only a single egg is laid, which is white in all the species. Both sexes take part in incubation, one remaining silently in the burrow all day whilst its mate ranges the ocean for food. Just at dusk the foraging birds begin to return and the sight of the return of the swarms of birds from the sea to the breeding-grounds is a remarkable one. At the same time cries, shrieks and wails break out from the ground in all directions as the brooding birds welcome their mates. Turmoil continues throughout the night as birds come and go and fly round overhead, but at daybreak the foragers once more depart to sea and quiet reigns again. The young remain in the nest for a number of weeks. They are densely covered with down and become very fat, and in this stage some species are collected for food, *e.g.*, Fulmars at St. Kilda I. (formerly) and Shearwaters (Mutton-birds) in the islands of Bass Strait. The old birds feed their young or their sitting mates by disgorging an oily fluid consisting of half-digested marine organisms. The fully-fed young birds are left in the nest by the parents and live for some time on their accumulated fat, while feathers are growing beneath the down. When fully fledged they emerge from their burrows and fly off to sea.

Petrels all have a characteristic musky scent which clings to their feathers for years in collections of skins.

Naturally it is very strong on their breeding grounds and their holes can be recognized by this scent even during the season when the birds are absent. The name Fulmar, meaning "foul mew" or gull, was given to the large Petrel of St. Kilda, owing to this scent.

In all Petrels, except the Giant Petrel, the plumage of immature birds substantially resembles that of adults, and in no species can the sex of an individual be told from its plumage. In many forms with a wide range, breeding on widely separated oceanic islands, birds from each breeding colony differ from those of all other colonies. When the differences are comparatively slight it is usual to regard them as races of a single species, but it is by no means easy to decide where to draw the line in this process and it is not surprising that authorities differ, especially as the numbers of some forms available for study in museums are small.

In addition to this geographical variation which affects chiefly the size and form of the bill, the dimensions, and the shade of the plumage, there are certain species which present striking differences in colour, independent of age or sex. The Kermadec Petrel, Trinidad Petrel and Herald Petrel may have the under surface entirely white or entirely dark and are sometimes intermediate, partly white and partly dark. In the two former species birds of all types appear to be met with in each breeding colony, but this is not the case with the Herald Petrel. The dark-breasted birds of this species are almost confined to Henderson I., where during the Whitney South Sea Expedition Mr. R. H. Beck found that over 99% of the breeding birds have this plumage. Similar birds were found in the breeding colonies at Ducie I. and at Uapu in the Marquesas, where however they formed less than 1% of the population. On adjacent islands and elsewhere in the South Pacific no dark-breasted birds were found.

The Giant Petrel is sometimes dark grey, some-

19

times white with dark spots, but white birds are hardly ever seen in south temperate latitudes. Their numbers increase as one proceeds toward the south till around the Antarctic continent they are the dominant form.

The common Fulmar of northern oceans has two phases, one silver grey above with white underparts, the other entirely dusky brownish-grey. The dusky form is practically unknown in the eastern Atlantic and in the eastern Bering Sea except about the Aleutian Is., but on the western sides of both Atlantic and Pacific oceans dusky birds are found mingling with the pale ones, and in some colonies they vastly predominate. They have also been found to predominate in the eastern Pacific in summer though no breeding colonies are known in that area.

The Black-capped Petrel of the West Indies formerly bred in Haiti, Guadeloupe and Dominica where it was known as the "diablotin." All the known specimens from these islands have white breasts. In Jamaica a dusky bird was formerly found agreeing precisely in form and dimensions with the Black-capped Petrel and like it having the base of the tail white. As these birds are almost or entirely extinct it can perhaps never be decided whether they were really distinct species or whether they were two phases of one species, whose proportions were different on different islands, as in the case of the Herald Petrel. It is noteworthy, however, that the most detailed early account of the hunting of the "diablotin" refers to it as a black bird.

Colour variations, such as those referred to above, increase the difficulty of identifying birds met with at sea. A few kinds of petrels are so distinctively marked that they can always be recognised. A considerable proportion can be identified if a good view is obtained, and the identity of others can be surmised if they are seen in numbers off islands where they are known to breed. But in a number of instances where two or more similar species frequent the same region their determination at sea is impossible.

In the following pages Petrels are grouped partly according to their size and partly according to their colouring. Apart from the Giant Petrel which is very much larger than any other member of the family, with a wing 20 inches long, most of the species are either large, with the wing from 11 to 14.5 inches long, or small, with the wing from 6.5 to 9.5 inches long. There are a few medium-sized species, with the wing from 9.5 to 11 inches long. The best known and most easily recognised of these is the Cape Pigeon or Pintado Petrel with its chequered upperparts. Any Petrel decidedly larger than a Cape Pigeon is here called "large," any species decidedly smaller is called "small."

The groups of Petrels here adopted are as follows:—

   I. Very large, with plumage either dark, or white with dark spots (Species 1).

  II. Large or medium-sized, with dark plumage (Species 2–14).

 III. Small, with dark plumage (Species 15–17).

 IV. Small or medium-sized, entirely dark above with the under surface of the body white (Species 18–30).

  V. Large, mainly or entirely dark above, with the under surface of the body white (Species 31–45).

 VI. Medium-sized, with dark head, chequered upperparts and white underparts (Species 46).

VII. Large, with upperparts, throat and foreneck dark and abdomen white (Species 47–48).

VIII. Medium-sized, with upperparts and abdomen dark, and throat and breast white (Species 49).

 IX. Medium-sized, with upperparts dark, and underparts white with a dark band across the breast (Species 50–51).

X. Large, with pale grey upperparts and white underparts (Species 52–53).

XI. Small, with pale grey upperparts and white underparts (Species 54–60).

XII. Medium-sized, with plumage entirely white (Species 61).

I. VERY LARGE PETRELS WITH PLUMAGE EITHER DARK, OR WHITE WITH DARK SPOTS

1. **Giant Petrel** (*Macronectes giganteus* = *Ossifraga gigantea*). (*Plates 12 and 13*)

Adult.—Dark grey with a lighter head, or white, usually more or less spotted with dark brown; bill large, pale straw-colour or greyish green; feet silvery brown or sooty black; length 33–36 ins.; wing 20; tail 6.5; bill 3.7–5; tarsus 3.5; span of wings about 8 feet. *Young.*—Slaty black fading to dark chocolate brown.

Range.—Southern oceans from the Antarctic Continent to the tropic of Capricorn and even further north on the west coast of South America. Breeds in Antarctica, the South Shetlands, South Orkneys and South Georgia, the Falkland Is., Bouvet I. and Gough I., Prince Edward I., Marion I., Crozet Is., Kerguelen, Heard I., Stewart I., the Chatham Is. and the sub-antarctic islands of New Zealand. *Egg-dates:* Aug.–Jan.

Notes.—Known to seamen and whalers as the "Nelly" or "Stinker"; much the largest member of the family; a scavenger, which also kills penguins and small petrels. Distinguished from the dark Albatrosses by its stouter form, shorter wings and large pale bill. The dark phase is much the commoner in temperate seas, the white phase being almost confined to the neighbourhood of the Antarctic ice.

II. LARGE OR MEDIUM-SIZED PETRELS WITH DARK PLUMAGE

(In dull weather most of these birds look quite black, whilst in bright sunlight the majority appear rich chocolate brown. In addition to the thirteen species placed in this group there are dark phases of the Kermadec, Trinidad, Herald and Soft-plumaged Petrels which may be confused with them, and the Fulmar has a dusky phase.)

2. White-chinned Petrel (*Procellaria aequinoctialis*)

Adult.—Sooty black, tending to chocolate brown on the mantle and underparts; chin white, the white sometimes extending to the sides of the face and crown, sometimes entirely absent; bill greenish white, marked with black; feet black; length 21.5 ins.; wing 14.5; tail 5.3; bill 1.7; tarsus 2.5.

Range.—Southern oceans from Antarctica to about 30° S. and on the west coast of South America to northern Peru; occasionally to Brazil, Angola and Mozambique. Breeds at South Georgia, the Falkland Is., the Crozet Is., Marion I. and Kerguelen (*P. a. aequinoctialis*), Tristan da Cunha (*P. a. conspicillata*), the Auckland Is., Antipodes I., Campbell I. and Macquarie I. (*P. a. steadi*). *Egg-dates:* Aug.–Feb.

Notes.—The "Cape Hen," as this species is called by sailors, is one of the commonest Petrels of the southern ocean and constantly follows ships. Its large size, almost black plumage and very pale bill are diagnostic, even if the white on the chin cannot be distinguished.

3. Black Petrel (*Procellaria parkinsoni*)

Adult.—Sooty black; shafts of primaries white beneath; bill yellowish horn-colour with black tip; feet black; length 18 ins; wing 13.2–15; tail 3.5–4.7; bill 1.6–2.0; tarsus 1.9–2.6.

Range.—South Pacific Ocean, from eastern Australia to the Galápagos Is. Breeds in both islands of New Zealand

(*P. p. parkinsoni*) and in Westland, South Island (*P. p. westlandica*). *Egg-dates:* Nov.–Feb. and May–June.

Notes.—A rare bird, smaller than the White-chinned Petrel but not easily distinguished in life. The Westland race, recently discovered, is larger than the more widely distributed form and breeds in winter, whilst the other race breeds in summer.

4. **Wedge-tailed Shearwater** (*Puffinus pacificus = P. cuneatus*)

Adult.—Upper surface dark chocolate-brown, deepening into black on primaries and tail; tail strongly wedge-shaped; face and throat, dark brownish grey; rest of under surface greyish-brown (dark phase), or white (light phase); bill reddish flesh-colour, darker on middle line and at tip; feet yellowish flesh-colour; length 15.5 ins.; wing 11.5; tail 6; bill 1.6; tarsus 1.9.

Range.—Warmer parts of the Indian and Pacific Oceans. Breeds in the Indian Ocean at the Seychelle Is., Mauritius and Reunion, on the western and eastern coasts of Australia and at many island groups in the Pacific Ocean from Lord Howe and Norfolk Is. to the Revillagigedo Is. (*P. p. chlororhynchus*), at the Kermadec Is. (*P. p. pacificus*), and at the Pescadores, Bonin and Hawaiian Is. (*P. p. cuneatus*). *Egg-dates:* May–Aug. (northern hemisphere), Sept.–Dec. (southern hemisphere).

Notes.—A dark shearwater with rather long, wedge-shaped tail and pale bill and feet. Decidedly smaller than the Pale-footed Shearwater, from which it can hardly be distinguished in life.

5. **Christmas Shearwater** (*Puffinus nativitatis*)

Adult.—Chocolate-brown, somewhat lighter below, slightly greyish on the throat; tail wedge-shaped; bill and feet black; length 14 ins; wing 9.8; tail 3.6; bill 1.6; tarsus 1.6.

Range.—Tropical Pacific. Breeds at the Hawaiian Is., Marcus I., Christmas I., Phoenix Is., Marquesas Is., Tuamotu Is. and Austral Is. *Egg-dates:* April–July.

Notes.—Smaller than the Wedge-tailed Shearwater, from which it is readily distinguished by its dark bill and feet. It nests on the ground under bushes.

6. **Short-tailed Shearwater** (*Puffinus tenuirostris* = *P. brevicaudus*)

Adult.—Sooty-brown, much paler on under surface; under wing-coverts greyish; bill blackish brown, tinged olive; feet vinous grey, outer toe blackish, webs sometimes yellowish flesh-colour; length 13 ins; wing 10.4; tail 3.2; bill 1.8; tarsus 2.1.

Range.—Pacific Ocean from Australia, New Zealand and Tuamotu Is. north in the (southern) winter to the Okhotsk and Bering Seas. Breeds on islands in Bass Strait and on the coasts of Victoria, South Australia and Tasmania. *Egg-dates:* Nov.–March.

Notes.—The "Muttonbird" of Bass Strait, where it is the main support of the islanders, and the "Whale bird" of Alaska. Smaller than the Sooty Shearwater and darker on the under surface of the wings.

7. **Sooty Shearwater** (*Puffinus griseus*)

Adult.—Upperparts blackish-brown; underparts greyish-brown, paler on the chin; under wing-coverts greyish-white; bill blackish; feet slate-grey, outer toe blackish, webs sometimes yellowish; length 16–20 ins; wing 10.5–12.5; tail 3.5–4.3; bill 1.5–2.1; tarsus 2.1–2.4.

Range.—Pacific and Atlantic Oceans from about 60° S. north in the (southern) winter to Kamchatka, Alaska, Labrador, Greenland and the Faroe Is. Breeds on Tasman I. off Tasmania, in New Zealand, Stewart I., the Snares Is., Chatham Is., Auckland Is., Macquarie Is., in the Andes of northern Chile, on islands off Cape Horn and in the Falkland Is. *Egg-dates:* Nov.–April.

Notes.—This is the "Mutton-bird" of New Zealand seas, distinguished from other dark-coloured petrels of similar size by its whitish under wing-coverts, and from all but the Short-tailed and Christmas Shearwaters by its dark bill and feet.

8. Pale-footed Shearwater (*Puffinus carneipes*). (*Plate 16*)

Adult.—Chocolate black; bill fleshy white with a line down the centre and the tip brown; feet yellowish flesh-colour; length 19.5 ins.; wing 12.5; tail 4.3; bill 1.8; tarsus 2.3.

Range.—Indian and Pacific Oceans from Australian seas north in the (southern) winter to Ceylon, Japan and California, and occasionally east to Juan Fernandez. Breeds on the south coast of Western Australia, the North Island of New Zealand, and Lord Howe I. *Egg-dates:* Sept.–Jan.

Notes.—Larger than the Wedge-tailed Shearwater, with a very pale bill, but hardly distinguishable in life.

9. Reunion Petrel (*Pterodroma aterrima*)

Adult.—Dark greyish-brown; bill very stout, black; feet dark reddish flesh-colour, outer toe and webs black; length 14 ins.; wing 9.4–9.7; tail 4; bill 1.4–1.5; tarsus 1.5.

Range.—Western Indian Ocean from the Mascarene Islands north to the Gulf of Aden. Breeds at Reunion.

Notes.—Considerably smaller than the Wedge-tailed Shearwater from which it is also distinguished by its short, black bill.

10. Great-winged Petrel (*Pterodroma macroptera*)

Adult.—Dark brown; patch round the bill, and throat, grey; wing quills and tail black; bill and feet black; length 15–16.3 ins.; wing 12–13; tail 4.5; bill 1.6; tarsus 1.7.

Range.—Southern Oceans between 50° S. and 30° S. lat. Breeds at Tristan da Cunha, the Crozet Is., Marion I., and Kerguelen (*P. m. macroptera*), the south coast of Western Australia (*P. m. albani*) and North Island, New Zealand (*P. m. gouldi*). *Egg-dates:* June–Sept.

Notes.—A wide-spread common species, which is often seen in the southern oceans flying swiftly past, but which pays no attention to ships. The very long wings and pale throat are the distinguishing features.

11. **Solander's Petrel** (*Pterodroma solandri*). (*Plate 11*)

Adult.—Upper parts slate-grey, inclining to dark brown on head, wings and tail; forehead and throat whitish; a black patch before the eye; underparts brownish-grey; base of primaries beneath and some of under wing-coverts white, forming a white patch in the centre of the under surface of the wings; bill black; feet flesh-colour, outer toe black; length 16 ins.; wing 12; tail 5.5; bill 1.7; tarsus 0.7.

Range.—South Pacific Ocean from east coast of Australia to Ducie I. Breeds at Lord Howe I., Tuamotu Is. and Austral Is. *Egg-dates:* May-June.

Notes.—The greyish colour of the back and the white patch on the under-surface of the wings are characteristic features.

12. **Murphy's Petrel** (*Pterodroma ultima*)

Adult.—Above and below blackish-brown, brownest on crown and nape, paler and slightly slater on the back, scapulars and coverts; a dark patch before and under the eye; a narrow-white infraorbital line; feathers of forehead and lores with greyish or whitish margins; throat mottled with white; inner webs of primaries and secondaries grey; bill black; feet fleshy or bluish white margined with black; wing 10.6–11.6 ins.; tail 4.1–4.8; bill 1.1–1.2; tarsus 1.4–1.6.

Range.—Central South Pacific Ocean. Breeds in the Tuamotu Is., Austral Is., Oeno and Ducie I.

Notes.—Resembles Solander's Petrel but is smaller and darker and lacks the white patch on the under-surface of the wing.

13. **Jamaica Petrel** (*Pterodroma caribbaea* = *P. jamaicensis*)

Adult.—Sooty-brown, darker on back, paler on under surface, greyer on forehead and throat; upper tail-coverts whitish; tail sooty-black, outer feathers whitish at base (dark phase)—a light phase, which is greyer, also occurs; feet black; length 14 ins.; wing 11; tail 4.5; bill 1.5; tarsus 1.4.

Range.—Only known from Jamaica, where it formerly bred.

Notes.—This rare, probably extinct, species is perhaps a dark form of the Black-capped Petrel, with which it agrees in dimensions and form of bill. All known specimens from Jamaica are dark, while all those known from other West Indian islands are white-breasted.

14. Kerguelen Petrel (*Pterodroma brevirostris*)

Adult.—Slaty-grey, paler on face and throat, darker on wings and tail; bill and feet black; length 13 ins.; wing 10–10.1; tail 3.6–4.2; bill 1; tarsus 1.4–1.5.

Range.—South Atlantic and Indian Ocean, from 70° S. to about 30° S., occasionally east to New Zealand. Breeds at Gough I., Kerguelen and Marion I. *Egg-dates:* Oct.–Dec.

Notes.—This wholly dark grey species can scarcely be confused with any other petrel.

III. SMALL PETRELS WITH DARK PLUMAGE

15. Heinroth's Shearwater (*Puffinus heinrothi*)

Adult.—Brownish-black, underparts somewhat paler than upper surface; throat and chin grey; under wing-coverts whitish; bill greyish-black; feet flesh-coloured with blackish margins; length 7.5 ins.; wing 7.6; tail 3.3.; bill 1.2; tarsus 1.3.

Range.—Known only from a single specimen from the coast of New Britain.

Notes.—Similar in colouring to the Short-tailed Shearwater but much smaller. Its relatively long, slender bill distinguishes it from Bulwer's Petrel, to which it approximates in size.

16. Bulwer's Petrel (*Bulweria bulwerii*)

Adult.—Sooty-black, rather paler on chin and edges of greater wing-coverts; tail long, wedge-shaped; bill black, feet flesh-coloured, outer toe and webs black; length 10.5–

11 ins.; wing 7.5–8.3; tail 3.9–4.4; bill 0.8–1.2; tarsus 1–1.2.

Range.—Pacific and Atlantic Oceans. Breeds on the coast of China, the Bonin Is., Volcano Is., western Hawaiian Is., Marquesas Is., Madeira, the Salvage Is., Canary Is., and Cape Verde Is. *Egg-dates:* May–July.

Notes.—A small entirely dark petrel with rather long wedge-shaped tail and short legs, widely distributed over both oceans, but rarely seen at sea. It is smaller than any other dusky petrel (except Heinroth's Shearwater) and slightly larger than any of the dark Storm-Petrels.

17. Macgillivray's Petrel (*Bulweria macgillivrayi*)

Adult.—Similar to Bulwer's Petrel but larger and uniformly sooty black, with a much larger bill; length 11.5 ins.; wing 8; tail 3.3; bill 1.3; tarsus 1.4.

Range.—Fiji Is.

Notes.—Only known from a single specimen captured on Ngau I.

IV. SMALL OR MEDIUM-SIZED PETRELS ENTIRELY DARK ABOVE WITH THE UNDER SURFACE OF THE BODY WHITE

18. Manx Shearwater (*Puffinus puffinus = P. anglorum*)

Adult.—Upper surface slaty-black or blackish-brown; sides of head and neck mottled with grey or brownish; underparts, including under surface of wings, white; sides of breast, flanks and abdomen more or less brownish in Mediterranean birds; outer under tail-coverts dark; axillaries with dark tips; bill leaden-black, bluish-grey at base; feet pinkish flesh-colour, outer edge brownish-black, webs grey-blue; length 14–15 ins.; wing 8.8–10.2; tail 2.7–3.3; bill 1.3–1.9; tarsus 1.7–2.

Range.—Atlantic Ocean and Mediterranean Sea, south (in winter) to Argentina. Breeds in the Bermudas, Iceland, Faroe Is., British Is., Brittany, Azores and Madeira (*P. p.*

puffinus), the Balearic Is. (*P. p. mauretanicus*) and Aegean Is. (*P. p. yelkouan*). *Egg-dates:* March–June.

Notes.—A rather small Shearwater almost black above, white below, with long, narrow wings. Larger than the Dusky Shearwater and in flight resembling the larger forms, gliding with outspread rigid wings and only occasionally giving a few rapid flaps.

19. Dusky Shearwater (*Puffinus assimilis = P. obscurus*)

Adult.—Upperparts slaty-black; sides of face and neck and underparts, including under surface of wings, white; sides of breast bluish-grey; under tail-coverts white or partly black and partly white; bill blackish, bluish at base; feet slate-blue, outer toe black; length 10.5–12 ins.; wing 6.5–8; tail 2.7–3.2; bill 0.9–1.5; tarsus 1.3–1.6.

Range.—Atlantic, Indian and S. Pacific Oceans, chiefly in subtropical latitudes. In the Atlantic occasionally north to the British Is. and Denmark and south to the South Orkneys. Breeds in the Azores, Madeira, Salvage Is. and Canary Is. (*P. a. baroli*), Cape Verde Is. (*P. a. boydi*), Tristan da Cunha and Gough I. (*P. a. elegans*), islets off coasts of S. W. Australia (*P. a. tunneyi*), Lord Howe I. and Norfolk I. (*P. a. assimilis*), New Zealand (*P. a. haurakiensis*), Chatham Is. (*P. a. munda*) and Kermadec Is. (*P. a. kermadecensis*). *Egg-dates:* Throughout the year depending on the locality.

Notes.—Also known as the Little Shearwater. Smaller than the Manx Shearwater and in flight usually flapping its wings frequently and only gliding for brief periods except in a strong wind. It does not seem normally to range far from its breeding grounds. From Audubon's Shearwater it can probably not be distinguished at sea but is usually slaty-black rather than brownish-black above and with more white on the under tail-coverts, while the feet are bluish. The downy nestling is also differently coloured.

20. Audubon's Shearwater (*Puffinus lherminieri*)

Adult.—Upperparts dark sooty brownish-black; underparts white; under tail-coverts black or partly white and partly black; bill black; feet flesh-colour or yellowish-white, outer toe black; length about 12 ins; wing 7.8–8.1; tail 3.3–3.8; bill 1.1–1.2; tarsus 1.5–1.7.

Range.—Tropical Indian, Pacific and West Atlantic Oceans, in the Atlantic occasionally north to Long Island and southern England. Breeds in Mauritius, Reunion and Seychelle Is. (*P. l. bailloni*), Bonin Is. (*P. l. bannermani*), New Hebrides (*P. l. nugax*), Phoenix Is. and Christmas I. (*P. l. dichrous*), Samoan, Society, Tuamotu and Marquesas Is. (*P. l. polynesiae*), Galápagos Is. (*P. l. subalaris*), West Indies, Bahamas and Bermuda (*P. l. lherminieri*). *Egg-dates:* March–May.

Notes.—Almost confined to the tropics in the vicinity of the islands where it breeds. For distinction from the Dusky Shearwater see under that species.

21. Black-vented Shearwater (*Puffinus opisthomelas*)

Adult.—Upperparts sooty-black; sides of the head dark far below the eye, freckled where they shade into the white of the under surface; under wing-coverts white, bend of wing and axillaries mottled blackish; flanks and under tail-coverts black; bill blackish, yellowish or reddish-brown at sides; feet yellowish flesh-colour, outer toe brownish-black; length 12 ins.; wing 9; tail 3.8; bill 2; tarsus 1.8.

Range.—Pacific Coast of North America from British Columbia to Mexico. Breeds on the west coast of Lower California. *Egg-dates:* April.

Notes.—Very similar to the Dusky Shearwater in general colouring, habits and flight, but with black cheeks and a markedly longer tail.

22. Townsend's Shearwater (*Puffinus auricularis*)

Adult.—Upperparts nearly black; black on sides of head extending below the eye to the level of the gape, mottled at the edge; underparts, including axillaries and flanks, white; under tail-coverts black; bill and feet black; length 12.5 ins.; wing 9.2; tail 3.2; bill 1.2; tarsus 1.8.

Range.—Pacific Ocean off the west coast of Mexico from Cape San Lucas to Clipperton I. Breeds at the Revillagigedo Is. *Egg-dates:* April.

Notes.—Very similar to the Black-vented Shearwater but with white flanks and axillaries, shorter tail and smaller bill. It appears to have a very limited range. The bird named *P. newelli,* which formerly bred on Lanai and Molokai in the Hawaiian group, was probably a form of Townsend's Shearwater.

23. Fluttering Shearwater (*Puffinus gavia = P. reinholdi*)

Adult.—Above blackish-brown; sides of head and neck mottled grey; region below eye and lores dark; below white, including under wing-coverts and under tail-coverts; axillaries dusky with white tips; bill blackish; feet flesh-colour, outer toe dark; length 12–14.6 ins.; wing 7.1–9; tail 2.3–2.8; bill 1.2–1.5; tarsus 1.4–1.8.

Range.—Australasian seas in the neighbourhood of New Zealand and Southern Australia. Breeds in both islands of New Zealand (*P. g. gavia*) and at Snares I. (*P. g. huttoni*). *Egg-dates:* Sept.–Oct.

Notes.—Resembles the Dusky Shearwater but has more black on sides of head. Except in very strong winds the flight is almost entirely by rapid wing-beats, and the birds spend much time on the water.

24. Persian Shearwater (*Puffinus persicus*)

Adult.—Head and nape sooty-brown; upperparts blackish-brown, almost black on primaries, rump, upper tail-coverts and tail; chin, throat, breast and abdomen white; a narrow white ring round eye, extending backwards as a white streak; sides, axillaries, flanks, lesser under wing-coverts and longer under tail-coverts brown; rest of under wing-coverts white; bill dusky-brown bluish at base; feet pinkish-white, outer toe black; length 12–13 ins.; wing 7–7.8; tail 2.9; bill 1.3; tarsus 1.5.

Range.—Arabian Sea and coasts of Persia, Baluchistan and N. W. India. Breeding grounds unknown.

Notes.—A little-known bird which probably resembles the Fluttering Shearwater in habits.

25. Bonin Petrel (*Pterodroma hypoleuca*)

Adult.—Upperparts slaty-black; middle of back, wing-coverts and upper tail-coverts grey, the feathers of the back with white edges; forehead, cheeks and underparts white; under surface of wings either white or black or white with black axillaries; bill black; feet flesh-coloured, outer toe and end of webs black; length 12–13 ins.; wing 8.3–9; tail 3.8–4.6; bill 1–1.3; tarsus 1.1–1.2.

Range.—Western Pacific Ocean. Breeds at Liu Kiu Is., Bonin Is., and western Hawaiian Is. (*P. h. hypoleuca*), at the Kermadec Is. (*P. h. nigripennis*), and the Chatham Is. (*P. h. axillaris*). *Egg-dates:* Nov.–Feb.

Notes.—This species resembles Gould's Petrel and Cook's Petrel, but is larger with a much stouter bill and with comparatively stout flesh-coloured and black feet. The black axillaries of the Chatham Is. race are conspicuous in flight.

26. Gould's Petrel (*Pterodroma leucoptera*)

Adult.—Upperparts slaty-black, middle of back, upper wing-coverts and upper tail-coverts dark grey; area before eyes black; primaries black, inner webs white at base; tail slaty-black, the outer feathers grey with white mottling on the inner web; face, throat and underparts white, forehead and sides of neck with blackish spotting; under surface of wings white with black edges; axillaries white; bill black; feet bluish-white, outer toe and ends of webs black; length 12 ins.; wing 8.5; tail 3.8; bill 1.3; tarsus 1.2.

Range.—South-western Pacific, breeding at Cabbagetree I., Port Stephens, New South Wales (*P. l. leucoptera*), and in New Caledonia, the New Hebrides and Fiji Is. (*P. l. brevipes*). *Egg-dates:* Nov.–Dec.

Notes.—This species resembles Cook's Petrel but has a smaller bill and is darker above, appearing in flight to be a dark bird with a grey area extending across the back and wings.

27. Cook's Petrel (*Pterodroma cooki*)

Adult.—Upperparts grey; wings black, the primaries with the inner webs white almost to the tip; lower back blackish; tail grey, the outer feathers nearly white; forehead and underparts white; a black area before the eye; under surface of wings, including axillaries white, the edges of the wings black; bill black; feet blue, outer toe and end of webs black; length 10–10.5 ins.; wing 8.8–9.4; tail 3.2–3.6; bill 1.1; tarsus 1.1–1.2.

Range.—Pacific Ocean from New Zealand and Chile north to Mexico. Breeds at Little Barrier I., New Zealand (*P. c. cooki*), and at Juan Fernandez, S. Felix I. and S. Ambrose I. (*P. c. defilippiana*). *Egg-dates:* Oct–Nov.

Notes.—In flight the upper parts appear light grey, with a conspicuous band like an inverted W across the wings and back. Distinguished from Gould's Petrel by its lighter upperparts, larger size and longer bill.

28. Stejneger's Petrel (*Pterodroma longirostris*)

Adult.—Upperparts slaty-black, middle of back, wing-coverts and upper tail-coverts light grey with white edges; primaries black, the inner webs white at the base; tail greyish black, outer feathers light grey; forehead, cheeks and underparts white; under surface of wings white with narrow dark edges; bill rather long and slender, black; feet blue, outer toe black, webs whitish; length 9.3–9.7 ins.; tail 3.8–4; bill 0.9–1; tarsus 1.1–1.2.

Range.—Pacific Ocean from New Zealand and Juan Fernandez north to Japan and California. Breeds in New Zealand (*P. l. pycrofti*) and Mas Afuera, Juan Fernandez (*P. l. longirostris*).

29. Collared Petrel (*Pterodroma brevipes* = *P. torquata*)

Adult.—Upperparts slaty-black, middle of back, wing-coverts and upper tail-coverts grey; primaries black; tail greyish black, outer feathers light grey; forehead, cheeks and throat white; under surface of body usually white, with the sides of the breast slaty-grey, this colour sometimes extends as a band across the breast, sometimes the whole under surface except the throat is grey; under surface of wings white with black edges; bill black; feet blue, outer toe and end of webs black; length 11.5 ins.; wing 8.2–8.9; tail 3.7–4; bill 0.9–1.3; tarsus 1–1.2.

Range.—South Pacific Ocean from the New Hebrides to the Galápagos Is. Breeds in New Hebrides and Fiji Is. *Egg-dates:* May.

Notes.—Closely resembles Gould's Petrel, but may be distinguished by the partial or complete grey band across the breast. Smaller than the Soft-plumaged Petrel from which it differs in its white under wing-coverts.

30. Soft-plumaged Petrel (*Pterodroma mollis*)

Adult.—Back of head and upper surface slate-grey; wings dark brown; tail dark grey, outer feathers mottled with greyish-white; forehead freckled grey and white; face and throat white; a black patch before and below the eye; underparts sometimes dark grey, usually white with a band of slaty-grey, often not quite complete, across the chest; under surface of wings dark brown; bill black; feet flesh-coloured, outer toe and ends of webs black; length 13.5–14 ins.; wing 9.8–10; tail 4.5–5; bill 1.1–1.4; tarsus 1.3–1.6.

Range.—Atlantic and Indian Oceans, south to 50° S. lat. Breeds at Madeira and the Cape Verde Is. (*P. m. feae*) and at Tristan da Cunha, Gough I., Kerguelen and St. Paul I. (*P. m. mollis*). *Egg-dates:* June–July, Oct.–Nov.

Notes.—The dark under surface of the wings, dark spot about the eye, and grey band on each side of the chest distinguish this species. It is rather a common bird, usually seen in small companies, flying rapidly over the water and paying no attention to ships.

35

V. LARGE PETRELS MAINLY OR ENTIRELY DARK ABOVE WITH THE UNDER SURFACE OF THE BODY WHITE

(In addition to the fifteen species listed below the Wedge-tailed Shearwater has a phase with white underparts.)

31. Hawaiian Petrel (*Pterodroma phaeopygia*). (*Plate 11*)

Adult.—Upperparts brownish-black, the feathers with concealed white bases; wings and tail black with concealed white patches; cheeks and region round the eye black; forehead and underparts white; under surface of wings white with dark edges; tail wedge-shaped; bill black; feet yellowish, end of webs black; length 17 ins.; wing 12; tail 5.5; bill 1.6; tarsus 1.6.

Range.—Tropical Eastern Pacific. Breeds at the Hawaiian Is. (*P. p. sandwichensis*) and Galápagos Is. (*P. p. phaeopygia*). *Egg-dates:* June–July.

Notes.—A wide-spread species in the Eastern Pacific. The white forehead, black patch round the eye and brown back contrasting with the black wings and tail are characteristic.

32. White-necked Petrel (*Pterodroma externa*)

Adult.—Crown and nape brownish-black; a greyish-white collar on the back of the neck; upperparts greyish-black, the feathers of the back with grey edges; wings and tail black; cheeks and region round the eye dark grey; forehead and underparts, including under surface of wings, white; tail wedge-shaped; bill black; feet yellowish, outer toe and end of webs black; length 16–19 ins.; wing 11.5; tail 5–5.2; bill 1.7–1.8; tarsus 1.5.

Range.—Pacific Ocean from the Kermadec Is. and Juan Fernandez north to Mexico, and South Atlantic. Breeds at the Kermadec Is. (*P. e. cervicalis*), and Masafuera, Juan Fernandez (*P. e. externa*). *Egg-dates:* Oct.–March.

Notes.—The black crown, whitish collar and grey back distinguish this species from other Pacific Petrels.

33. Black-capped Petrel (*Pterodroma hasitata = P. diabolica*)

Adult.—Crown brown-black; forehead and nape whitish; upperparts sooty-brown; upper tail-coverts and base of tail white or greyish; underparts white; under surface of wings white in centre with broad dark margins; sides of breast greyish or brownish; bill black; feet flesh-coloured, end of webs black; length 16 ins.; wing 10.3–11.5; tail 5–6.5; bill 1.2–1.7; tarsus 1.4–1.6.

Range.—North Atlantic and Caribbean Sea. Formerly bred at Haiti, Guadeloupe and Dominica. Now probably only (a few) in Dominica. *Egg-dates:* Nov.–Jan.

Notes.—Resembles the Greater Shearwater, but distinguished by whitish nape and upper tail-coverts. Formerly known as the "Diablotin." The Jamaica Petrel was perhaps a dark form of this species but as far as is known was confined to that island.

34. Bermuda Petrel (*Pterodroma cahow*)

Adult.—Upper-parts sooty, grayish on the back and upper tail-coverts; forehead, lores and under-parts white; sides of breast grey; under surface of wings white in centre with broad, dark margins; bill black; feet pink margined with black; length 13.7–14.8 ins.; wing 10.2–10.3; tail 4.6–4.8; bill 1.1; tarsus 1.3–1.4.

Range.—Only known from Bermuda, where it breeds. *Egg-dates:* Dec.–Feb.

Notes.—Formerly abundant at Bermuda, where it was known as the "Cahow." Long thought to be extinct but recently rediscovered breeding on outlying rocky islets. From the Black-capped Petrel it differs in its smaller size, proportionately longer tail, absence of white on the rump and the fact that the crown is not darker than the back and not separated from it by a nuchal band of lighter feathers.

Resembles the Soft-plumaged Petrel but has a white central area on the under surface of the wings.

35. Herald Petrel (*Pterodroma heraldica*)

Adult.—Upperparts dark brown, feathers of back indistinctly edged grey; wings and tail blackish with concealed white patches at base of feathers; forehead and cheeks white, mottled with brown; underparts very variable, sometimes entirely dark brown, except for some whitish feathers on the throat, more usually white, with grey lines on the sides of the neck, breast and flanks, occasionally with a dark band across the chest; under wing-coverts chiefly blackish, partly white in the middle line; bill black; feet flesh-coloured, end of webs black; tail wedge-shaped; length 14 ins.; wing 11.3; tail 4.5; bill 1.5; tarsus 1.4.

Range.—Warmer parts of South Pacific Ocean. Breeds at the Chesterfield Is., Tonga Is., Marquesas Is. and Tuamotu Is. (*P. h. heraldica*), also at Easter I. (*P. h. paschae*).

Notes.—Very similar to the Kermadec Petrel, but distinctly smaller, and with black shafts to the primaries. The very dark birds are chiefly found at Henderson I. near the Tuamotu group. It seems probable that *P. magentae*, based on a single bird captured at sea near Pitcairn I., is only a form of this variable species.

36. Kermadec Petrel (*Pterodroma phillipii = P. neglecta*). (*Plates 14 and 15*)

Adult.—Upperparts brown; head and underparts sometimes white, sometimes brown, sometimes partly white and partly brown; primaries blackish-brown, the bases of the inner webs and adjoining shafts white; under surface of wings brown with a white patch towards the tip; bill black; feet black or yellow with end of webs black; length 15.5 ins.; wing 11–11.8; tail 3.9–4.3; bill 1.1–1.3; tarsus 1.5–1.7.

Range.—Pacific Ocean from the Kermadec Is. and Juan Fernandez north to Mexico. Breeds at Lord Howe I., the

Kermadec Is., Austral Is., Tuamotu Is., San Antonio I. and Juan Fernandez. *Egg-dates:* Throughout the year.

Notes.—Very similar to the Herald Petrel but larger, with a distinct white area towards the tip of the under surface of the wings and white shafts to the primaries. The closely related Trinidad Petrel of the South Atlantic and Indian Oceans has the primary shafts black. This species nests on the surface of the ground under bushes or ferns.

37. **Trinidad Petrel** (*Pterodroma arminjoniana = P. wilsoni = P. trinitatis*)

Adult.—Above blackish-brown; shafts of primaries black; underparts very variable, sometimes entirely blackish-brown, sometimes white with a mottled collar of grey crossing the chest and dark-brown flanks, sometimes with the whole breast also dark grey; under surface of wings dark brown with a white patch towards the tip; bill black; feet black or flesh-coloured with ends of webs black; length 16 ins.; wing 11.1; tail 4.4; bill 1.5; tarsus 1.35.

Range.—Tropical Atlantic and western Indian Ocean. Breeds at South Trinidad I., off Brazil and Round I., off Mauritius. *Egg-dates:* Throughout the year.

Notes.—Closely related to the Kermadec Petrel, which it resembles in habits, but apparently always distinguished by having black shafts to the primaries. The striking white-backed bird described as *P. chionophara* is clearly a partial albino, remarkable in that the white area is symmetrical.

38. **Greater Shearwater** (*Puffinus gravis = P. major*). (Plates 11 and 16)

Adult.—Upperparts brown, darker on wings and tail, darkest on head; neck white nearly all round; most of the feathers of the back with pale edges; longer upper tail-coverts tipped with whitish; underparts white, flecked with sooty on the abdomen and under tail-coverts; under wing-coverts streaked with brown; bill dark horn-colour;

feet brown, webs yellowish flesh-colour; length 18-21 ins.; wing 12-13; tail 4.2–4.8; bill 1.7–2.3; tarsus 2.2–2.4.

Range.—Atlantic Ocean from Cape Horn and the Cape of Good Hope north in the (southern) winter to the Arctic circle. Breeds at Tristan da Cunha and Cough I. *Egg-dates:* Nov.

Notes.—A common species in the North Atlantic in summer, usually seen in large flocks. Distinguished from the Black-capped Petrel by its longer and more slender bill, also by the dark colouring of the back of the neck, dark flecks on the abdomen and smaller amount of white at the base of the tail; from the Mediterranean Shearwater by its darker crown, whiter cheeks and dusky bill; from the Brown Petrel by the white at base of tail and white under wing-coverts.

39. Mediterranean Shearwater (*Puffinus kuhli*)

Adult.—Upperparts brown, darker on the head, wings and tail, the feathers of the back and wing-coverts with paler edges; outer primaries in the Mediterranean race with white at base forming a white wing patch; longer upper tail-coverts whitish or mottled; cheeks and sides of neck grey mottled with white; underparts white, including under surface of wings except at the edge; bill yellow with paler tip; feet yellow, darker on outer side; length 18–22 ins.; wing 11.3–14.5; tail 4.5–6.5; bill 1.5–2.8; tarsus 1.7–2.3.

Range.—Atlantic Ocean, from Newfoundland and England to Brazil and the Cape of Good Hope, Mediterranean Sea and Indian Ocean, occasionally to New Zealand. Breeds on islands in the Mediterranean (*P. k. kuhli*), on the coast of Portugal and in the Salvage Is., Canary Is., Madeira and Azores (*P. k. borealis*), and the Cape Verde Is. (*P. k. edwardsi*). *Egg-dates:* May-Sept.

Notes.—The largest Atlantic Shearwater. Similar to the Greater Shearwater but may be distinguished by its light brown crown not sharply separated from the white throat and by its pale bill. Its white under wing-coverts and whitish colour at base of tail distinguish it from the Brown Petrel. Sometimes known as Cory's Shearwater.

40. Pink-footed Shearwater (*Puffinus creatopus*)

Adult.—Upper surface dark greyish brown; under surface white, sides of neck, flanks and under wing-coverts mottled with grey; axillaries and under tail-coverts greyish-brown; bill and feet yellowish; length 20 ins.; wing 13; tail 4.4; bill 2.5; tarsus 2.2.

Range.—Eastern portions of Pacific Ocean from southern Chile north in the (southern) winter to Alaska. Breeds in the Juan Fernandez Is. and at Mocha I., Chile. *Egg-dates:* Dec.–March.

Notes.—Very nearly related to the Mediterranean Shearwater, of which it may be only a race. Distinguished from the white-breasted phase of the Wedge-tailed Shearwater by its larger size, and the lighter and greyer colouring of its upper surface.

41. Brown Petrel (*Adamastor cinereus*). (*Plate 11*)

Adult.—Upperparts dark brownish-grey, darker on the head, wings and tail; sides of the face and neck pale grey; throat, chest and abdomen white; under wing-coverts, some feathers on the flanks and under tail-coverts grey; bill greenish yellow with black lines; feet bluish-brown, outer toe darker, webs tinged with yellow; length 18–19.5 ins.; wing 12.8; tail 4.3; bill 2.1; tarsus 2.2.

Range.—Southern Oceans from about 55° S. lat. to about 30° S. and on the west coast of South America to Peru. Breeds at Tristan da Cunha, Gough I., Kerguelen, Marion I., Macquarie I., Campbell I. and Antipodes I. *Egg-dates:* March–May.

Notes.—This is one of the familiar petrels of the southern oceans, frequently following ships, and sometimes called the "Pediunker" or "Cape Dove" by sailors. It is distinguished from the Greater, Mediterranean and Pink-footed Shearwaters by the dark colour beneath the wings and tail. It dives much more frequently than many other petrels and shearwaters.

42. Grey-backed Shearwater (*Puffinus bulleri*)

Adult.—Crown, back of the neck, lesser wing-coverts, primaries and tail sooty-black; back and greater wing-coverts grey, the coverts edged with white; region before and below the eye mottled with greyish white; under-parts, including under-surface of wings white; under tail-coverts edged with grey; bill blue or bluish-grey; feet flesh-colour, outer toe black; length 16.5 ins.; wing 11.3; tail 5,2; bill 2.6; tarsus 2.0.

Range.—Pacific Ocean from New Zealand and Chile north in the (southern) winter to California. Breeds on islands off the North Island, New Zealand. *Egg-dates:* Dec.

Notes.—The dark brown head, wings and tail contrast conspicuously with the pale grey mantle and upper tail-coverts. The dark brown feathers on the wing-coverts and back form a wide inverted W when the wings are spread.

43. White-faced Shearwater (*Puffinus leucomelas*)

Adult.—Upper surface brown, feathers of back and wings with pale edges; front and sides of head, neck and underparts, including undersurface of wings, white, feathers of face and neck and edge of wing with dark streaks; primaries black; tail cuneate, brown; bill horn-colour; feet flesh-colour; length 19 ins.; wing 13; tail 5.6; bill 2.1; tarsus 2.

Range.—North-western Pacific Ocean from Korea and Japan south in winter to Philippine Is., Borneo, Molucca Is., and New Guinea; occasionally to Ceylon. Breeds at the Pescadores Is., near Formosa and Oh-sima I., N. Japan. *Egg-dates:* May–June.

Notes.—A large petrel easily recognised by its white face streaked with black.

44. White-headed Petrel (*Pterodroma lessoni*). (*Plate 11*)

Adult.—Front of head, throat, under surface of body and tail white; hinder part of head, back of neck and upper tail-coverts grey; round and before the eye a black mark; back greyish-brown; wings blackish-brown; under wing-coverts dark grey, each feather edged with white; quills grey below; bill black; feet fleshy white, end of webs black; length 18 ins.; wing 12.2; tail 5; bill 1.9; tarsus 1.8.

Range.—Southern Oceans from Antarctica to about 33° S. lat. Breeds at Kerguelen (*P. l. lessoni*), the Auckland Is., Antipodes I. and Macquarie Is. (*P. l. australis*). *Egg-dates:* Dec.–Jan.

Notes.—Easily recognised by its comparatively large size, white tail, and the large amount of white on the head. The "Muttonbird" of Kerguelen.

45. Antarctic Petrel (*Thalassoica antarctica*)

Adult.—Above brown, the inner secondaries and greater wing-coverts white; upper tail-coverts white, central feathers tipped with brown; tail white, brown at tip; primaries outwardly brown, shafts and inner webs white; throat and sides of neck pale brown; rest of underparts, including under surface of wing except the margin, white; bill blackish; feet yellowish; length 17 ins.; wing 12; tail 4.2; bill 2; tarsus 1.7.

Range.—Antarctic seas from the ice-barrier to 50° S. Breeds on the Antarctic continent. *Egg-dates:* Nov.–Dec.

Notes.—The brown colour, with large patches of white on the wings and tail make this species unmistakable.

VI. MEDIUM-SIZED PETRELS WITH DARK HEAD, CHEQUERED UPPERPARTS AND WHITE UNDERPARTS

46. Pintado Petrel (*Daption capensis*). (*Plates 11 and 13*)

Adult.—Head, chin, back and sides of neck, upperpart of the back, lesser wing-coverts, edge of the under surface of the wings; and primaries, sooty-brown; wing-coverts, back and upper tail-coverts white, each feather tipped with sooty-brown; base of tail white, tip sooty brown; underparts, including under surface of wing except the edge, white; under tail-coverts tipped with sooty brown; beneath the eye a small white streak; bill blackish-brown; feet dark brown; length 14 ins.; wing 10.5; tail 4.0; bill 1.3; tarsus 1.8.

Range.—Southern Oceans, from Antarctica north to Brazil, Angola, Mozambique, Australia, the Marquesas Is. and Peru; occasionally to Mexico and Ceylon, and even to the United States and Europe. Breeds in Antarctica, and at the South Shetlands, South Orkneys, South Georgia, Heard I., the Crozets and Kerguelen (*D. c. capensis*) and at the Snares, Antipodes and Bounty Is. (*D. c. australis*). *Egg-dates:* Nov.–May.

Notes.—The "Cape Pigeon," as this species is called by sailors, is one of the commonest petrels of the southern hemisphere and often follows ships. Its chequered mantle makes it quite unmistakable.

VII. LARGE PETRELS WITH UPPERPARTS THROAT AND FORENECK DARK AND ABDOMEN WHITE

47. Schlegel's Petrel (*Pterodroma incerta*). (*Plates 11 and 15*)

Adult.—Upperparts brown, darker on the rump, paler on the back of the neck, the feathers of the back and wing-coverts edged with a paler shade; throat and foreneck brown, the throat paler; lower neck, breast and abdomen white; under surface of wings dark brown; under tail-coverts brown, central ones mottled with white; bill black; feet yellow, end of webs black; length 17.5–18 ins.; wing 12.5–12.7; tail 5.3–5.5; bill 1.6–2; tarsus 1.7.

Range.—South Atlantic and South Indian Oceans from the Straits of Magellan and coast of Uruguay to the Cape of Good Hope and 96° E. long. north to about 30° S. lat. Breeds at Tristan da Cunha.

Notes.—The brown throat and under tail-coverts and blackish-brown under surface of wings make this species unmistakable. It is common in the South Atlantic.

48. Tahiti Petrel (*Pterodroma rostrata*)

Adult.—Underparts, sides of head, neck and breast, under surface of wings, and tail, deep blackish-brown; chin, throat, upper breast and flanks rather paler brown; abdomen and under tail-coverts white; bill black; legs yellowish flesh-colour, feet black; length 14 ins.; wing 11; tail 4.8; bill 1.4; tarsus 1.8.

Range.—South-western Pacific Ocean. Breeds in New Caledonia (*P. r. trouessarti*) and the Society and Marquesas Is. (*P. r. rostrata*). *Egg-dates*: Oct.

Notes.—This distinctly coloured species, with head, neck, upper breast and under surface of wings dark, is little known and apparently does not range far from its breeding grounds.

VIII. MEDIUM-SIZED PETRELS WITH UPPERPARTS AND ABDOMEN DARK AND THROAT AND BREAST WHITE

49. Peale's Petrel (*Pterodroma inexpectata* = *P. gularis* = *P. scalaris* = *P. fisheri*). (*Plate 11*)

Adult.—Upperparts dark grey; back, scapulars, wings and tail blackish; a black patch round the eye; forehead, throat, breast and under tail-coverts white; face, sides of breast and flanks mottled with grey; abdomen brownish-grey; axillaries black; under surface of wings white with broad black margins; bill black; feet yellow, ends of webs black; length 14 ins.; wing 10; tail 4; bill 1; tarsus 1.2.

Range.—Pacific Ocean, from 68° S. north in the (southern) winter to the Aleutian Is. and Alaska. Breeds in both islands of New Zealand, the Chatham Is. and the Bounty Is. *Egg-dates*: Dec.–Jan.

Notes.—This is the "Rain-bird" of New Zealand. It is easily distinguished by its dark-grey upperparts, the black area round the eye, the large dark patch on the abdomen, and the black undersurface of the wings with narrow white central stripe.

IX. MEDIUM-SIZED PETRELS WITH UPPERPARTS AND BREAST DARK AND UNDERPARTS WHITE

50. Phoenix Petrel (*Pterodroma alba*). (*Plate 17*)

Adult.—Sooty black above; a dark band across the upper breast; under surface of wings dark; throat, lower breast, axillaries, abdomen and under tail-coverts white; flanks mottled with brown; tail wedge-shaped; bill black; feet yellow, end of webs black; length 15 ins.; wing 10.5; tail 4.2; bill 1.5; tarsus 1.3.

Range.—Tropical Pacific Ocean. Breeds at Christmas I., Phoenix Is., Marquesas Is., Tonga Is. and Tuamotu Is. *Egg-dates:* Jan., June–July.

Notes.—This is the only species which invariably has a dark band across the breast, but three larger species, the Herald, Kermadec and Trinidad Petrels, and two smaller species, the Collared and Soft-plumaged Petrels, frequently have a similar dark band. Of these the Herald, Kermadec and Collared Petrels occur in the Pacific Ocean and may be confused with the Phoenix Petrel. The bird named *P. wortheni* from a single specimen captured near the Galápagos Is. is probably of this species, possibly also *P. oliveri*, named from a single bird from the Kermadec Is.

51. Beck's Petrel (*Pterodroma becki*)

Adult.—Head, neck, breast and upperparts blackish-brown; abdomen white, flanks washed with blackish-brown; under tail-coverts white mottled with blackish-brown; bill black; feet particoloured, flesh-colour and black; wing 9.6 ins.; tail 3.9; bill 1.4; tarsus 1.4.

Range.—Only two specimens known, captured at sea north of the Solomon Is.

Notes.—Similar to the Tahiti Petrel in colouring but much smaller with a relatively weaker bill. In size similar to the Phoenix Petrel but browner, with throat dark and larger legs and feet.

X. LARGE PETRELS WITH PALE GREY UPPERPARTS AND WHITE UNDERPARTS

52. Fulmar (*Fulmarus glacialis*). (*Plate 18*)

Adult.—Head, neck and underparts white; a dusky spot in front of the eye; mantle, upper tail-coverts and tail pearl-grey; primaries slate-grey; an obscure pale spot near the tip of the wing (light phase); sometimes the whole plumage is ashy-brown, paler beneath (dark phase); bill grey, greenish or yellow; feet pale flesh-colour or greyish; length 19–20 ins,; wing 12–13.3; tail 4.6–5.3; bill 1.4–1.8; tarsus 2–2.2.

Range.—North Pacific and North Atlantic Oceans and adjacent Arctic seas, south in winter to Japan, Lower California, Massachusetts and France. Breeds in the Kurile Is., Commander Is., Kamchatka and eastern Siberia, Wrangel I., Herald I., St. Lawrence I. and the Pribilof Is. (*F. g. rodgersi*) Baffin Land, north Greenland, Spitzbergen, Franz Josef Land, Novaya Zemblya, Iceland, Norway, the Faroe Is. and the British Is. (*F. g. glacialis*). *Egg-dates:* May–Aug.

Notes.—The commonest oceanic bird of northern seas. The dark phase is unlike any other seabird. The commoner light phase has a superficial resemblance to a gull but lacks any black tip to the wings. Its usual gliding flight, rarely interrupted by a few flaps of the wings, at once distinguishes it from any gull, and in light airs, when it flaps much more frequently, the stiffness with which it holds its wings is still distinctive.

53. Silver-grey Petrel (*Fulmarus glacialoides*)

Adult.—Upper surface and tail pale grey, paler on the head and back of the neck; wing-quills slaty-black; a light mark near the tip of the wing; a dark spot in front of the eye; forehead, cheeks and under surface, including under wing-coverts, white; bill pinkish or yellowish, tip and a

47

line down middle, black; feet pale flesh-colour; length 18 ins.; wing 12.6; tail 5.1; bill 2.1; tarsus 1.8.

Range.—Southern Oceans from Antarctica north to St. Helena, New Zealand and Peru. Breeds in Antarctica, the S. Shetlands, S. Orkneys, Bouvet I. and Kerguelen. *Egg-dates:* Nov.–Dec.

Notes.—This is the southern representative of the Fulmar, which it closely resembles in colouration and habits.

XI. SMALL PETRELS WITH PALE GREY UPPERPARTS AND WHITE UNDERPARTS

(Stejneger's and Cook's Petrels are darker grey above than the members of this group.)

54. Blue Petrel (*Halobaena caerulea*)

Adult.—Back of the neck, sides of the chest, back, wings and tail grey, the secondaries, scapulars and six middle tail-feathers tipped with white, the two outer tail-feathers almost wholly white and the tail square; forehead, cheeks, throat, centre of the chest and all the under surface white; narrow space beneath the eye, shoulders and the outer webs of the first primaries deep brownish-black; bill dull blackish-brown, with a stripe of blue-grey along the lower mandible; feet blue, webs flesh-white traversed by red veins; length 11 ins.; wing 8.5; tail 3.6; bill 1.4; tarsus 1.3.

Range.—Southern Oceans from Antarctica north to 40° S. and occasionally to Tristan da Cunha, the Cape of Good Hope, New Zealand and Fiji. Breeds at the Falkland Is., Heard I., the Crozets, Kerguelen and Macquarie I. *Egg-dates:* Oct.–Nov.

Notes.—In colouration this species closely resembles the Prions from which it may be distinguished by its square, white-tipped tail.

55. Broad-billed Prion (*Pachyptila vittata*)

Adult.—Upper surface delicate blue-grey; space round eyes and ear-coverts, edge of shoulders, scapulars, outer primaries and tips of middle tail-feathers black; lores, line over eye and under surface white, stained with blue on flanks and under tail-coverts; bill very broad at base and with large lamellae on the sides of the palate, greyish-blue, with black tip and a black line along the side of the lower mandible; feet light blue; tail wedge-shaped; length 12 ins.; wing 7.6; tail 3.8; bill 1.5 long, 0.7–0.8 broad at base; tarsus 1.3.

Range.—Southern Oceans between 60° S. and 40° S., occasionally north to Madagascar and Reunion. Breeds at Tristan da Cunha, Gough I., S. W. New Zealand, Stewart I., the Chatham Is. (*P. v. vittata*) and St. Paul I. (*P. v. macgillivrayi*). *Egg-dates:* Sept.–Oct.

56. Salvin's Prion (*Pachyptila salvini*)

Adult.—Similar to the Broad-billed Prion but smaller, with bill bluer and narrower.

Range.—Southern Indian Ocean and coasts of southern Australia and New Zealand. Breeds at Marion I. (*P. s. salvini*) and the Crozet Is. (*P. s. crozeti*). *Egg-dates:* Nov.–Dec.

57. Dove Prion (*Pachyptila desolata*)

Adult.—Similar to the Broad-billed Prion with bill equally long but decidedly narrower, 0.5–0.6 in. broad at base.

Range.—Southern Oceans between 66° S. and 35° S., occasionally north to the Malay Archipelago. Breeds at Cape Denison on the Antarctic continent and at Kerguelen and Macquarie I. (*P. d. desolata*) at Heard I., the Auckland Is. (*P. d. alter*) and at South Georgia (*P. d. banksi*). *Egg -dates:* Dec.–Feb.

58. Thin-billed Prion (*Pachyptila belcheri*)

Adult.—Similar to the Dove Prion but with bill scarcely enlarged at the base, 0.3 in. wide.

Range.—Off the coasts of Patagonia, Argentina, the Falkland Is., Australia and New Zealand. Breeds at Kerguelen and the Falkland Is. *Egg-dates:* Nov.–Dec.

59. Fairy Prion (*Pachyptila turtur-*= *P. ariel*)

Adult.—Similar to the Dove Prion but paler on the crown, more white on the face and with a broader dark band on the tail; bill shorter and stouter, 0.9 in. long, 0.4 in. wide at base.

Range.—Southern Oceans between 60° S. and 35° S., occasionally north to Madeira. Breeds on islands in Bass Strait, New Zealand and the Chatham Is. (*P. t. turtur*), and at Stewart I., New Zealand, and Akaroa, Chatham Is. (*P. t. fallai*). *Egg-dates:* Oct.–Dec.

60. Thick-billed Prion (*Pachyptila crassirostris*)

Adult.—Similar to the Fairy Prion but with a much stouter bill.

Range.—New Zealand seas and southern Indian Ocean. Breeds at Heard I., Kerguelen and Antipodes I. (*P. c. eatoni*), the Bounty Is. (*P. c. crassirostris*) and the Chatham Is. (*P. c. pyramidalis*). *Egg-dates:* Nov.–Dec.

Notes.—The six species of Prion cannot be distinguished at sea, hardly differing except in the shape of the bill. From the Blue Petrel they differ in their wedge-shaped tails with black tips to the central feathers. They are commonly seen in flocks, flying swiftly, alternately showing their white breasts and grey backs. When their upper surfaces only are visible they almost disappear against the background of the sea. To seamen they are known as "Whale-birds" or "Ice-birds."

XII. MEDIUM-SIZED PETRELS WITH PLUMAGE ENTIRELY WHITE

61. Snow Petrel (*Pagodroma nivea*)

Adult.—Pure white; bill black; feet dark grey; length 14–16 ins.; wing 9.8–11; tail 4.3–5.1; bill 1.4–1.6; tarsus 1.3–1.5.

Range.—Antarctic Seas north to 50° S. lat. Breeds in Antarctica, the South Shetlands, South Orkneys and South Georgia. *Egg-dates:* Nov.–Dec.

Notes.—Snow Petrels are almost confined to the Antarctic ice-barrier and have the most southerly range of any birds except the Emperor Penguin and McCormick's Skua.

CHAPTER III

~~~~~~~~~~~~~~~~~~~~~~~~~~~

Storm-Petrels

(Order *Procellariiformes:* Family *Hydrobatidae* =
Thalassidromidae)

~~~~~~~~~~~~~~~~~~~~~~~~~~~

THE STORM-PETRELS are the smallest of sea-birds,
ranking in size with such land-birds as starlings,
swallows and martins. They are commonly known to
seamen as "Mother Carey's Chickens," Mother Carey
being a corruption of "Mater Cara," an appellation
of the Blessed Virgin Mary. They are characterised
by their rather slender hooked beaks, on the upper
surface of which the nostrils open within a single
median tube. Their slender legs are frequently very
long in proportion to the size of the bird, and the toes
are united by webs. Their wings are fairly long but
not so narrow in proportion as those of the larger
Petrels and Albatrosses, and their tails are usually
either square or forked. Most of them are dusky in
colouring, a few grey; many have a patch of white at
the base of the tail, and some have white areas on the
under surface. All species have the bill and legs black,
but in a few the webs are partly yellow.

In structure Storm-Petrels do not differ very much
from the larger Petrels described in the last chapter
and some authorities do not consider them entitled
to rank as a separate family. Sometimes the short-
legged forms are grouped with the larger petrels,
whilst the long-legged species are separated. Recent

researches have however tended to show that the short-legged and long-legged Storm-Petrels are more closely related than was formerly supposed.

In their habits the Storm-Petrels do not differ greatly from their larger relatives. In the breeding season they congregate on small islands, and either excavate burrows in soft soil or beneath matted vegetation, or utilise natural crevices among rocks or the burrows of other birds. For some days before the egg is laid both birds are found together in their burrow but later they take it in turns to incubate. The single, oval, white egg is rather frequently marked, especially at the larger end, with small red, purple or black spots. The young bird is densely covered with grey or brownish down. When full-fed it is considerably larger than its parents, which then leave it, and when the feathers have replaced the down the young fledgling follows them to sea.

Like those of their larger relatives which breed in burrows Storm-Petrels are nocturnal in their habits when on the breeding ground. During the daytime thousands may be brooding just below the surface on an island but no sound indicates their presence. After dark, however, when the birds from sea return to relieve their mates or to feed their young, various twittering, crooning or cooing notes are uttered. Sometimes also, at sea, these usually silent birds utter chirping or squealing notes when congregated to feed on some unusually bountiful supply, such as the fat from a dead whale or seal or the refuse from a ship's galley. Any oily food appears to attract them specially but their normal diet is no doubt composed of small plankton organisms obtained from the surface of the sea.

In spite of their association with the Queen of Heaven, the appearance of Mother Carey's Chickens round a ship is regarded by superstitious mariners as foreboding a storm. It seems clear that they are more often to be seen about a ship in stormy weather, but this is probably because the passage of a ship commonly leaves an area of calmer water in which it is easier for them to obtain food. Their habit of flying to and fro across the wake of a steamer is perhaps chiefly owing to the fact that the propeller kills many small organisms which then float up to the surface, though at times they will also pick up some of the smaller fragments of galley refuse.

When flying close over the surface, especially in calm weather and when feeding, Storm-Petrels often assist their progress or support themselves on the surface by patting the water with their feet. Generally both feet are brought down together and the birds spring along the surface in a series of hops, keeping their wings spread; less frequently the feet are used alternately so that they may be said to run or walk on the water, supporting the supposed origin of their name from St. Peter; occasionally one foot alone is used, the other leg being trailed backwards. On land their legs are not strong enough to support them and the wings have to be used to assist their progress.

The flight of Storm-Petrels is usually very erratic and has been compared to the flight of butterflies, bats, martins or swifts. Sometimes they seem to behave almost exactly like insectivorous birds catching flying insects, but there is no evidence that insects ever form part of their diet. They do not often settle on the water, but when they do they float buoyantly. Sometimes they dive from the air and obtain food a short depth below the surface, but this is an unusual occurrence.

For purposes of identification Storm-Petrels may be arranged in the following colour-groups:—

I. Mainly or entirely sooty-black, above and below. (Species 1–6.)
II. Mainly or entirely sooty-black, except for a white patch on the rump. (Species 7–13.)

III. Mainly sooty-black above; largely white below.
(Species 14–18.)

IV. Partly or entirely grey above; grey, partly white
or entirely white below. (Species 19–21.)

I. STORM-PETRELS MAINLY OR ENTIRELY SOOTY-BLACK, ABOVE AND BELOW

(Besides the six species described below, Bulwer's Petrel,
the smallest member of the preceding family is entirely
black.)

1. Least Storm-Petrel (*Halocyptena microsoma*)

Adult.—Dark sooty black, under surface browner, greater
wing-coverts paler; tail wedge-shaped; length 5.5–6 ins.;
wing 4.6–5.1; tail 2–2.3; bill 0.4–0.6; tarsus 0.8–0.9.

Range.—Pacific coast of tropical America from Lower
California to Ecuador. Breeds on San Benito Is., Lower
California. *Egg-dates:* July–Sept.

Notes.—As its name implies this is the smallest of the
Petrels. It is also the only Storm-Petrel with a wedge-
shaped tail, in this feature resembling Bulwer's Petrel,
which is, however, twice its size.

2. Ashy Storm-Petrel (*Oceanodroma homochroa*)

Adult.—Sooty black, edges of wing-coverts paler, under
wing-coverts edged with whitish; tail forked; length 7.5
ins.; wing 5.3; tail 3.1; bill 0.7; tarsus 0.9.

Range.—Coast of California. Breeds at the Farallon and
Sta. Barbara Is. *Egg-dates:* May–July.

Notes.—Larger than the Least Storm-Petrel, from which
it also differs in having a forked tail. Smaller than the
Black Storm-Petrel and with much shorter legs. Very
similar to Swinhoe's Storm-Petrel but with shorter wings
and the under wing-coverts with whitish edges.

3. Swinhoe's Storm-Petrel (*Oceanodroma monorhis*)

Adult.—Upper parts sooty brown, forehead and upper
wing-coverts paler; upper tail-coverts in the American race

grey, the lateral ones frequently white; under parts, including under surface of wings, sooty grey; tail forked; length 6.8–7.6 ins.; wing 5.6–6; tail 2.9; bill 0.6–0.8; tarsus 0.8–0.9.

Range.—North Pacific Ocean from Japan and California south to Java and the Galápagos Is. Breeds on islands off Formosa (*O. m. monorhis*) and off Lower California (*O. m. socorroensis*). *Egg-dates:* June–Sept.

Notes.—Nearly related to Leach's Storm-Petrel, of which some authorities regard it as a race. The Asiatic form appears always to have the upper tail-coverts dark, but in the American form they are light and the lateral ones are often white.

4. Sooty Storm-Petrel (*Oceanodroma markhami*). (*Plate 19*)

Adult.—Sooty brown; face, wing-coverts, lower rump and under surface of wings somewhat paler; wing-quills sooty black; tail deeply forked; length 9–10 ins.; wing 7–7.5; tail 3.7–4.4; bill 0.7–0.9; tarsus 0.9–1.2.

Range.—Pacific Ocean from Japan to the Hawaiian Is. and seas off the west coast of Central and South America. Breeds at the Hawaiian Is. (*O. m. owstoni*). *Egg-dates:* Jan.

Notes.—A large species with a long forked tail. The southern race (*O. m. markhami*) is common off the coasts of Peru and Chile but its breeding grounds are unknown. The northern race has been called *O. fuliginosa* and *O. tristrami*, but it is not certain that the birds to which these names were originally applied were of this species.

5. Black Storm-Petrel (*Loomelania melania*)

Adult.—Sooty black; underparts somewhat paler; upper wing-coverts pale greyish sooty brown; tail strongly forked; length 9 ins.; wing 7; tail 3.5; bill 0.8; tarsus 1.2.

Range.—Eastern Pacific Ocean from California south to Peru. Breeds on islands off the coast of Lower California. *Egg-dates:* May–Sept.

Notes.—Decidedly larger than the Ashy Storm-Petrel and somewhat smaller than the Sooty Storm-Petrel. Distinguished from both by its relatively much longer legs.

6. Samoan Storm-Petrel (*Nesofregetta moestissima*)

Adult.—Sooty black; wings and tail rather blacker; tail deeply forked; length 9.5 ins.; wing 9.1; tail 4.2; bill 0.7; tarsus 1.9.

Range.—Samoa Is.

Notes.—Only known from a single specimen, but the long wings and very long flattened legs at once distinguish it from the other dark Storm-Petrels.

II. STORM-PETRELS MAINLY OR ENTIRELY SOOTY-BLACK, EXCEPT FOR A WHITE PATCH ON THE RUMP

(In addition to the seven species described below, Swinhoe's Storm-Petrel sometimes has white patches at the sides of the rump.)

7. British Storm-Petrel (*Hydrobates pelagicus*)

Adult.—Sooty black, slightly browner below; a whitish band across the wing above, and a small patch of whitish on the under wing-coverts; upper tail-coverts white, longer feathers with black tips; under tail-coverts mixed with white; tail nearly square; length 5.5–7.5 ins.; wing 4.1–4.9; tail 2.0–2.5; bill 0.4–0.5; tarsus 0.8–0.9.

Range.—Eastern North Atlantic and Mediterranean Sea, in winter south to the Red Sea and west coast of Africa, occasionally to Greenland, Labrador, Newfoundland, Nova Scotia, the Cape of Good Hope and Zanzibar. Breeds in Iceland, Norway, the British Is., Brittany and the Mediterranean countries east to Malta. *Egg-dates:* May–Oct.

Notes.—Rather smaller and darker than the Madeiran, Leach's and Wilson's Storm-Petrels. From the two former it is also distinguished by its square tail and shorter wings, from the latter by its shorter legs and black feet. None of these features are very obvious at sea unless the species are seen together, but the weaker, more fluttering flight is a further aid to recognition, and the white patch below the wing is diagnostic.

8. Galápagos Storm-Petrel (*Oceanodroma tethys*)

Adult.—Sooty-black; upper wing-coverts paler; upper tail-coverts white; tail very slightly forked; length 6.4–6.7 ins.; wing 5.1–5.7; tail 2.1–2.6; bill 0.4–0.6; tarsus 0.8–0.9.

Range.—Pacific Ocean adjacent to west coast of America, from Lower California to northern Chile. Breeds in the Galápagos Is. (*O. t. tethys*) and on islands off the coast of Peru (*O. t. kelsalli*). *Egg-dates:* May–June.

Notes.—Resembles the British Storm-Petrel and may be distinguished from similar birds by the same features, and by the form of the white patch on the rump, which is triangular.

9. Madeiran Storm-Petrel (*Oceanodroma castro*)

Adult.—Sooty black, wing coverts slightly browner; upper tail-coverts white with black tips; forming an even broad white band across the rump; bases of outer tail-feathers white; flanks and outer under tail-coverts partly white; tail somewhat forked; length 7.1–8.1 ins.; wing 5.6–6.5; tail 2.5–3.6; bill 0.6–0.7; tarsus 0.7–1.

Range.—Eastern North Pacific and Eastern Atlantic, near its breeding grounds, occasionally to the United States, England, Denmark and Japan. Breeds in the Hawaiian Is. (*O. c. cryptoleucura*), Cocos I. and the Galápagos Is. (*O. c. bangsi*), Madeira, the Azores, the Salvage Is., Cape Verde Is., Ascension and St. Helena (*O. c. castro*). *Egg-dates:* Throughout the year.

Notes.—Larger than the British and Galápagos Storm-Petrels and with tail distinctly forked, though less markedly than in Leach's Storm-Petrel. From the latter it also differs in the even band across the rump and the greater amount of white on the flanks and under tail-coverts. From Wilson's Storm-Petrel it differs in its longer wings and shorter legs.

10. Leach's Storm-Petrel (*Oceanodroma leucorhoa*). (*Plates 19 and 20*).

Adult.—Upper parts sooty black, wings and tail darker; wing-coverts greyish-brown; upper tail-coverts white, centre feathers largely sooty; underparts sooty-brown; a few white feathers on flanks; tail deeply forked; length 8.0–8.8 ins.; wing 5.6–6.5; tail 2.4–3.6; bill 0.5–0.7; tarsus 0.7–1.

Range.—Bering Sea, North Pacific and North Atlantic Oceans, south in winter to Japan, Mexico, Brazil and Sierra Leone, occasionally to New Zealand, the Galápagos Is. and the Cape of Good Hope. Breeds on the Kurile Is., Commander Is., Aleutian Is., coasts of Alaska, Maine, Nova Scotia, Newfoundland, South Greenland, Iceland, Faroe Is. and British Is. (*O. l. leucorhoa*), coasts of southeastern Alaska, British Columbia, Washington and California (*O. l. beali*), and Guadalupe I., Lower California (*O. l. kaedingi*). *Egg-dates:* May–Aug.

Notes.—About the size of the Madeiran Storm-Petrel, but the tail is more deeply forked, and the white area on the rump is nearly interrupted in the middle, widening on each side. The wings are noticeably longer than in the British and Wilson's Storm-Petrels and the flight correspondingly more rapid and darting.

11. Guadalupe Storm-Petrel (*Oceanodroma macrodactyla*)

Adult.—Upperparts slaty-black; wing-coverts greyish brown; upper tail-coverts white, the feathers with very broad dusky tips; underparts dark greyish-brown; under wing-coverts light greyish-brown; tail deeply forked; length 8.4 ins.; wing 6.4; tail 3.9; bill 0.6; tarsus 0.9.

Range.—Pacific coast of Lower California. Breeds at Guadalupe I. *Egg-dates:* March.

Notes.—Very similar to Leach's Storm-Petrel but paler under the wings. Probably extinct.

12. Wilson's Storm-Petrel (*Oceanites oceanicus = O. wilsoni*). (Plates 19 and 21)

Adult.—Upperparts sooty-black, darkest on wings and tail; wing-coverts greyish margined with whitish; longer upper tail-coverts white, shorter ones marked with sooty-black; underparts somewhat lighter than back; flanks and

59

under tail-coverts partly white; tail square; inner portion of the web between the toes bright yellow; length 7.0–7.5 ins.; wing 5.3–6.2; tail 2.6–2.8; bill 0.5; tarsus 1.3–1.5.

Range.—Southern Oceans, north in the (southern) winter to California, Labrador, the British Is., Arabia, India, New Guinea and Japan. Breeds in Antarctica and the South Shetlands (*O. o. exasperatus*), islets off Cape Horn and the Falkland Is. (*O. o. magellanicus*), the South Orkneys and South Georgia (*O. o. oceanicus*), and Kerguelen and Heard I. (*O. o. parvus*). *Egg-dates:* Dec.–Feb.

Notes.—The most widespread and common of the Storm-Petrels. The square tail and pale band in the wing with the very long legs and yellow webs are distinctive. In flight when the legs are extended backwards the feet project beyond the middle feathers of the tail.

13. Elliot's Storm-Petrel (*Oceanites gracilis*)

Adult.—Similar to Wilson's Storm-Petrel but smaller and has the middle of the abdomen white; length 5.8 ins.; wing 5.0; tail 2.2; bill 0.6; tarsus 1.

Range.—Pacific coast of South America. Breeds at the Galápagos Is. (*O. g. galapagoensis*). *Egg-dates:* Undoubtedly June–July, but it has not actually been found nesting.

Notes.—The white patch on the abdomen is distinctive but difficult to observe at sea. The breeding place of the southern race (*O. g. gracilis*) is unknown.

III. STORM-PETRELS MAINLY OR ENTIRELY SOOTY-BLACK ABOVE, LARGELY WHITE BELOW

(In addition to the five species described below, the British Storm-Petrel has some white under the wing, and Elliot's Storm-Petrel some white on the abdomen.)

14. Hornby's Storm-Petrel (*Oceanodroma hornbyi*). (Plate 19)

Adult.—Upper surface dusky brown, paler and greyer on the upper back; hind neck greyish white, forming with the white throat a cervical collar; top and sides of head black; forehead, and under surface white; a dark band across the breast; wings black, coverts greyish sooty; under wing-coverts pale greyish-sooty; tail dusky brown, deeply forked; length 8.8 ins.; wing 6.7; tail 3.9; bill 0.9; tarsus 0.9.

Range.—West coast of South America from Ecuador to Chile (32° S.). Breeds in the Chilean Andes.

Notes.—The white collar and dark band across the breast distinguish this species.

15. White-throated Storm-Petrel (*Nesofregetta albigularis*)

Adult.—Sooty-black, the greater wing-coverts somewhat paler; upper tail-coverts short, white, forming a narrow band across the rump; a broad sooty band across the chest; throat, lower breast and abdomen white, sometimes with black streaks on the flanks, occasionally with black streaks on the throat, breast and abdomen; under tail-coverts white with sooty tips; under surface of wings sooty white; tail long, deeply forked; the legs and toes remarkably flattened; length 8.7 ins.; wing 7.8; tail 3.7–4.2; bill 0.6–0.8; tarsus 1.6–1.7.

Range.—Pacific Ocean. Breeds at Christmas I., the Phoenix Is., Marquesas Is., Fiji Is., and New Hebrides. *Egg-dates:* Jan.–Feb., June, Sept.–Oct.

Notes.—Resembles Hornby's Storm-Petrel but lacks the white collar, has a white band on the rump and much longer legs.

16. Striped Storm-Petrel (*Fregetta lineata*)

Adult.—Head black; upper parts dark sooty-black; breast somewhat lighter sooty; upper tail-coverts white; abdomen and under tail-coverts white striped with sooty-brown; greater under wing-coverts whitish ash; tail almost square; length 8 ins.; wing 6.5; tail 2.9; bill 0.5; tarsus 1.5.

Range.—South Pacific Ocean. Said to breed on Upolu, Samoan group.

Notes.—A very rare species only known from four specimens. Rather larger than the White-bellied Storm-Petrel, with the whole breast dark and bolder dark streaks on the abdomen.

17. White-bellied Storm-Petrel (*Fregetta grallaria = F. leucogaster = F. segethi*). (*Plate 19*)

Adult.—Head and neck deep sooty-black; back greyish-black, each feather margined with white; wings and tail black; upper tail-coverts, lower breast, abdomen, inner under wing-coverts and under tail-coverts white; flanks sometimes streaked with black; the longer under tail-coverts broadly tipped with sooty; tail almost square; length 7.2–7.7 ins.; wing 6.5; tail 3.0; bill 0.6; tarsus 1.5.

Range.—Southern Oceans, north to the tropics. Breeds at Lord Howe I. (*F. g. insularis*), Rapa, Austral Group (*F. g. titan*), and Masatierra, Juan Fernandez group (*F. g. grallaria*), also at Tristan da Cunha and Gough I. *Egg-dates:* Dec.–Feb.

Notes.—Rather smaller than the Striped Storm-Petrel with considerably more white below, and the dark stripes on the abdomen, when present, not so bold.

18. Black-bellied Storm-Petrel (*Fregetta tropica*). (*Plate 19*)

Adult.—Sooty-black, darkest on head and primaries, wing-coverts rather paler; upper tail-coverts, flanks, sides of the abdomen and middle of under surface of wings white; frequently some white feathers on the throat; tail almost square; length 7.5–8.2 ins.; wing 6.1; tail 2.7; bill 0.6; tarsus 1.5.

Range.—Southern Oceans, north to the tropics. Breeds at the South Shetlands, South Orkneys, South Georgia, Crozet Is., Kerguelen and the Auckland, Antipodes and Bounty Is. *Egg-dates:* Dec.

Notes.—The large white areas on the sides of the abdomen, which leave only a longitudinal dark band in the centre, at once distinguish this species, but are not always easy to observe.

IV. STORM-PETRELS PARTLY OR ENTIRELY GREY ABOVE, GREY, PARTLY WHITE OR ENTIRELY WHITE BELOW

19. Fork-tailed Storm-Petrel (*Oceanodroma furcata*)

Adult.—Pearly-grey, wing-coverts edged with greyish-white; area below eye black; under surface pale grey, nearly white on throat and under tail-coverts; under wing-coverts and axillaries greyish black, edged with white; tail forked, grey, darker towards tip, edged with white; length 8.0 ins.; wing 6.2; tail 3.4; bill 0.8; tarsus 1.0.

Range.—Kotzebue Sound, Bering Sea and the North Pacific Ocean, south to Japan and California. Breeds on the Kurile Is., Commander Is., Aleutian Is., coasts of southern Alaska, Washington, Oregon and northern California. *Egg-dates:* May–July.

Notes.—A common species in the North Pacific, at once distinguished by its light grey plumage, nearly white beneath.

20. Grey-backed Storm-Petrel (*Garrodia nereis*)

Adult.—Upperparts slaty-black, darkest on the head, and becoming lighter on the rump and upper tail-coverts, which are silvery-grey; tail-feathers silvery-grey, broadly tipped with black; median wing-coverts ashy-grey, these as well as some feathers of the back and upper tail-coverts narrowly edged with white on the tips; head, neck and chest sooty-grey; underparts from breast to under tail-coverts, and inner under wing-coverts white; flanks streaked with grey; tail almost square; length 6.5–7.2 ins.; wing 5.2; tail 2.5; bill 0.5–0.6; tarsus 1.2.

Range.—Southern Oceans. Breeds at South Georgia, the Falkland Is., Gough I., Kerguelen, the Chatham Is., Antipodes I. and Auckland Is. *Egg-dates:* Nov.–Jan.

Notes.—Readily distinguished from the White-faced Storm-Petrel by its dark breast and smaller size.

21. White-faced Storm-Petrel (*Pelagodroma marina*). (*Plate 19*)

Adult.—Forehead, face, line over the eye, and all the under surface, including under wing-coverts, white; crown and nape, a broad patch beneath the eye, and the ear-coverts, slate-colour; sides of the chest, back of the neck and upper part of the back dark grey, gradually passing into the dark brown of the back and wings; upper tail-coverts light grey; primaries and tail black; tail almost square; webs between the toes yellow; length 8 ins.; wing 5.5–6.5; tail 2.5–3.1; bill 0.7–0.9; tarsus 1.6–1.8.

Range.—Atlantic, Indian and South Pacific Oceans north in the Pacific to Cocos I. off Costa Rica. Breeds at the Salvage Is., Canary Is., and Cape Verde Is. (*P. m. hypoleuca*), Tristan da Cunha (*P. m. marina*), western and southern coasts of Australia (*P. m. dulciae*), New Zealand, the Auckland Is., Chatham Is. and Kermadec Is. (*P. m. maoriana*). *Egg-dates:* March–April (northern hemisphere), Oct.–Dec. (southern hemisphere).

Notes.—Distinguished from all other species by its entirely white under surface.

CHAPTER IV

Diving-Petrels

(Order *Procellariiformes:* Family *Pelecanoididae*)

THE SMALL BIRDS which constitute this family are confined to the southern hemisphere where they have a somewhat remarkable range. Between the latitudes of 35° S. and 55° S. they occur from South America through the southern Atlantic and Indian Oceans to the seas of southern Australia and New Zealand, but they are not found in the corresponding latitudes of the South Pacific between the Chatham Islands and the coast of Chile. One species ranges northward into the tropics on the west coast of South America in the cold waters of the Humboldt current.

The four species of Diving-Petrels now recognised have a close resemblance to one another and a remarkable superficial likeness to the Little Auk or Dovekie of Arctic seas. Their general colour is black above and white below. They have short, stout necks, comparatively small wings and short legs placed far back. Their legs are very much compressed and their toes webbed. Their bills are short, broad at the base and hooked at the tip. The nostrils open upwards side by side at the base of the upper mandible. Their openings are surrounded by short vertical tubes, and their passages are partly divided by a flap projecting from the side. Between the diverging sides of the lower mandible there is a distensible pouch, only covered with feathers towards the throat.

Diving-Petrels are sometimes met with at considerable distances from land but are more frequent near the coasts and islands on which they breed. They are usually found singly or in small scattered flocks, resting on the surface of the water, or diving for their food, which consists of small fishes, crustacea and other marine organisms. When disturbed by a passing boat they sometimes dive, but more often flutter along the surface of the water using their feet to assist them to rise. Once clear of the surface they usually fly swiftly and straight for a few hundred yards close over the waves, with rapidly beating wings, then suddenly drop down into the water and promptly dive. Occasionally they fly higher and travel longer distances. Their wings are used beneath the water as in the air, and not infrequently they emerge from the water flying or fly through a wave.

The Diving-Petrels breed in burrows which they scratch out in the soil or under rocks on islands, sometimes at a considerable elevation and some miles inland. They lay a single pure white egg. Throughout their period on land they are nocturnal, excavating their burrows and feeding their chicks at night, though of course when incubating the egg one bird remains in the burrow during the daytime. They are comparatively silent birds, but when breeding utter croaking notes like those of frogs or mewing sounds like those made by cats.

The four species are so similar that only one, the Magellan Diving-Petrel, can be distinguished by its colouring. The Peruvian Diving-Petrel is decidedly larger than its southern relatives. To separate the remaining species it is necessary to examine the bill, the shape of which is diagnostic. As the breeding ranges of the different species hardly overlap the locality in which a bird is seen is generally sufficient clue to its identity, unless it is far from any coast.

The breeding ranges of the different species tend to lie in concentric circles round the Antarctic continent. Most southerly are the Georgian and Magellan species with breeding grounds about 55° S. The former is remarkable in that it is only known to breed at two island groups, both in this latitude but almost exactly on opposite sides of the Antarctic continent. The Common species has a much wider latitudinal range breeding on islands between 35° S. and 52° S. It is probable that the temperature of the water is the actual controlling factor and this of course is only partly dependent on latitude.

1. Common Diving-Petrel (*Pelecanoides urinatrix*)

Adult.—Upperparts black; scapulars dark grey with a whitish terminal bar; underparts white; sides of neck and breast dark grey; foreneck sometimes mottled with grey forming an indistinct collar; under wing-coverts whitish, more or less washed with grey; axillaries, sides, flanks and thighs grey; bill black, the sides of the lower mandible nearly parallel for the greater part of their length, converging sharply towards the tip; feet cobalt-blue, webs bluish-white or blackish; length 6.4–10 ins.; wing 4.1–5.2; tail 1.3–1.8; bill 0.5–0.7 long, 0.25–0.35 wide at base; tarsus 0.9–1.1.

Range.—Southern Oceans from the coasts of South America eastward to New Zealand seas, between 35° S. and 55° S. Breeds at the Falkland Is. (*P. u. berard*), Tristan da Cunha and Gough I. (*P. u. dacunhae*), islands of Bass Strait, coasts of Victoria, Tasmania and New Zealand (*P. u. urinatrix*), Chatham Is., Bounty Is., Antipodes I., Snares I. and Auckland Is. (*P. u. chathamensis*), Crozet Is., Marion I., Heard I., Kerguelen and Auckland Is. (*P. u. exsul*). *Egg-dates:* July–Jan.

Notes.—This species appears to travel further from its breeding grounds than other members of the family, the Falkland race visiting the coast of Argentina. A form (*P. u. coppingeri*) occurs on the southern coast of Chile, between Ancud and Trinidad Channel, whose breeding area is not known. The Common Diving-Petrel has a more northerly range than the other species, except the Peruvian, but it meets the Magellan Diving-Petrel on the Chilean coast at Trinidad Channel and the Georgian Diving-Petrel at Kerguelen.

2. Georgian Diving-Petrel (*Pelecanoides georgicus*). (Plate 22)

Adult.—Similar in colour to the Common Diving-Petrel, but somewhat smaller; bill black, proportionately wider at the base and tapering more sharply than in other species; feet cobalt-blue, webs black; length 7–8.4 ins; wing 4.1–4.8; tail 1.3–1.7; bill 0.5–0.6 long, 0.35–0.4 wide at base; tarsus 0.8–1.

Range.—Seas adjacent to South Georgia, Kerguelen, Heard I., Auckland Is. and Macquarie Is., where it breeds. *Egg-dates:* Nov.–Feb.

Notes.—Inhabits islands south of the range of the other insular species, but meets the Common Diving-Petrel at Kerguelen, Heard I. and the Auckland Is. It can only be distinguished by the form of its bill.

3. Magellan Diving-Petrel (*Pelecanoides magellani*)

Adult.—Similar in size and general colouring to the Common Diving-Petrel but the wings are proportionately longer; feathers of mantle (in fresh plumage) have white tips; a conspicuous white patch on each side of the neck forms an interrupted collar; the foreneck is always pure white (never crossed by a mottled band); bill blackish, comparatively long and slender; feet bluish, webs black; length 7.5–8.8 ins.; wing 4.7–5.2; tail 1.3–1.7; bill 0.6–0.7 long, 0.35–0.4 wide at base; tarsus 1–1.2.

Range.—Coasts and channels of southern Chile, Patagonia and Tierra del Fuego, from Cape Horn north to Chiloé I. and Port Desire. Breeds on the coasts of the Straits of Magellan. *Egg-dates:* Dec.

Notes.—The common species of the Straits of Magellan, distinguished by the shape of the bill, but most readily identified by the white half-collar on the sides of the neck. Its range is more southerly than that of the Common Diving-Petrel but they meet at Trinidad Channel on the coast of Chile and perhaps also on the coast of Patagonia.

4. Peruvian Diving-Petrel (*Pelecanoides garnoti*)

Adult.—Similar in colouring to the Common Diving-Petrel but decidedly larger; the band on the foreneck absent or only represented by faint grey mottling; bill black, comparatively long and slender; feet bluish, webs black; length 8.2–9.3 ins.; wing 5.1–5.6; tail 1.3–1.7; bill 0.7–0.9 long, 0.35–0.4 wide at base; tarsus 1.2–1.3.

Range.—Coasts of Peru and Chile, from Payta to Coronel. Breeds on islands off the coast. *Egg-dates:* Throughout the year.

Notes.—The largest species, with a much more northern range than any other. It appears to be strictly limited to the cool inshore waters of the Humboldt Current, and was formerly of some importance as a guano bird.

CHAPTER V

Gulls

(Order *Charadriiformes*: Family *Laridae*)

THE MEMBERS of this family are long-winged sea-
birds of moderate or fairly large size, ranging in
length of body from one foot to two feet six inches.
They have short necks and rather short legs with
webbed feet, which are sometimes hidden in the feathers when they are flying, but more often carried under
the tail. Their bills are slender and tapering in the
smaller forms, but in some of the larger species they
are stout and wedge-shaped, the upper mandible being almost hooked at the tip and the lower mandible
having a conspicuous blunt angle, often marked with
a red spot, near the tip. The nostrils open on the sides
of the upper mandible nearly half way to the tip, the
openings being oval slits without any covering. This
feature at once distinguishes them from Petrels and
Albatrosses, which have tubular nostrils. The tails of
most species of gulls are nearly square at the end, but
in two the tail is decidedly forked and in one it is
wedge-shaped.

In adult plumage nearly all gulls have the body and
tail white and the wings and back grey or black. In
many species the head is white, but a number acquire
a dark hood which is worn during the breeding season. Young gulls in some cases do not differ very

greatly from their parents, but in the majority of species the young are partly or entirely dusky in colour. A few adult gulls are also dusky, but immature birds may almost always be recognised as such by the fact that their dark plumage is mottled, streaked or spotted with lighter shades. Gulls appear to be long-lived birds and they take rather a long period to reach maturity. The smaller species attain their full plumage in the second year but the larger species take three or even four years in the process. The gradual changes from the dark plumage to the light adult plumage are puzzling and make the identification of young gulls a matter of difficulty.

As in other sea-birds the plumage of gulls mainly presents black, grey, brown and white tints, but a number of species have the white parts more or less tinged with a beautiful rosy colour in the breeding season. The bills and feet of gulls may be black, brown, greenish, yellow, pink, red or combinations of these colours, and there is sometimes a bright yellow or red ring round the eye.

The sexes are outwardly similar in all species, though males are usually a trifle larger than females and often have stronger bills.

Gulls are probably the best known of all sea-birds and those unacquainted with ornithology often call any bird seen at sea a Sea-Gull. In actual fact however gulls are pre-eminently birds of the coast. The flock of sea-gulls which usually follows a ship as it leaves harbour rapidly melts away as the land is left behind and, except in the North Atlantic, no other gulls are likely to be seen until land is sighted once more. In the North Atlantic throughout the winter and spring months the Common Kittiwake may be seen astern of the ship every day, often in large flocks. It seems possible that individual birds of this species actually follow ships right across the ocean since in two different years birds marked with rings as nestlings in the Farne Islands off the northeast coast of Eng-

71

land have been captured on the opposite side of the Atlantic, once in Newfoundland and once on the coast of Labrador, suggesting that they had followed steamers from England bound for Canada by the northern route. Glaucous-winged Gulls are said to have followed ships from San Francisco to the Hawaiian Islands on several occasions.

Gulls are specially characteristic of the coasts, harbours and lakes of the northern hemisphere. Several species breed within the Arctic circle and the Ivory Gull has been found in the polar sea at 85° N., the most northerly record for any bird. Twenty-nine of the forty-four species of gulls breed in the northern hemisphere; one of these, Franklin's Gull, regularly migrates across the equator to spend the winter south of the line, and many others make considerable southward journeys in autumn returning in spring. Northern Black-headed Gulls marked as nestlings in Prussia have been captured in Barbados and on the east coast of Mexico, and one marked in England was found in the Azores. Several Lesser Black-backed Gulls marked as nestlings in the British Isles have been recovered on the north-west coast of Africa, and one marked in Germany was obtained in Egypt.

Gulls are sociable in habits at all times and breed in colonies. Frequently a colony may contain nests of several different species, and gulls may often be found nesting in colonies of Terns. The Kittiwake Gull commonly breeds on the same cliffs as Murres and Razorbills. The nests of gulls are usually fairly substantial structures composed of seaweed, grass, weeds or sticks and are placed in a variety of situations. They may be on ledges of cliffs, on low islands, sand-hills or beaches, on tussocks in lakes and swamps, and even occasionally in bushes or trees. Many species breed far from the sea, but all visit the sea coasts during the rest of the year.

Gulls usually lay two or three eggs, sometimes only one or four, occasionally five. The eggs may be light brown, greenish or bluish in ground colour and are usually spotted or blotched with black, brown or purplish. The young when hatched are covered with mottled down, yellow, brown, grey or black. Though they may leave the nest at an early age, they are dependent on their parents for food until they can fly.

In their feeding habits gulls are primarily scavengers, picking up dead animals and refuse from the surface in coastal waters. They are thus of considerable value in preventing the pollution of harbours. They also obtain molluscs, worms and other organisms on the shore as well as in swampy places or on ploughed fields inland, and many of the species which breed inland feed largely on insects. When the Mormons established their earliest settlement in Utah, their first crops were almost destroyed by myriads of black crickets. In the following season the crickets again appeared and the settlers were in despair, as the failure of their second crop would have meant starvation. Then Sea-Gulls came in thousands and devoured the insects so that the fields were freed from them. The settlers regarded this as a heaven-sent miracle and the event is commemorated at Salt Lake City by a monument erected at a cost of $40,000. Unfortunately the eggs and young of other birds are also devoured by Gulls when opportunity offers, and in islands and reserves where birds are protected Gulls show a marked tendancy to increase at the expense of Terns, Puffins, Cormorants and other sea-birds.

Gulls settle freely on the surface of the water, where they ride buoyantly, but they very rarely dive. Occasionally they may be seen to swoop down from the air and disappear for a brief period below the surface. When feeding they are distinctly quarrelsome, pursuing any fortunate individual which has secured booty until it is forced to drop the desired morsel. Then another bird seizes the treasure and the chase begins again. Their flight is extremely buoyant and graceful and they can twist and turn in the air with great ease and dexterity. Unlike the narrow-winged Albatrosses and Petrels which glide for long periods through the air with rigid wings, Gulls are constantly adjusting their wings to every gust. At one moment they may be hanging in the air without effort over the stern of a moving ship or circling swiftly round her. Then they will observe something of interest on the water and swooping swiftly down will suddenly stop at the desired point and settle gracefully on the surface. In fine weather they sometimes rise high in the air and soar round in great circles.

The notes of Gulls are usually harsh or querulous and most species utter them constantly when feeding and especially at their breeding grounds. Mew and Kittiwake are names given to certain species in imitation of their calls. But to quote Dr. F. M. Chapman "the voices of Gulls possess a certain, indescribable human quality which adds in no small degree to the impression created when storms rule and these wild cries are heard above the tumult of wind and wave."

The arrangement of the Gulls in groups to facilitate their identification is a matter of great difficulty owing to the comparative uniformity of their plumage, especially in winter. The primary division here adopted is into large, medium and small size groups. The large Gulls are those with wings more than 16 inches long; medium-sized Gulls have wings between 13 and 16 inches long; whilst those with wings under 13 inches long are considered small. In each of these sections the species are grouped according to their colouration in breeding plumage. It should be borne in mind that whilst the colour of the mantle and tail are always the same in non-breeding plumage, that of the head is usually different. Some white-headed Gulls have pure white heads throughout the year, but a number which have white heads in the breeding season have the heads streaked or spotted with brown, grey or black in winter. On the other hand Gulls which assume dark hoods in the breeding season invariably lose most of the dark colour in winter, when the head becomes white with patches or spots of darker colour.

The identification of immature specimens of large Gulls seen on the wing is frequently difficult and in some cases impossible. Some of the small Gulls however are more easily identified in immature plumage than in the adult state.

Several of the smaller Gulls sometimes have the white parts tinged with a rosy colour in the breeding season.

In the following pages the Gulls are arranged in twelve groups according to their size and colouring. In all the species except the members of Group V the underparts and tail are white, but in the members of Group VI and one species in Group I the tail is crossed by a black band. The groups are as follows:—

    I. Large, with white head and very dark mantle (Species 1–6).

   II. Large, with white head and grey mantle (Species 7–12).

  III. Large, with black head and grey mantle (Species 13).

  IV. Large, with grey head, grey-and-white mantle and forked tail (Species 14).

   V. Medium-sized, with dark mantle and grey underparts (Species 15–18).

  VI. Medium-sized, with white head and dark mantle (Species 19–20).

 VII. Medium-sized, with brown head and breast and grey-brown mantle (Species 21).

VIII. Medium-sized, with white head and grey mantle (Species 22–24).

  IX. Medium-sized, with dark head and grey mantle (Species 25–27).

   X. Medium-sized, with plumage entirely white (Species 28).

  XI. Small, with dark head and grey mantle (Species 29–38).

XII. Small, with white head and grey mantle (Species 39–44).

The following arrangement of gulls according to the colours of their bills and feet should assist in their identification.

I. BILL YELLOW OR YELLOWISH; FEET YELLOW OR YELLOWISH

(1) Pacific, (2) Southern Black-backed, (6) Lesser Black-backed, (9) Yellow-legged and (22) Mew Gulls (adult); (41) Slender-billed Gull (young).

II. BILL YELLOW OR YELLOWISH; FEET PINK OR FLESH-COLOURED

(3) Great Black-backed, (4) Slaty-backed, (5) Western, (7) Herring, (10) Glaucous-winged, (11) Glaucous and (12) Iceland Gulls (adult).

III. BILL YELLOW OR YELLOWISH; FEET BLACK OR DUSKY

(28) Ivory and (39) Common Kittiwake Gulls (adult).

IV. BILL YELLOW OR YELLOWISH; FEET RED

(40) Red-legged Kittiwake (adult).

V. BILL YELLOW OR GREENISH WITH BLACK BAND OR TIP; FEET YELLOWISH

(8) California, (13) Great Black-headed, (19) Japanese, (20) Siméon, (21) Aden and (23) Ring-billed Gulls (adult); (27) Grey-headed, (35) Northern Black-headed and (37) Indian Black-headed Gulls (young).

VI. BILL YELLOWISH WITH BLACK TIP; FEET GREYISH

(20) Siméon Gull (young).

VII. BILL RED OR REDDISH BLACK; FEET RED OR REDDISH BLACK

(15) Magellan, (18) Grey, (26) Andean (27) Grey-headed, (30) Franklin's, (34) Little, (35) Northern Black-headed, (36) Patagonian Black-headed, (37) Indian Black-headed, (41) Slender-billed and (42) Silver Gulls (adult).

VIII. BILL RED OR BLACKISH RED; FEET BROWN OR BLACK

(16) Heermann's, (17) Dusky and (25) Laughing Gulls (adult).

IX. BILL RED WITH BLACK BAND; FEET YELLOW-ISH, DARK RED OR BLACKISH

(24) Audouin's, (29) Red Sea Black-headed and (31) Mediterranean Black-headed Gulls (adult).

X. BILL BLACK OR BROWN; FEET RED OR REDDISH

(32) Chinese Black-headed, (33) Bonaparte's, (43) Buller's and (44) Ross's Gulls (adult), (31) Mediterranean Black-headed and (32) Chinese Black-headed Gulls (young).

XI. BILL BLACK OR BROWN; FEET BLACKISH, BROWN OR DUSKY

(38) Sabine's Gull (adult); (2) Southern Black-backed, (4) Slaty-backed, (5) Western, (6) Lesser Black-backed,

(8) California, (10) Glaucous-winged, (13) Great Black-headed, (14) Swallow-tailed, (16) Heermann's, (17) Dusky, (18) Grey, (25) Laughing, (26) Andean, (28) Ivory, (29) Red Sea Black-headed, (30) Franklin's, (38) Sabine's, (40) Red-legged Kittiwake, (42) Silver, (43) Buller's and (44) Ross's Gulls (young).

XII. BILL BLACK OR BROWN; FEET FLESH-COLOURED, PALE BROWN OR YELLOWISH

(3) Great Black-backed, (7) Herring, (9) Yellow-legged, (33) Bonaparte's, (34) Little and (39) Common Kittiwake Gulls (young).

XIII. BILL FLESH-COLOURED OR BROWNISH WITH BLACK BAND OR TIP; FEET FLESH-COLOURED OR BROWNISH

(1) Pacific, (7) Herring, (11) Glaucous, (12) Iceland, (15) Magellan, (19) Japanese, (22) Mew, (23) Ring-billed and (36) Patagonian Black-headed Gulls (young).

XIV. BILL GREY WITH PALE TIP; FEET PINKISH RED

(14) Swallow-tailed Gull (adult).

I. LARGE GULLS WITH WHITE HEAD AND VERY DARK MANTLE

1. Pacific Gull (*Gabianus pacificus*)

Adult.—Head, neck and underparts white; mantle black; primaries black with small apical white spots except on first two; secondaries black with broad white tips; tail white with a subterminal black band, broadest on central feathers; bill compressed, very deep, yellow with a red spot at the angle; feet yellow; length 25 ins.; wing 17.5–18; tail 8; bill 2.8; tarsus 2.9. *Young.*—Brown, the feathers mottled and with pale edges; face whitish; primaries and tail brownish-black; bill flesh-coloured with a subterminal black band; feet brownish.

Range.—Tasmania and coasts of southern Australia north to Geraldton and Rockhampton. Breeds throughout its range. *Egg-dates:* Sept.–Jan.

Notes.—The large gull of Australian coasts, distinguished by the black tail-band and very large bill from the Southern Black-backed Gull found in New Zealand.

2. Southern Black-backed Gull (*Larus dominicanus*)

Adult.—Head, neck, underparts and tail white; mantle sooty-black; wing-quills, except the first primaries, with white tips; bill yellow with a red spot at the angle; feet yellowish; length 23 ins.; wing 16.5; tail 7; bill 2.2; tarsus 2.4. *Young.*—Brown, more or less mottled with white; head whitish streaked with brown; wing-quills and tail blackish; bill black; feet brownish.

Range.—Coast of South America from Cape Horn north to the Gulf of Guayaquil and Rio de Janeiro, the Falkland Is., South Shetlands, South Orkneys and South Georgia, coasts of South Africa from Walvisch Bay to Lourenço Marques and Madagascar, Marion I., the Crozet Is., Kerguelen, Heard I., New Zealand, the Chatham Is. and Macquarie Is. Breeds throughout its range. *Egg-dates:* Oct.–Jan. in the south, throughout the year in the tropics.

Notes.—The only large black-backed gull in the southern hemisphere with a pure white tail. This distinguishes it from the Siméon Gull, which is also decidedly smaller. It is sometimes called the "Kelp Gull."

3. Great Black-backed Gull (*Larus marinus*). (*Plate* 27)

Adult.—Head and neck white in summer, streaked with dusky in winter; mantle sooty black; underparts and tail white; wing-quills sooty with white tips; bill yellow with a red spot at the angle; feet pale flesh-colour; length 27–30 ins.; wing 18.3–20; tail 7.3–8; bill 2.3–2.7; tarsus 2.9–3. *Young.*—Head and neck whitish streaked with greyish;

mantle brownish, feathers margined and marked with buff; underparts whitish streaked or barred with greyish; primaries brownish black, inner ones with small white tips; tail largely white, mottled with blackish; bill blackish; feet pale flesh-coloured.

Range.—Coasts of the North Atlantic south in winter to Cuba, the Azores, Canary Is., Senegal, the Mediterranean and the Black Sea. Breeds on the coasts of Nova Scotia, Newfoundland, Labrador, Greenland, Iceland, the British Is., Scandinavia and northern Russia. *Egg-dates*: April–July.

Notes.—The largest of the gulls, distinguished by its black mantle and flesh-coloured feet.

4. Slaty-backed Gull (*Larus schistisagus*)

Adult.—Head and neck white in summer, streaked with grey in winter; underparts and tail white; mantle dark slate-colour; wing-quills black, outer primaries with white spots, inner primaries, secondaries and tertials with broad white tips; bill yellow with a red spot at the angle; feet pinkish flesh-colour; length 24–25 ins.; wing 17.2–18.5; tail 7–7.7; bill 2.1–2.6; tarsus 2.3–2.8. *Young.*—Light brown above, the feathers with dark streaks and light margins; a conspicuous drab bar on the wing; chin white; underparts grey; tail dark brown, mottled at base; bill black; feet brown.

Range.—Coasts of north-eastern Asia, south to China and Japan and east to Alaska. Breeds on the shores of the Sea of Okhotsk and in Kamchatka, the Kurile Is. and northern Japan. *Egg-dates*: May–June.

Notes.—The young bird is paler than any other immature large gull except young Glaucous and Iceland Gulls. The adult is distinguished from the Herring Gull by its much darker mantle and from the Yellow-legged Gull by its pink feet.

5. Western Gull (*Larus occidentalis*)

Adult.—Head and neck white, sometimes lightly streaked with grey in winter; underparts and tail white; mantle leaden-grey (lighter in the northern race); wing-quills grey with white tips, the first four primaries with black outer webs and the first with a white subterminal spot; bill yellow with a red spot at the angle; feet flesh-coloured; length 21–22 ins.; wing 14.5–17.6; tail 5.7–7; bill 2–2.3; tarsus 2.3–2.6. *Young.*—Greyish-brown the upperparts spotted with greyish-white; wing-quills and tail dull black; bill black; feet brownish.

Range.—Pacific coast of North America from Vancouver I. to Cape Corrientes, Mexico, and the Revillagigedo Is. Breeds on the coasts of Washington, Oregon, and northern California (*L. o. occidentalis*), of southern California and Lower California (*L. o. wymani*) and on islands in the Gulf of California (*L. o. livens*). *Egg-dates:* April–July.

Notes.—The adult differs from the Herring and California Gulls by its darker mantle, and from the latter also by its flesh-coloured feet.

6. Lesser Black-backed Gull (*Larus fuscus*). (*Plate 49*)

Adult.—Head, neck, underparts and tail white, mantle sooty black or slate-grey (darkest in the Scandinavian race); wing-quills black, the first primary with a white spot near the tip, the secondaries and tertials with broad white tips; bill yellow with a red spot at the angle; feet yellow; length 20–24.2 ins; wing 16–17.4; tail 5.7–7; bill 1.8–2.7; tarsus 2.2–2.8. *Young.*—Head, neck and underparts white mottled with dusky brown; mantle ash-brown, the feathers with light edges and dark streaks; wing-quills and tail blackish-brown, the outer tail-feathers mottled with white; upper tail-coverts white; bill black; feet brown.

Range.—Coasts of Europe, western Asia and northern Africa, south in winter to Sierra Leone, Lake Nyasa, Somaliland, western India and Ceylon. Breeds in Scandinavia and on the shores of the Baltic (*L. f. fuscus*) and in the British Is. (*L. f. graellsii*). *Egg-dates:* May–July.

Notes.—A migratory species deserting the northern parts of its range in winter. Distinguished from the Great Black-backed Gull by its smaller size, greyer mantle and yellow feet, from the Herring Gull by its darker mantle and yellow feet and from the Yellow-legged Gull by its darker mantle.

II. LARGE GULLS WITH WHITE HEAD AND GREY MANTLE

7. Herring Gull (*Larus argentatus*). (*Plates 23, 25, and 26*)

Adult.—Head and neck white in summer, in winter streaked with dusky grey; underparts, rump and tail white; mantle grey; primaries black with white tips, outermost also with white subterminal spot; secondaries with white tips; bill yellow with a red spot at the angle; feet pinkish flesh-colour; length 22–24.5 ins.; wing 16.7–18; tail 6.7–7.5; bill 2.2–2.3; tarsus 2.5–2.7. *Young.*—Head greyish-brown, streaked with greyish-white and pale buff; mantle darker, the feathers edged and barred with pale buff; underparts greyer, mottled; primaries brownish-black; tail brownish-black, more or less barred and spotted with white, especially towards the base; bill blackish; feet fleshy-brown.

Range.—Coasts of Europe, Asia and North America, south in winter to the Canary Is., northern Africa, the Black Sea, Gulf of Tonquin, Bonin Is., Mexico, Cuba and the Bahamas. Breeds on the coasts of northern Europe from northern France and the British Is. to Scandinavia and the Baltic (*L. a. argentatus*), in northern Russia, Kolguev and north-west Siberia (*L. a. antelius*), on the Taimyr Peninsula and islands in the Arctic Sea (*L. a. birulai*), in north-east Siberia and Kamchatka (*L. a. vegae*), on the southern coast of Alaska and the coast of British Columbia and across North America to Hudson Bay and the Atlantic coast from Labrador to Maine (*L. a. smithsonianus*), also in arctic Canada from Banks Land to Ellesmere Land (*L. a. thayeri*). *Egg-dates:* April–Aug.

Notes.—The most widespread and commonest gull of the northern hemisphere, distinguished from other large gulls with grey mantles and black primaries by its pink

PLATE I

Photo by Dr. A. O. Gross

BROWN PELICANS FEEDING.   PANAMA BAY

PLATE 2

Fig. 1

Photo by Dr. R. C. Murphy

WANDERING ALBATROSSES. FEMALE ON NEST. MALE
STANDING. SOUTH GEORGIA

Fig. 2

Photo by Dr. R. C. Murph

WANDERING ALBATROSS ON NEST. SOUTH GEORGIA

PLATE 3

Fig. 1   Photo by E. F. Pollock

WANDERING ALBATROSS.   SOUTH PACIFIC OCEAN

Fig. 2   Photo by W. R. B. Oliver

SHY ALBATROSSES.   STEWART I., NEW ZEALAND

PLATE 4

From drawings by the author

ALBATROSSES

2. WANDERING ALBATROSS: (a) ADULT MALE; (b) ADULT FEMALE; (c) IMMATURE; (e) ADULT FROM BELOW;

From drawings by the author

ALBATROSSES

4. SHY ALBATROSS: (a) ADULT; (b) ADULT FROM BELOW.   6. BLACK-BROWED ALBATROSS: (a) ADULT;
(b) ADULT FROM BELOW; (c) YOUNG; (d) YOUNG FROM BELOW.   7. YELLOW-NOSED ALBATROSS: (a) ADULT;
(b) ADULT FROM BELOW. 10. WAVED ALBATROSS.

PLATE 6

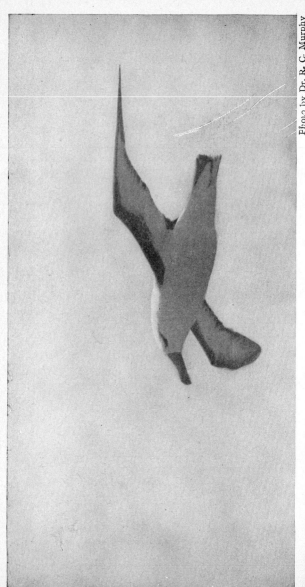

Photo by Dr. R. C. Murphy

PLATE 7

Photo by R. H. Beck

Black-browed Albatross and Young in Nest. Falkland Is.

PLATE 8

BLACK-FOOTED ALBATROSSES NESTING, LAYSAN, HAWAIIAN ISLANDS

PLATE 9

Photo A. M. Bailey
BLACK-FOOTED ALBATROSS AND YOUNG.
LAYSAN, HAWAIIAN IS.

PLATE 10

Fig. 1   Photo by Dr. R. C. Murphy

LIGHT-MANTLED SOOTY ALBATROSS.
SOUTH ATLANTIC OCEAN

Fig. 2   Photo by Dr. R. C. Murphy

LIGHT-MANTLED SOOTY ALBATROSS AND YOUNG.
SOUTH GEORGIA

PLATE II

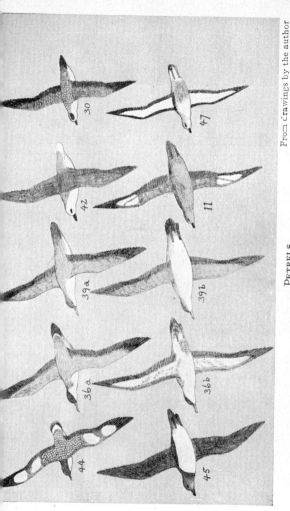

From drawings by the author

PETRELS

11. SOLANDER'S PETREL (FROM BELOW). 30. HAWAIIAN PETREL. 36. GREATER SHEARWATER: (a) FROM ABOVE; (b) FROM BELOW. 39. BROWN PETREL: (a) FROM ABOVE; (b) FROM BELOW. 42. WHITE-HEADED PETREL. 44. PINTADO PETREL OR CAPE PIGEON. 45. SCHLEGEL'S PETREL (FROM BELOW). 47. PEALE'S PETREL (FROM BELOW).

PLATE 12

Photo by R. H. Beck

GIANT PETRELS NESTING   FALKLAND ISLANDS

PLATE 13

Fig. 1   Photo by Dr. R. C. Murphy

PINTADO PETREL OR CAPE PIGEON.
SOUTH ATLANTIC OCEAN

Fig. 2   Photo by Dr. R. C. Murphy

GIANT PETREL (WHITE PHASE) ON NEST.
SOUTH GEORGIA

PLATE 14

PLATE 15

Fig. 1   Photo by Dr. R. C. Murphy

SCHLEGEL'S PETREL. SOUTH ATLANTIC OCEAN

Fig. 2   Photo by R. H. Beck

KERMADEC PETREL (LIGHT PHASE) AND YOUNG.
JUAN FERNANDEZ IS.

PLATE 16

Fig. 1   Photo by H. K. Job

GREATER SHEARWATER.   COAST OF MASSACHUSETTS

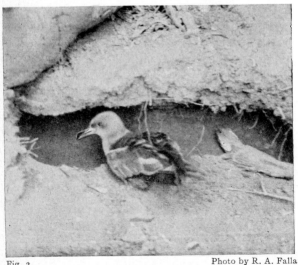

Fig. 2   Photo by R. A. Falla

PALE-FOOTED SHEARWATER IN EXCAVATED BURROW SHARED
BY TUATERA LIZARD.   MERCURY I., NEW ZEALAND

PLATE 17

Photo by R. H. Beck

PHOENIX PETREL AT ENTRANCE TO ITS NESTING BURROW.
MARQUESAS IS.

PLATE 18

Fig. 1   Photo by C. H. Wells

FULMAR AT NEST. ST. KILDA I., SCOTLAND

Fig. 2   Photo by N. Rankin

FULMAR. SPITZBERGEN

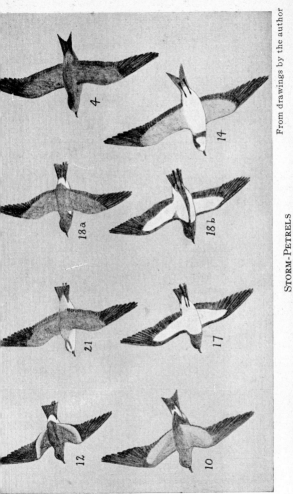

From drawings by the author

STORM-PETRELS

4. SOOTY STORM-PETREL. 10. LEACH'S STORM-PETREL. 12. WILSON'S STORM-PETREL. 14. HORNBY'S STORM-PETREL (FROM BELOW). 17. WHITE-BELLIED STORM-PETREL (FROM BELOW). 18. BLACK-BELLIED STORM-PETREL: (a) FROM ABOVE; (b) FROM BELOW. 21. WHITE-FACED STORM-PETREL.

PLATE 20

Photo by W. L. Finley

PLATE 21

Photo by Howard H. Cleaves

WILSON'S STORM-PETRELS FEEDING ON OILY GROUND-BAIT OR "CHUM"
THROWN OVERBOARD BY FISHERMEN. OFF SANDY HOOK, NEW JERSEY

PLATE 22

GEORGIAN DIVING-PETREL.   SOUTH GEORGIA

PLATE 23

Photo by J. D. Rattar

HERRING GULLS.   SHETLAND ISLANDS

PLATE 24

Fig. 1

Photo by H. K. Job

LAUGHING GULLS.   LOUISIANA

Fig. 2

Photo by J. D. Rattar

YOUNG ICELAND GULL.   SHETLAND IS.

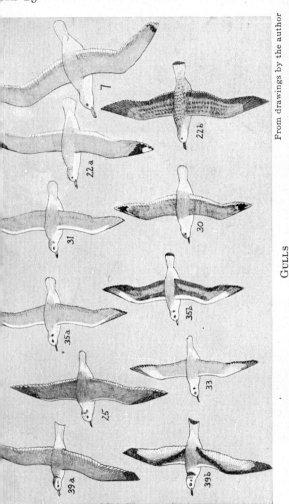

From drawings by the author

GULS

7. Herring Gull. (Adult in Winter). 22. Mew Gull: (a) Adult in Winter; (b) Young. 25. Laughing Gull (Adult in Winter). 30. Franklin's Gull (Adult in Winter). 31. Mediterranean Blackheaded Gull (Adult in Winter). 33. Bonaparte's Gull (Adult in Winter). 35. Northern Blackheaded Gull: (a) Adult in Winter; (b) Young. 30. Common Kittiwake: (a) Adult in Winter; (b) Young.

PLATE 26

Photo by Dr. A. O. Gross

HERRING GULL   GREAT DUCK I., MAINE

PLATE 27

Fig. 1

Photo by Howard H. Cleaves

GREAT BLACK-BACKED GULLS, ADULT AND YOUNG. LAKE GEORGE, NOVA SCOTIA

Fig. 2

Photo by Howard H. Cleaves

GREAT BLACK-BACKED GULLS. LAKE GEORGE, NOVA SCOTIA

PLATE 28

Fig. 1

Photo by J. D. Rattar

YOUNG GLAUCOUS GULL WITH YOUNG HERRING GULLS.
SHETLAND ISLANDS

Fig. 2

Photo by A. C. Bent

GLAUCOUS-WINGED GULLS.   PRIBILOF ISLANDS

PLATE 29

Fig. 1   Copyright Photo by Seton Gordon

MEW GULL AT NEST. SCOTLAND

Fig. 2   Photo by C. H. Wells

NORTHERN BLACK-HEADED GULL ON NEST. ENGLAND

PLATE 30

Photo by R. H. Beck

Magellan Gulls with Patagonian Black-headed Gulls and Magellan
Penguins. Falkland Islands

PLATE 32

Fig. 1   Photo by W. G. Fargo

LAUGHING GULL IN WINTER PLUMAGE. FLORIDA

Fig. 2   Photo by S. C. Arthur

LAUGHING GULL. COAST OF LOUISIANA

PLATE 33

Fig. 1   Photo by N. Rankin

SABINE'S GULL ON NEST.   SPITZBERGEN

Fig. 2   Photo by N. Rankin

IVORY GULL.   SPITZBERGEN

PLATE 34

Photo by Dr. F. M. Chapman

COMMON KITTIWAKES AND YOUNG. BIRD ROCK, QUEBEC

PLATE 35

Photo by H. K. Job

ARCTIC TERNS. MATINICUS ROCK, MAINE

PLATE 36

Fig. 1   Photo by N. Rankin

ARCTIC TERN ON NEST.   SPITZBERGEN

Fig. 2   Photo by C. H. Wells

LITTLE TERN ON NEST.   ENGLAND

From drawings by the author

TERNS

1. CASPIAN TERN (FROM BELOW). 6. CRESTED TERN. 8. GULL-BILLED TERN. 25. SOOTY TERN. 26. BROWN-WINGED TERN. 30. COMMON NODDY. 34. BLACK TERN. 35. WHITE-WINGED BLACK TERN. 36. LITTLE TERN. 42. BLACK-NAPED TERN.

PLATE 38

Fig. 1

CASPIAN TERN.   LOUISIANA

Fig. 2

CASPIAN TERN.   OREGON

Photo by A. C. Bent

ROYAL TERNS NESTING. LOUISIANA

PLATE 40

PLATE 41

Fig. 1
Photo by S. C. Arthur

ROYAL TERN. LOUISIANA

Fig. 2
Photo by Dr. F. M. Chapman

COMMON NODDY. BAHAMA ISLANDS

PLATE 42

Fig. 1   Photo by Dr. R. C. Murphy

SWALLOW-TAILED TERN AT NEST.   SOUTH GEORGIA

Fig. 2   Photo by Dr. F. M. Chapman

SOOTY TERNS.   BAHAMA IS.

PLATE 43

Fig. 1   Photo by W. E. Hastings

COMMON TERN

Fig. 2   Photo by A. C. Bent

COMMON TERN ON NEST. MASSACHUSETTS

PLATE 44

Fig. 1   Photo by H. S. Cottrell
WHITE-FRONTED TERNS NESTING.   NAPIER, NEW ZEALAND

Fig. 2   Photo by J. Richardson
BLACK TERN AT NEST.   MINNESOTA

PLATE 45

WHITE-CAPPED NODDIES. CLIPPERTON ISLAND, PACIFIC OCEAN

Photo by R. H. Beck

PLATE 46

PLATE 47

Fig. 1

Photo by S. C. Arthur

BLACK SKIMMER ON NEST. LOUISIANA

Fig. 2

Photo by S. C. Arthur

BLACK SKIMMERS. COAST OF LOUISIANA

PLATE 48

SOUTHERN SKUA.   SOUTH GEORGIA

SOUTHERN SKUA EATING A PENGUIN.   SOUTH GEORGIA

From drawings by the author

SKUAS AND GULLS

1. GREAT SKUA. 6. POMARINE JAEGER: (a) DARK PHASE; (b) LIGHT PHASE FROM BELOW. 7. PARASITIC JAEGER OR ARCTIC SKUA: (a) DARK PHASE; (b) LIGHT PHASE FROM BELOW. 8. LONG-TAILED JAEGER (FROM BELOW). G6. LESSER BLACK-BACKED GULL. G38. SABINE'S GULL.

PLATE 50

Photo by N. Rankin

PARASITIC JAEGER OR ARCTIC SKUA AT NEST   SPITZBERGEN

PLATE 51

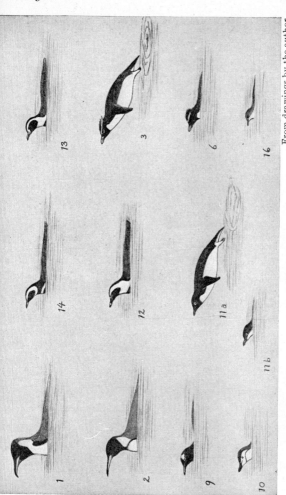

PENGUINS

From drawings by the author

1. EMPEROR PENGUIN. 2. KING PENGUIN. 3. ROCK-HOPPER PENGUIN. 6. MACARONI PENGUIN.
9. GENTOO PENGUIN. 10. BEARDED PENGUIN. 11. ADELIE PENGUIN: (a) ADULT; (b) YOUNG. 12. JACKASS
PENGUIN. 13. HUMBOLDT PENGUIN. 14. MAGELLAN PENGUIN. 16. LITTLE PENGUIN.

PLATE 52

Fig. 1   Photo by Dr. R. C. Murphy

KING PENGUIN INCUBATING EGG.
SOUTH GEORGIA

Fig. 2   Photo by Dr. R. C. Murphy

KING PENGUINS INCUBATING. SOUTH GEORGIA

PLATE 53

Photo by Dr. R. C. Murphy

KING PENGUINS MARCHING. SOUTH GEORGIA

PLATE 54

Fig. 1 Photo by R. H. Beck

ROCK-HOPPER PENGUINS NESTING. FALKLAND ISLANDS

Fig. 2 Photo by Dr. R. C. Murphy

GENTOO PENGUINS NESTING. SOUTH GEORGIA

PLATE 55

Photo by R. H. Beck

GENTOO PENGUINS NESTING. FALKLAND ISLANDS

PLATE 56

MAGELLAN PENGUINS. FALKLAND ISLANDS

PLATE 57

Fig. 1   Photo by Dr. G. Murray Levick

ADELIE PENGUINS NESTING. ANTARCTICA

Fig. 2   Photo by Dr. G Murray Levick

EMPEROR PENGUIN. ANTARCTICA

PLATE 58

Photo by N. Rankin

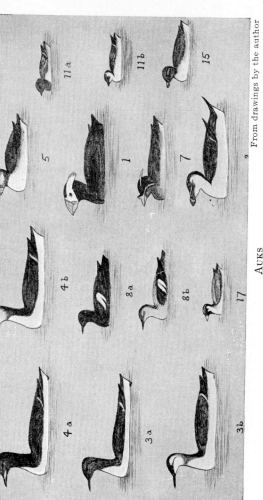

AUKS

From drawings by the author

1. TUFTED PUFFIN (SUMMER). 2. RAZOR-BILLED AUK (WINTER). 3. COMMON MURRE OR GUILLEMOT:
(a) SUMMER; (b) WINTER. 4. BRUNNICH'S MURRE OR GUILLEMOT: (a) SUMMER; (b) WINTER. 5. HORNED
PUFFIN (SUMMER). 7. RHINOCEROS AUKLET (SUMMER). 8. PIGEON GUILLEMOT: (a) SUMMER; (b) WINTER.
11. DOVEKIE OR LITTLE AUK: (a) SUMMER; (b) WINTER. 15. PAROQUET AUKLET (SUMMER). 17. ANCIENT
MURRELET (SUMMER).

PLATE 60

Fig. 1   Photo by W. B. Alexander

RAZOR-BILLED AUK.   HANDA I.,
SCOTLAND

Fig. 2   Photo by C. H. Wells

RAZOR-BILLED AUK.   ISLE OF MAN

PLATE 61

Fig. 1   Photo by W. B. Alexander
COMMON MURRES OR GUILLEMOTS.
RAMSEY I., WALES

2
Photo by A. C. Bent
ÜNNICH'S MURRE OR GUILLEMOT.   BOGOSLOF I., ALASKA

PLATE 62

Photo by N. Rankin

Fig. 1

ATLANTIC PUFFINS.   SCOTLAND

Photo by A. C. F

Fig. 2

ATLANTIC PUFFINS.   BIRD ROCK, QUEBEC

PLATE 63

Copyright Photo by Seton Gordon

BLACK GUILLEMOT CARRYING FISH TO NESTING HOLE. SCOTLAND

PLATE 64

Fig. 1 Photo by N. Rankin

DOVEKIE OR LITTLE AUK.   SPITZBERGEN

Fig. 2 Photo by N. Rank

DOVEKIE OR LITTLE AUK.   SPITZBERGEN

PLATE 65

Fig. 1   Copyright Photo by Seton Gordon

BLACK GUILLEMOT WITH A FISH. SCOTLAND

Fig. 2   Photo by A. C. Bent

PAROQUET AUKLET. ST. MATTHEW I., BERING SEA

PLATE 66

Fig. 1   Photo by H. K. Job

MAGNIFICENT FRIGATE-BIRD (FEMALE).   FLORIDA KEYS

Fig. 2   Photo by Dr. F. M. Chapman

MAGNIFICENT FRIGATE-BIRDS.   BAHAMA IS.

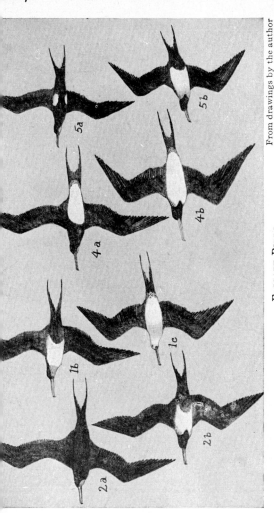

FRIGATE-BIRDS

From drawings by the author

1. GREAT FRIGATE-BIRD: (b) FEMALE; (c) YOUNG.   2.   MAGNIFICENT FRIGATE-BIRD: (a) MALE; (b) FEMALE.
4. CHRISTMAS FRIGATE-BIRD: (a) MALE; (b) FEMALE.   5.   LESSER FRIGATE-BIRD: (a) MALE; (b) FEMALE.   ALL
SEEN FROM BELOW.

PLATE 68

Photo by R. H. Beck

PLATE 69

Photo by W. L. Finley

AMERICAN WHITE PELICANS AND DOUBLE-CRESTED CORMORANTS. OREGON

PLATE 70

Photo by R. H. Beck

BROWN PELICAN ON NEST. GALÁPAGOS IS.

PLATE 71

Fig. 1   Photo by Dr. F. M. Chapman

BROWN PELICAN. FLORIDA

Fig. 2   Photo by Dr. F. M. Chapman

BROWN PELICANS NESTING. PELICAN I., FLORIDA

PLATE 72

Fig. 1   Photo by Dr. R. C. Murphy

CHILEAN PELICANS. COAST OF PERU

Fig. 2   Photo by W. L. Finley

AMERICAN WHITE PELICANS NESTING. OREGON

PLATE 73

Photo by W. R. B. Oliver

AUSTRALIAN GANNETS NESTING.   WHITE ISLAND, NEW ZEALAND

PLATE 74

Fig. 2
Photo by N. Rankin
NORTHERN GANNETS NESTING. BASS
ROCK, SCOTLAND

Fig. 1
Photo by R. H. Beck
RED-FOOTED BOOBY (BROWN PHASE) ON

GANNETS

From drawings by the author

1. NORTHERN GANNET: (a) ADULT; (b) YOUNG. 2. CAPE GANNET. 3. AUSTRALIAN GANNET. 4. RED-FOOTED BOOBY: (a) ADULT; (b) BROWN PHASE (IMMATURE?). 5. BLUE-FACED BOOBY. 6. PERUVIAN BOOBY. 8. BLUE-FOOTED BOOBY. 9. BROWN BOOBY: (a) ADULT; (b) ADULT FROM BELOW; (c) YOUNG.

PLATE 76

Fig. 1   Photo by Dr. R. C. Murphy

PERUVIAN BOOBIES.   COAST OF PERU

Fig. 2   Photo by Dr. F. M. Chapman

BROWN BOOBIES.   BAHAMA IS.

PLATE 77

Photo by Dr. F. M. Chapman

BROWN BOOBY AT NEST. BAHAMA IS.

PLATE 78

Photo by W. L. Finley

BRANDT'S CORMORANTS AT NEST. THREE ARCH ROCKS, OREGON

PLATE 79

Fig. 1   Copyright Photo by Seton Gordon

GREEN CORMORANTS OR SHAGS.   SCOTLAND

Fig. 2   Photo by Dr. R. C. Murphy

BIGUA CORMORANTS.   PARACAS BAY, PERU

PLATE 80

Fig. 1

Photo by Dr. R. C. Murphy

GUANAY CORMORANTS. PISCO BAY, PERU

Fig. 2

Photo by A. C. Bent

RED-FACED CORMORANTS AT NEST. WALRUS I., ALASKA

PLATE 81

BLUE-EYED CORMORANTS NESTING. FALKLAND IS.

PLATE 82

Fig. 1   Photo by R. A. Falla

PIED CORMORANTS.   BAY OF PLENTY, NEW ZEALAND

Fig. 2   Photo by Dr. R. C. Murphy

BLUE-EYED CORMORANTS AT NEST.   SOUTH GEORGIA

Photo by R. H. Beck

MAGELLAN CORMORANTS NESTING. FALKLAND IS.

PLATE 84

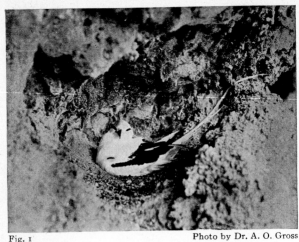

Fig. 1   Photo by Dr. A. O. Gross

WHITE-TAILED TROPIC-BIRD ON NEST.   BERMUDA IS.

Fig. 2   Photo by Dr. A. O. Gross

WHITE-TAILED TROPIC-BIRD (YOUNG).   BERMUDA IS.

PLATE 85

Photo by R. H. Beck

RED-TAILED TROPIC-BIRD ON NEST. CHRISTMAS I., PACIFIC OCEAN

PLATE 86

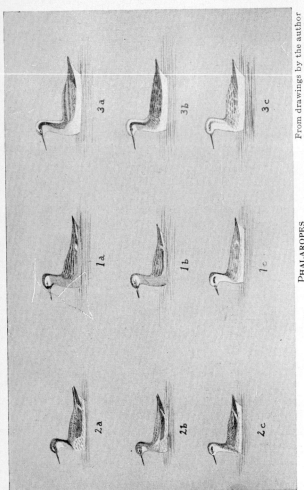

From drawings by the author

PHALAROPES

... (a) FEMALE IN SUMMER; (b) MALE IN SUMMER; (c) ADULT IN WINTER. 2...

PLATE 87

Fig. 1

Photo by F. Harper

NORTHERN (OR RED-NECKED) PHALAROPE (FEMALE IN SUMMER PLUMAGE). ATHABASKA DELTA, ALBERTA

Fig. 2

Photo by N. Rankin

RED (OR GREY) PHALAROPE (SUMMER PLUMAGE). SPITZBERGEN

PLATE 88

) Phalarope (Male) at Nest. Scotland

feet and in winter by its streaked head. The immature may be recognised by its very dark plumage.

8. California Gull (*Larus californicus*)

Adult.—Similar to the Herring Gull in plumage; bill yellow, with a red spot at the angle, usually with a dusky subterminal band; feet greenish-yellow; length 20 ins.; wing 12.5–16.9; tail 4.8–6.6; bill 1.6–2.2; tarsus 1.8–2.5. *Young.*—Head, neck and underparts whitish, mottled with brown; upperparts coarsely spotted with greyish-brown and buffy-white; wing-quills dusky, tipped with white; tail blackish with white barring; bill black; feet dark brown.

Range.—In winter on the Pacific coast of North America from British Columbia to California, and sometimes to southern Alaska, Mexico and Texas. Breeds on inland lakes in western North America. *Egg-dates:* May–June.

Notes.—The adult differs from the Herring Gull in its greenish-yellow feet and partial dark bar on the bill. The immature bird is darker than the young Herring Gull with a paler rump and with the bill sharply black-tipped. In this feature it resembles the young Ring-billed Gull, which is decidedly smaller and has a light tail with a dark terminal band.

9. Yellow-legged Gull (*Larus cachinnans*)

Adult.—Similar to the Herring Gull in plumage but mantle slightly darker grey; bill yellow with a red spot at the angle; feet yellow; length 22–26 ins.; wing 16.7–18.5; tail 7.7; bill 1.9–2.4; tarsus 2.5–2.8. *Young.*—Similar to the young Herring Gull but somewhat paler; bill black; feet yellowish.

Range.—In winter on the coasts of the Mediterranean, Red Sea, Persian Gulf, India, China and Japan, occasionally to the Atlantic coasts of Europe. Breeds on the Murman coast and coasts and islands of the White Sea (*L. c. omissus*), in northern Siberia (*L. c. heuglini*), on the lakes of central Asia (*L. c. mongolicus*), in southern Russia and on the shores of the Black and Caspian Seas (*L. c. cachinnans*), on islands in the Adriatic and off the coasts of

Spain and Portugal (*L. c. michahelles*) and in the Canary Is., Madeira and the Azores (*L. c. atlantis*). *Egg-dates:* April–June.

Notes.—The various races here treated as forms of the Yellow-legged Gull are by some authorities regarded as forms of the Herring Gull, by others as forms of the Lesser Black-backed Gull, whilst others consider these two birds conspecific and also unite with them the California, Glaucous-winged and Iceland Gulls. Admittedly these forms are all closely related and the colouring of the mantle in different races grades from the very pale grey of the Iceland Gull to the slaty-black of the darkest race of the Lesser Black-backed Gull. The birds here treated as the Yellow-legged Gull are rather slimmer than the typical Herring Gulls with the mantle slaty-grey rather than blue-grey, with yellow feet as a rule, though occasionally pink-footed birds occur in some races, and with little or no dark streaking on the head in winter. From the forms of the Lesser Black-backed Gull they are distinguished by their paler mantle. They are less maritime in their habits than their congeners.

10. Glaucous-winged Gull (*Larus glaucescens*). (*Plate 28*)

Adult.—Similar to the Herring Gull but mantle somewhat paler; primaries dark grey subterminally with white tips, the outermost also with a white subterminal spot; secondaries grey with white tips; bill yellow with a red spot; feet flesh-coloured; length 25–26 ins.; wing 16.2–17.8; tail 6.7–7.3; bill 2.1–2.4; tarsus 2.1–2.8. *Young.*—Drab-grey; feathers of the black with light edges; throat and vent white; tail dark grey, slightly barred or mottled at the base; bill blackish; feet light brown.

Range.—Bering Sea and coasts of North Pacific, south in winter to northern Japan and Lower California and occasionally to the Hawaiian Is. Breeds on the coasts of Kamchatka and north-eastern Siberia, the Commander and Aleutian Is. and the northwest coast of America from Norton Sound, Alaska, to Washington. *Egg-dates:* May–July.

Notes.—The adult resembles a pale coloured Herring Gull, the mantle being lighter and the primaries grey, not black. The immature bird differs from every other species in its drab-grey wings and tail.

11. Glaucous Gull (*Larus hyperboreus = L. glaucus*). (Plate 28)

Adult.—Head and neck white in summer, in winter streaked with greyish; underparts, rump and tail white; mantle pale grey; primaries and secondaries pale grey with white ends; bill yellow with a red spot at the angle; feet pinkish flesh-colour; length 28 inches; wing 16.7–18.7; tail 6.8–8.1; bill 1.9–2.6; tarsus 2.1–2.9. *Young.*—Greyish white; head and neck streaked with pale brownish-grey; upperparts mottled with brownish-grey more or less tinged with buff; tail pale brownish-grey more or less mottled with whitish; bill pinkish-white with a blackish-brown terminal band; feet pinkish-white. In intermediate plumage the birds are white, usually with pale buff or greyish mottlings and frecklings.

Range.—Arctic seas, in winter south to the British Is., Baltic Sea, Japan, California and New England, occasionally to the Azores, Madeira, the Mediterranean and Red Seas, the Hawaiian Is., Texas, Cuba and Bermuda. Breeds in Iceland, Spitzbergen, Bear I., northern Russia, northern Siberia, Alaska, Hudson's Bay, Newfoundland, Labrador and Greenland. *Egg-dates:* May–July.

Notes.—Almost equal in size to the Great Black-backed Gull; its very light colouring and the white ends of its primaries distinguish it from all other large gulls. Nelson's Gull (*L. nelsoni*) is probably a hybrid between the Glaucous Gull and the Herring Gull.

12. Iceland Gull (*Larus leucopterus = L. glaucoides*). (Plate 24)

Adult.—Similar to the Glaucous Gull but considerably smaller and with proportionately longer wings; length 22 ins.; wing 16–16.5; tail 7; bill 2.4; tarsus 2.3. *Young.*—Similar to young Glaucous Gull but smaller.

Range.—Arctic seas, south in winter to Nova Scotia, Iceland, the British Is. and the Baltic, occasionally to Maryland and the Bay of Biscay. Breeds in arctic Canada, Greenland, Jan Mayen, Novaya Zemblya and northern Siberia. *Egg-dates:* May–July.

Notes.—Noticeably smaller than the Glaucous Gull and the longer wings give it a more buoyant flight. Its very pale colour distinguishes it from all other species. Kumlien's Gull (*L. kumlieni*) is probably a hybrid between this species and the Herring Gull, said to breed in Baffin Land.

III. LARGE GULLS WITH GREY MANTLE AND BLACK HEAD IN BREEDING SEASON

13. Great Black-headed Gull (*Larus ichthyaetus*)

Adult.—Head deep black in summer, in winter white with dusky streaks; small crescentic patches above and below eye white; mantle grey; primaries mainly white, the outer ones with subterminal black bands and white tips, the inner ones and secondaries grey with broad white tips; underparts and tail white; bill very stout towards tip, yellow with a subterminal black band; feet greenish yellow; length 27–29 ins.; wing 18.7–20; tail 7.5–7.7; bill 2.0–2.7; tarsus 2.6–3.4. *Young.*—Head white, mottled with brown; underparts and rump white; mantle dark brown, the feathers with pale edges; wing-quills dusky with pale tips; tail white with a broad subterminal blackish band; bill blackish; feet greyish-brown.

Range.—In winter on coasts of eastern Mediterranean, Red Sea, Persian Gulf, India and Ceylon, occasionally to England, Sicily, Nubia and Tenasserim. Breeds on the inland seas and lakes of south-eastern Russia and central Asia. *Egg-dates:* May–June.

Notes.—The only large gull with a dark hood in the breeding season. Its very large size and the colouring of the bill and feet distinguish the adult in winter, whilst the white tail with black band distinguishes the immature bird from the young Great Black-backed Gull.

IV. LARGE GULLS WITH FORKED TAIL, GREY AND WHITE MANTLE AND DARK GREY HEAD IN BREEDING SEASON

14. Swallow-tailed Gull (*Creagrus furcatus*). (*Plate 30*)

Adult.—Head and neck dark grey in summer with a white stripe on each side of the forehead, in winter whitish with an ill-defined grey collar and greyish-black rings round the eyes; eyelids crimson; mantle smoky-grey with a white line on each side of the back; outer webs of outer primaries black; inner primaries and adjacent secondaries grey and white; inner secondaries and wing-coverts white; throat and breast rosy white; abdomen, upper tail-coverts and tail white; bill greenish-grey with pale tip; feet pinkish-red; length 20 ins.; wing 15.4–17.1; tail 6.7–8.1; bill 1.8–2.1; tarsus 1.8–2.2. *Young.*—Head white, spotted and streaked with brown; neck and mantle barred with brown and white; tail white with terminal dull black band; bill blackish; feet greyish-white.

Range.—Confined to the Galápagos Is. where it breeds. *Egg-dates:* Throughout the year.

Notes.—This local species with its long wings and long forked tail resembles a large tern. It is much larger than Sabine's Gull, the only other fork-tailed species, and both in adult and immature plumage may be distinguished by the large triangular white patch on the wings. It lays a single egg in a slight hollow lined with stones.

V. MEDIUM-SIZED GULLS WITH DARK MANTLE AND GREY UNDERPARTS

15. Magellan Gull (*Gabianus scoresbyi*). (*Plate 31*)

Adult.—Head pale grey in summer, dusky in winter; neck and underparts pale grey; mantle slaty-black; under

surface of wings dark grey; wing-quills with white tips
tail white; bill and feet red; length 18 ins.; wing 13.2
tail 6; bill 1.7; tarsus 2. *Young.*—Mantle dark brown; head
neck and upper breast pale brown; upper tail-coverts
lower breast and abdomen yellowish white; tail white with
a broad black subterminal bar, broadest on central feath
ers; bill brownish with black tip, feet brownish. In inter
mediate plumage the head has a dark slaty-grey hood.

Range.—Coasts of southern South America and ad
jacent subantarctic islands, north to Chiloe I. and Sant
Cruz, Patagonia. Breeds at the Falkland Is. and Tierra de
Fuego. *Egg-dates:* Dec.–Jan.

Notes.—This gull is largely terrestrial in habits. From
the Grey Gull it is distinguished by its white tail and red
bill and feet.

16. Heermann's Gull (*Larus heermanni*)

Adult.—Head and upper neck white in summer, greyish-
brown in winter; mantle slate-coloured; lower neck, under
parts and upper tail-coverts pale grey; tail dull black
tipped with white; wing-quills mostly with white tips
under surface of wings greyish-brown; bill red; feet black
length 17 ins.; wing 13.3–14.8; tail 5.2–6.4; bill 1.5–2
tarsus 1.8–2.1. *Young.*—Deep brown with darker wings and
tail, the feathers with buff edges; bill and feet blackish.

Range.—Pacific coast of N. America from Vancouver I
to Guatemala. Breeds on coast of N. W. Mexico. *Egg-
dates:* April–June.

Notes.—This dark gull, with white head in adult plumage, cannot be confused with any other North American
species.

17. Dusky-Gull (*Larus fuliginosus*)

Adult.—Head black, eyelids white; mantle dark leaden-
grey; underparts, rump and tail grey, almost white on
abdomen; tips of secondaries almost white; bill red; feet
black; length 15–17.2 ins.; wing 12.1–14.1; tail 5.1–6.5;
bill 1.6–2; tarsus 2.0–2.3. *Young.*—Dark sooty-brown

feathers with lighter margins; head, wing-quills and tail almost black; rump and underparts greyer; bill and feet black.

Range.—Galápagos Is., where it doubtless breeds but has not yet been found nesting. *Egg-dates:* Only egg known taken from a bird shot in Nov.

Notes.—This local species with its very dark colouring cannot be mistaken.

18. Grey Gull (*Larus modestus*)

Adult.—Head white in summer, pale brown in winter; mantle lead-coloured; wings dull black, secondaries broadly tipped with white; tail grey with a broad, black band; rest of upper and underparts grey; bill and feet reddish-black; length 18 ins.; wing 13; tail 5.5; bill 2–2.1; tarsus 1.9. *Young.*—Brown, the feathers with pale edges; wings and tail brownish black; bill and feet black.

Range.—Pacific coast of S. America from the Gulf of Guayaquil to Chiloe I. Breeds in the deserts of Peru and Chile. *Egg-dates:* Nov.

Notes.—Peculiar to the Humboldt Current occurring in large flocks, this grey bird with whitish head and white band along the back of the wing cannot be mistaken.

VI. MEDIUM-SIZED GULLS WITH VERY DARK MANTLE AND TAIL WHITE WITH A BLACK CROSS-BAND

19. Japanese Gull (*Larus crassirostris*)

Adult.—Head white in summer, greyish-brown in winter; mantle slate-grey; first two primaries grey, rest black, all primaries and secondaries with white tips; tail white, with a black band near the end of the central feathers; bill yellowish with a black cross-band and red tip; feet yellowish; length 19 ins.; wing 15; tail 6; bill 2.4; tarsus 2. *Young.*—Dark brown, feathers with pale edges; wings and tail brownish black; face whitish; underparts pale brown; bill flesh-coloured with black tip; feet flesh-coloured.

Range.—Coasts of eastern Asia from Saghalien to Hong Kong. Breeds on the coasts of the Japan and China Seas. *Egg-dates:* May–June.

Notes.—Cannot be confused with any other Asiatic species.

20. Siméon Gull (*Larus belcheri*)

Adult.—Head white in summer, brownish-black in winter, eyelids white; mantle sooty black; primaries black, secondaries dark grey with broad white tips; underparts and rump white; tail white at base and tip, black in the middle; bill yellow, with a black crossband and red tip; feet yellow; length 20 ins.; wing 14.5; tail 6.3; bill 2.3; tarsus 2.4. *Young.*—Pale brown, the feathers with dark bars and light edges; abdomen whitish; primaries and tail dull black with whitish tips; bill yellowish with black tip; feet greyish.

Range.—Pacific coast of S. America from Chiclayo to Coquimbo. Breeds on islands off the coast of Peru. *Egg-dates:* Nov.–Dec.

Notes.—Somewhat resembles the Southern Black-backed Gull but smaller, with black band on tail and black bar on bill.

VII. MEDIUM-SIZED GULLS WITH BROWN HEAD AND BREAST AND GREYISH-BROWN MANTLE

21. Aden Gull (*Larus hemprichi*)

Adult.—Head, nape and throat coffee-brown in summer, in winter pale brown mottled with whitish, eyelids white; neck white all round in summer, grey in winter; mantle greyish-brown; primaries blackish-brown; secondaries and posterior primaries tipped with white; edge of wing white; breast pale brown, mottled with white in winter; abdomen, tail-coverts and tail white; bill greenish, with subterminal black cross-bar and red tip; feet yellowish; length 17.5–18.5 ins.; wing 13.2–13.7; tail 5.5; bill 1.8–2.2; tarsus 2–2.1. *Young.*—Brown, paler on head, whitish on abdomen, the feathers with conspicuous light edges; bill and feet greenish.

Range.—Arabian and Red Seas, ranging east to Bombay and south to Zanzibar. Breeds on east coast of Africa, in southern Red Sea, Gulf of Aden, Persian Gulf and on the Mekran coast. *Egg-dates:* June–Aug.

Notes.—The only gull with the mantle brown when adult. Distinguished from the Red Sea Black-headed Gull also by its brown hood and breast.

VIII. MEDIUM-SIZED GULLS WITH PALE GREY MANTLE AND HEAD WHITE IN BREEDING SEASON

22. **Mew Gull** (*Larus canus*). (*Plates 25 and 29*)

Adult.—Head white, in winter streaked with dusky; neck, underparts and tail white; mantle pale grey; outer primaries black with broad white tips, inner primaries and secondaries grey with white tips; bill and feet greenish yellow; length 18–18.5 ins.; wing 13.3–15; tail 5.3–5.9; bill 1.4–1.8; tarsus 1.8–2.2. *Young.*—Head and neck whitish mottled with greyish-brown; mantle brownish-grey, the feathers with pale brown edges; tail whitish mottled with brown, with a broad subterminal dusky band; underparts whitish mottled with brownish; bill brownish with a black subterminal bar; feet flesh-coloured.

Range.—Europe, northern Asia and northwestern North America, south to the Mediterranean, Persian Gulf, China, Formosa and California, occasionally to Quebec, Iceland and the Canary Is. Breeds, chiefly on inland lakes, in the British Is., Holland, Scandinavia and Russia (*L. c. canus*), in northern Asia (*L. c. kamtschatschensis*), in Alaska and western Canada (*L. c. brachyrhynchus*). *Egg-dates:* May–July.

Notes.—The "Common Gull" of British writers, but the epithet is usually only applicable in northern inland districts. The American race is called the "Short-billed Gull."

The adult resembles the Herring and California Gulls but is smaller, has more white on wing-tips and differently coloured bill and feet. From the adult Ring-billed Gull it differs chiefly in its white-tipped primaries and yellowish bill. Immature birds of these two species are indistinguishable in life.

23. Ring-billed Gull (*Larus delawarensis*)

Adult.—Head white, in winter streaked with greyish; neck, underparts and tail white; mantle pale grey; outer primaries black with white subterminal spot on the first and often on the second; inner primaries and secondaries grey with white tips; bill greenish yellow, crossed near the tip by a black band; feet yellow or greenish; length 18.5 ins.; wing 13.1–15.3; tail 5.2–6.3; bill 1.5–1.8; tarsus 1.8–2.4. *Young.*—Similar to the young Mew Gull.

Range.—In winter on both coasts of the United States south to Cuba, Texas and southern Mexico, occasionally visiting the Bermudas and Hawaiian Is. Breeds on lakes in Canada and the northern United States. *Egg-dates:* May–June.

Notes.—The adult resembles the Herring and California Gulls, but is decidedly smaller and its bill and feet are differently coloured. The immature bird is very much whiter than the young Herring Gull, but is indistinguishable from the young Mew Gull.

24. Audouin's Gull (*Larus audouini*)

Adult.—Head white, in winter streaked with greyish; neck, underparts and tail white; mantle pale grey; outer primaries black with white apical spot; inner primaries and secondaries grey with white tips; bill red, crossed near the tip by a black band; feet greyish-black; length 20 ins.; wing 15.7; tail 6.5; bill 2.3; tarsus 2.4. *Young.*—Head whitish grey, streaked; mantle greyish brown, spotted; tail whitish, more or less spotted with dusky; underparts whitish.

Range.—Mediterranean Sea. Breeds on the coasts of Syria, Tunisia, Sardinia, Corsica and Spain. *Egg-dates:* April–May.

Notes.—Confined to the Mediterranean Sea where it is a rare species. The adult may be distinguished from the large gulls of the Mediterranean by its smaller size, very pale mantle and the colouration of the bill. The young is probably indistinguishable from the young Lesser Black-backed Gull except by its smaller size.

IX. MEDIUM-SIZED GULLS WITH GREY MANTLE AND HEAD DARK IN BREEDING SEASON

25. Laughing Gull (*Larus atricilla*). (*Plates 24, 25 and 32*)

Adult.—Head and upper neck greyish-black in summer, in winter white mottled with brownish-grey on crown and sides of head; bars above and below eye, lower neck, underparts and tail white; mantle leaden-grey; five outer primaries black; inner primaries, secondaries and tertials grey with white tips; bill red in summer, blackish in winter; feet brown; length 16.5 ins.; wing 12.2–13.7; tail 4.6–5.3; bill 1.5–1.7; tarsus 1.8–2.1. *Young.*—Upperparts light greyish-brown, the feathers with pale buff edges; primaries and secondaries black, the latter with white edges; tail grey with a broad black subterminal band; underparts white with dusky mottlings; rump, upper and under tail-coverts white; bill black; feet brownish. In intermediate plumage the head is white with a dusky collar on the hindneck.

Range.—Atlantic coast of America from Maine to Venezuela, south in winter to Brazil and to the Pacific coast from Mexico to Peru. Breeds on the east coast of the United States and in the Gulf of Mexico and Caribbean Sea. *Egg-dates:* April–July.

Notes.—Larger than the other American dark-hooded gulls and with a darker mantle. The immature bird is characterized by its white rump and lower abdomen which contrast sharply with the brownish back and breast.

26. Andean Gull (*Larus serranus*)

Adult.—Head black in summer, in winter white with greyish markings; a small white semicircle behind the eye; mantle pale pearl-grey; primaries black, the first three with large white subterminal patches, the posterior ones with white tips; secondaries and under wing-coverts grey; neck, underparts and tail white, breast with a rosy tinge; bill and feet dark red; length 19 ins.; wing 14.2; tail 6; bill 1.9; tarsus 2.1. *Young.*—Crown, neck and mantle mottled with brown; secondaries largely brown; tail with a subterminal blackish bar; bill and feet brown.

Range.—In winter on the coasts of Peru. Breeds on Lake Titicaca and other lakes in the high Andes.

Notes.—Larger than the other dark-hooded South American gulls. Distinguished from the Laughing Gull by its pale grey mantle.

27. Grey-headed Gull (*Larus cirrocephalus*)

Adult.—Head and throat lavender-grey in summer, in winter white with a pale-grey half-hood; mantle grey; outer primaries black, with subterminal white patches; inner primaries and secondaries grey; neck, underparts and tail white; under wing-coverts grey; bill and feet crimson; length 16 ins.; wing 13; tail 5; bill 1.8; tarsus 2. *Young.*—Head white with dark patches; mantle mottled with ashy brown; outer primaries black; secondaries brown; tail white with brownish-black terminal band on central feathers; bill yellowish with dark tip; legs yellowish-brown.

Range.—In winter on the coasts of Peru, Argentina and southern Brazil, also on the coasts of western Africa from Gambia to Walvisch Bay and of east Africa from Madagascar to Port Elizabeth. Breeds inland in eastern South America (*L. c. cirrocephalus*) and in tropical Africa (*L. c. poiocephalus*). *Egg-dates:* June, Nov.–Dec.

Notes.—The only southern gull with a grey head in breeding plumage, and sufficient of this colour remains on the head in winter to aid in determination of the species. It is only slightly larger than the Patagonian Black-headed Gull.

X. MEDIUM-SIZED GULLS WITH WHOLE PLUMAGE WHITE

28. **Ivory Gull** (*Pagophila eburnea*). (*Plate 33*)

Adult.—Entirely white; bill light blue, greenish at base and reddish at tip; feet black; length 16–18 ins.; wing 11.8–14.3; tail 5–6.2; bill 1.2–1.4; tarsus 1.3–1.5. *Young.*—White with a few brownish marks on head, back and wings; tail with a narrow black, subterminal band; bill blackish.

Range.—Arctic regions from 85° N. lat., south in winter to Alaska, Hudson's Bay, Labrador, Iceland, the Baltic and White Seas, Kamchatka and the Aleutian Is., and occasionally to British Columbia, New York and France. Breeds on islands north of Canada, Europe and Siberia. *Egg-dates:* June–Aug.

Notes.—The most northerly of all birds, distinguished from young Glaucous and Iceland Gulls, which are sometimes pure white, by its smaller size and the colouring of its bill and feet.

XI. SMALL GULLS WITH GREY MANTLE AND DARK HEAD IN BREEDING SEASON

29. **Red Sea Black-headed Gull** (*Larus leucophthalmus*)

Adult.—Head, neck and throat deep black in summer, grizzled in winter; eyelids and hind-neck white; mantle, sides of breast and under surface of wings slate-colour, mantle brownish-black in winter; primaries black; secondaries broadly tipped with white; lower breast, abdomen and tail white; bill orange-red with black terminal band; feet yellowish; length 15.6 ins.; wing 12.3; tail 4.7; bill 2; tarsus 1.7. *Young.*—Brown with whitish rump, throat and abdomen; primaries and tail brownish-black; secondaries with white tips; bill black; feet greenish-grey.

Range.—Red Sea and coasts of Arabia and Somaliland. Breeds in the Gulf of Aden and southern Red Sea. *Egg-dates:* July–Sept.

Notes.—Distinguished from the Aden Gull by its smaller size, black hood and slaty mantle. In pattern the two are very similar. From the Northern and Indian Black-headed Gulls it differs in its black (not brown) hood and dark mantle, sides of breast and under surface of wings.

30. Franklin's Gull (*Larus pipixcan = L. franklini*) (*Plate 25*)

Adult.—Head with a deep black hood in summer, in winter with a dull black half-hood on forehead and crown; bars above and below eye, underparts and tail white; mantle blue-grey; wing-quills with white tips, five outer primaries subterminally black, other primaries and secondaries grey; bill dark reddish in summer, blackish in winter; feet reddish brown; length 13.5–14 ins.; wing 10.6–11.6; tail 3.7–4.3; bill 1.2–1.3; tarsus 1.5–1.6. *Young.*—Forehead white; crown and sides of head dusky, forming a half-hood; mantle greyish-brown; wing-quills tipped with white; upper tail-coverts white; tail pale grey with a broad subterminal blackish band; underparts white; bill and feet brownish.

Range.—Winters on the west coast of South America from Valparaiso northwards, on migration occurs in Central America and inland localities in North America; occasionally visits the West Indies, the Atlantic and Pacific coasts of the United States, the Galápagos Is. and Hawaiian Is. Breeds on lakes in the interior of North America. *Egg-dates:* May–June.

Notes.—The only gull which regularly migrates completely from its breeding grounds in the north to winter in the southern hemisphere. Its mantle is darker than that of other American dark-hooded gulls except the Laughing Gull, from which it may be distinguished by its smaller size and the white tips to its outer primaries.

31. Mediterranean Black-headed Gull (*Larus melano-cephalus*). (*Plate 25*)

Adult.—Head black in summer, in winter white streaked with blackish; small crescentic patches above and below eye white; mantle pearl-grey; primaries white at ends with grey bases, the first with a black line on the outer web; neck, underparts and tail white; bill very stout, coral red with a dusky terminal band; feet dark red; length 15.5–17 ins.; wing 11.5–12; tail 5; bill 1.6–1.8; tarsus 1.9. *Young.*—Head, neck and back mottled with brown; outer primaries dark brown with white areas towards the base; tail white with a subterminal brown band; bill brownish-black, yellow at the base; feet reddish-brown.

Range.—In winter on coasts of Bay of Biscay, Spain, Portugal, the Mediterranean and Black Seas, occasionally to England. Breeds in southeastern Europe, Asia Minor (*L. m. melanocephalus*) and in central Asia (*L. m. relictus*). *Egg-dates:* May–June.

Notes.—Distinguished from the Northern Black-headed Gull by its black (not brown) head in summer, stouter bill and white primaries. The young bird has brown (not white) band along edge of wings.

32. Chinese Black-headed Gull (*Larus saundersi*)

Adult.—Head bluish-black in summer, in winter white with dusky patches; a slender white ring round the eye interrupted in front; neck, underparts and tail white; mantle dark pearl-grey; wing-quills largely white, first primary with a narrow edge of black on outer web, outermost primaries with black inner webs merging into subterminal bars, except on the first; under wing-coverts grey; bill black; feet red; length 12.6 ins.; wing 11; tail 4.4; bill 1.4; tarsus 1.6. *Young.*—Crown and mantle brownish-grey mottled with brown and buff; outer primaries black at tips, the first two also on the outer webs; tail white with a narow black subterminal band; bill blackish; feet brownish-red.

Range.—In winter on coasts of eastern Siberia, Korea and China, occasionally to Japan and Formosa. Breeds on inland lakes in Mongolia and northern China.

Notes.—Distinguished from the Northern Black-headed Gull by its black (not brown) head in summer, darker mantle and largely white outer primaries.

33. Bonaparte's Gull (*Larus philadelphia*). (Plate 25)

Adult.—Head bluish-black in summer, in winter white with dusky patches; a narrow white ring round the eye interrupted in front; mantle pearl-grey; outer primaries black, with large areas of white on inner webs, all but first two with white tips; underparts, under wing-coverts, rump and tail white; bill black, sometimes reddish at base; feet reddish flesh-colour; length 14 ins.; wing 10.2; tail 4.5; bill 1.5; tarsus 1.4. *Young.*—Crown, nape and upper back greyish-brown; a dusky patch on the sides of the head; forehead, neck and underparts white; lower back and scapulars greyish-brown, the feathers with buff tips; tail white with a subterminal dusky band; bill dusky; feet pale brownish.

Range.—In winter on the coasts of Mexico and the United States, occasionally to Peru, the Hawaiian Is., Bermuda and the British Is.; on migration visits coasts of Alaska, Canada and Labrador. Breeds in the interior of Alaska and western Canada. *Egg-dates:* June–July.

Notes.—The smallest American Gull, distinguished by its black bill and reddish feet, and in flight by the white band near the front of the wing.

34. Little Gull (*Larus minutus*)

Adult.—Head and upper neck black in summer, in winter white with greyish-black patch on the crown and nape; lower neck, underparts and tail white, with a rosy tinge on the underparts; mantle pale grey; wing-quills grey with broad white edges; under surface of wings greyish-black; bill deep red; feet vermilion; length 10–12 ins.; wing 8.3–8.8; tail 3.3–3.7; bill 0.9–1.2; tarsus 0.9–1.1. *Young.*—Crown, nape and mantle dark brown, the feathers with pale tips; primaries mostly blackish on outer webs, with white on tips and inner webs; secondaries dark brown with white tips; tail white with a broad subterminal black band; bill brownish; feet dull flesh-colour.

Range.—In winter on coasts of western Europe, the Mediterranean, Black Sea, Sea of Okhotsk and Japan Sea, sometimes to British Is., occasionally to Bermuda, the United States and Mexico. Breeds in northern Europe and Siberia from Holland and Denmark to the Sea of Okhotsk. *Egg-dates:* May–June.

Notes.—Much smaller than any other Gull. Distinguished also by the very dark under surface of the wings and absence of black on the primaries.

35. Northern Black-headed Gull (*Larus ridibundus*).
(Plates 25 and 29)

Adult.—Head in summer coffee-brown with a narrow white ring round the eye interrupted in front, in winter white with dusky markings; neck, underparts and tail white, the under surface sometimes with a rosy tinge; mantle and under wing-coverts blue-grey; wing-coverts on edge and bend of wing white; outer primaries chiefly white, with black tips and black margins to the inner webs; inner primaries and secondaries grey; bill and feet deep red; length 15.5–17 ins.; wing 12–13.5; tail 4.7–5.5; bill 1.3–1.8; tarsus 1.7. *Young.*—Similar but back of head chiefly greyish-brown; mantle brown; some of the wing-coverts grey; outer primaries black all round with white centres; tail with a subterminal band of blackish brown; bill yellowish with a black tip; feet dull reddish-yellow.

Range.—In winter on coasts of Europe, northern Africa and Asia, south to Gambia, the Red Sea, Persian Gulf, India, the Philippines, China and Japan, occasionally to Iceland, the Azores, Madeira and Canary Is. Breeds, mostly inland, from the British Is. and western Europe to Turkestan and eastern Asia. *Egg-dates:* April–June.

Notes.—A common and widespread species in the eastern hemisphere, distinguished by its small size, red bill and feet and the broad white margin of the front edge of the black-tipped wings. In summer the dark brown head distinguishes it from all other northern Gulls.

36. Patagonian Black-headed Gull (*Larus maculipennis* = *L. glaucodes*). (*Plate 31*)

Adult.—Similar to the Northern Black-headed Gull but underparts generally rosy; outer primaries white at the ends; bill reddish black; feet reddish; length 14–15 ins.; wing 11–12; tail 4.8–5; bill 1.7; tarsus 1.8–2. *Young.*— Similar to young Northern Black-headed Gull but with more black on the primaries; bill brownish with a blackish tip; feet brownish.

Range.—South America north to northern Chile and southern Brazil. Breeds in the Falkland Is., Tierra del Fuego, Patagonia, S. Chile, Argentina and Uruguay. *Egg-dates:* July, Oct.–Dec.

Notes.—Distinguished from the Grey-headed Gull by its pale grey under wing-coverts, and when adult by its dark brown hood.

37. Indian Black-headed Gull (*Larus brunnicephalus*)

Adult.—Similar to the Northern Black-headed Gull but the hood is paler brown on the forehead and appears blacker where it joins the white neck; outer primaries black, with white patches towards the tips of the first two; bill deep red, feet vermilion; length 15.8–17 ins.; wing 11.5–13; tail 4.5–5.7; bill 1.9; tarsus 1.9. *Young.*—Similar to young Northern Black-headed Gull but outer primaries are sooty-brown, with white only at the base; bill yellowish-orange with a dusky tip; feet orange.

Range.—In winter on the coasts of southern Asia from Aden to Ceylon and Siam. Breeds in the highlands of central Asia from Turkestan to Mongolia and Tibet. *Egg-dates:* March, June–July.

Notes.—In winter when the two species may occur together, the Indian bird can readily be distinguished from its Northern relative by the large white patches on its primaries and by its larger size.

38. **Sabine's Gull** (*Xema sabini*). (*Plates 33 and 49*)

Adult.—Head and throat slate-coloured in summer, in winter white with dusky patches; neck, underparts and forked tail white; mantle pearl-grey; first primary black, next three black subterminally with white tips, remainder of primaries and secondaries grey with white tips; bill black with yellow tip; feet dusky; length 13–14 ins.; wing 10.2–11.3; tail 4.4–5.1; bill 0.9–1.1; tarsus 1.2–1.4. *Young.*—Upperparts ashy-brown, the feathers with light tips; forehead underparts and tail white, the latter with a broad, terminal, blackish bar; bill dusky; feet brownish.

Range.—Arctic regions, south in winter to West Africa and on the Pacific Coast of America to northern Chile, occasionally to Texas, Bermuda and France. Breeds in Alaska, northern Canada, Greenland, Spitzbergen and northern Siberia. *Egg-dates:* May–July.

Notes.—The only Arctic Gull with a dark hood, and the only Gull except the Swallow-tailed Gull, which is much larger, with a definitely forked tail. It may be distinguished from the Kittiwakes, which have slightly forked tails, by its black bill.

XII. SMALL GULLS WITH GREY MANTLE AND WHITE HEAD IN BREEDING SEASON

39. **Common Kittiwake** (*Rissa tridactyla*). (*Plates 25 and 34*)

Adult.—Head and neck white in summer, in winter crown and sides of head streaked with dark grey and back of neck grey like the back; underparts, under surface of wings and slightly forked tail white; mantle pearl-grey; outer margin of first primary and tips of next three black; remainder of primaries and secondaries grey with white tips; bill greenish yellow; feet dusky; length 15.5–16 ins.; wing 11.5–13; tail 4.5–5.6; bill 1.3–1.7; tarsus 1.2–1.4. *Young.*—Head white with grey patches on crown and nape; back of neck with numerous transverse blackish-grey crescentic bands; underparts and tail white, the latter with a black terminal band; mantle grey, the wings crossed by a conspicuous dark stripe; primaries dull black; bill black; feet pale brown.

Range.—Arctic Seas, North Pacific and North Atlantic, in winter south to Japan, Lower California, New Jersey, the Azores, Cape Verde Is., Mediterranean and Black Sea. Breeds on coasts of Bering Sea (*R. t. pollicaris*), in the Gulf of St. Lawrence and on the coasts of Labrador, arctic Canada, Greenland, arctic Europe, the British Is. and northern France (*R. t. tridactyla*). *Egg-dates:* April–July.

Notes.—The only truly oceanic gull, mostly found offshore except in the breeding season. The immature bird is characterized by the striking black band across the wings and the dark streaks on the sides of the neck, the adult by its slightly forked tail, yellow bill and black feet, in winter also by its streaked head.

40. Red-legged Kittiwake (*Rissa brevirostris*)

Adult.—Similar to the Common Kittiwake but mantle leaden-grey; bill yellow; feet red; length 15 ins.; wing 11.8–12.8; tail 4.5–5.2; bill 1.1–1.3; tarsus 1.1–1.3. *Young.*—Similar to the adult but mantle somewhat browner; nape crossed by a broad band of greyish-black; sides of head and spot in front of eye blackish; primary coverts and outer webs of three or four outer primaries black; bill dusky; feet brownish.

Range.—Southern portion of Bering Sea, occasionally to Alaska. Breeds on Commander Is., western Aleutian Is. and Pribilof Is. *Egg-dates:* June–July.

Notes.—The adult differs from the Common Kittiwake in its darker mantle and red legs; the young is the only immature Gull with a wholly white tail and is without the black band on the wing so characteristic of the Common Kittiwake.

41. Slender-billed Gull (*Larus genei = L. gelastes*)

Adult.—Head, neck, underparts and tail white, all except the head suffused with rosy; mantle pearl-grey; inner primaries and secondaries grey; first four primaries largely white tipped with black, the outermost with the outer web black; axillaries and under wing-coverts grey; bill slender, red; feet red; length 15.5–18.5; wing 11.5–12.2; tail 4.5–5; bill 1.9–2.2; tarsus 1.6–2. *Young.*—Similar to the adult but the crown and nape marked with grey; mantle ashy-brown, the feathers with pale edges; tail white with a terminal blackish band; underparts without rosy tinge; bill orange-yellow; feet lemon-yellow.

Range.—Coasts of south-western Europe, north-western Africa, the Mediterranean, Black and Red Seas, Persian Gulf and Mekran coast to Karachi. Breeds in Spain, Asia Minor and Egypt and on coasts of Black, Azof and Caspian Seas, Persia and Baluchistan. *Egg-dates:* April–July.

Notes.—Resembles the Northern Black-headed Gull but is rather larger and always has a white head.

42. Silver Gull (*Larus novaehollandiae*)

Adult.—Head, neck, underparts and tail white; mantle grey; two or three outer primaries black with a large spot of white near the tip, most of the other primaries white with a black band near the tip, all but first two tipped with white; bill and feet red; length 14–15 ins.; wing 10.8–12; tail 4.7–5.5; bill 1.6–1.8; tarsus 1.7–2. *Young.*—Similar but mantle mottled with brown; first two primaries almost entirely brownish-black; tail with a narrow subterminal brown band; bill brownish; feet greyish.

Range.—Coasts of South Africa from Namaqualand to Natal, Australia, Tasmania, New Caledonia, New Zealand, the Chatham Is. and Auckland Is. Breeds in western Cape Colony (*L. n. hartlaubii*), western and southern Australia (*L. n. novaehollandiae*), Queensland and New Caledonia (*L. n. forsteri*), Tasmania (*L. n. gunni*), New Zealand and the Chatham Is. (*L. n. scopulinus*). *Egg-dates:* April–Dec.

Notes.—The New Zealand form is commonly called the "Mackerel Gull" and may be distinguished from Buller's Gull by its red bill and differently marked primaries. In Australia it is the only small Gull. "Hartlaub's Gull," the

South African form, may be distinguished from the Grey-headed Gull by its pure white head.

43. Buller's Gull (*Larus bulleri*)

Adult.—Similar in size and general colouring to the Silver Gull; white underparts sometimes tinged with rose; outer primary white with black edges towards the base, next three largely white but with a subterminal black band; bill black; feet red; length 14.5 ins.; wing 11.8–12; tail 4.8; bill 1.8; tarsus 1.7. *Young.*—Similar to young Silver Gull but all primaries with small white tips.

Range.—New Zealand. Breeds on lakes and rivers in both islands. *Egg-dates:* Dec.

Notes.—A rare species most readily distinguished from the Silver Gull by its black bill.

44. Ross's Gull (*Rhodostethia rosea*)

Adult.—Head and neck white in summer with a narrow black collar, in winter pale bluish-grey; eyelids vermilion; mantle and wing-quills pearl-grey, the outer web of the first primary black, secondaries tipped with rosy white; under wing-coverts grey; underparts, rump and wedge-shaped tail rosy white; bill black; feet red; length 13.5–14 ins.; wing 9.5–10.5; tail 3.9–5.2; bill 0.7–0.9; tarsus 1.1–1.2. *Young.*—Crown, neck and mantle brownish-black, the feathers with buff edges; forehead and sides of head dull white, with dusky spots round and behind the eye; outer primaries black, inner primaries partly white the amount increasing to the secondaries which are wholly white; a blackish band on the lesser coverts and tertials; tail white, with a broad black terminal band on the inner feathers; underparts white; bill black; feet fleshy purple.

Range.—Arctic regions, occasionally south in winter to western Europe. Breeds in north-eastern Siberia. *Egg-dates:* June.

Notes.—This small arctic gull differs from all other species in the black ring round the neck, wedge-shaped tail and rosy colouring. The young bird is distinguished by its sharply contrasted black and white plumage.

CHAPTER VI

Terns or Sea Swallows and Noddies

(Order *Charadriiformes*: Family *Sternidae*)

THE MEMBERS of this family are long-winged sea-birds of rather small size with tapering pointed bills, straight or slightly curved at the tip. Their legs are very short and their webbed feet are small. The majority of the species have long forked tails, the outer tail-feathers being exceptionally elongated in some of the marine species. In those which live mainly on fresh-water lakes and swamps the tail is much less forked, whilst in the tropical Noddies the tail is forked in the centre but the outer feathers become progressively shorter, so that it may be described as wedge-shaped with a V cut out of the centre.

Terns are mainly birds of the coasts of the warmer parts of the world, but a number of species migrate into the north temperate regions during the summer to breed, and the Arctic Tern breeds in northern and arctic regions to within 8° of the North Pole. This species performs the most extensive migration of any bird as it spends the northern winter in antarctic seas. One marked when 10 days old in Turnavik Bay, Labrador, in July, 1928, was recovered near Shepstone, Natal, in November, 1928. It has been computed that some Arctic Terns probably enjoy continuous daylight for eight months of the year. Several other species which breed in the northern hemisphere winter south of the equator.

Terns are generally sociable in habits and often breed in large colonies. Most of the species lay their eggs in a mere hollow on sandy or shingly beaches, either by the sea or on rivers or lakes, usually on islands. The Whiskered, Black and White-winged Black Terns, which breed in swamps, make a nest of floating water-weeds and reeds lined with finer materials; the Noddies make rude nests of seaweed on bushes or the branches of trees; the Brown-winged and Inca Terns lay their eggs in a cave or under tangled vegetation, often almost in the dark; whilst the White Terns lay their single egg on bare rocks or on a slight hollow or crotch of a tree-trunk, or even the rib of a palm leaf, where it often seems impossible that it should remain without rolling off.

The eggs of Terns are large in proportion to the size of the bird. The Noddies, White Terns, Sooty Tern and several other tropical and subantarctic species only lay one, but the majority lay two or three and occasionally clutches of four or even five may be found. Tern's eggs are either white, pale greenish, buff or yellowish in ground colour, blotched, spotted, streaked or scrawled with grey, brown, chocolate, red or black markings. There is great individual variation in the eggs of most of the species. The chicks when hatched are covered with down, usually yellowish with darker markings. Both eggs and young harmonise so well with their usual surroundings on beaches that they are generally difficult to discover and the young behave as if conscious of this resemblance, lying motionless on the ground when danger threatens. The parents are usually very bold when their breeding grounds are invaded, hovering in the air over the intruder, uttering loud screams and at intervals swooping down within a few inches of his head.

The young birds are dependent on their parents for food until they are fledged, and for some time remain in their nests or the slight hollows which serve as such. When almost fledged they begin to wander about and frequently swim about near the shore in shallow water. Curiously enough, adult Terns, though their feet are webbed, rarely settle on the water, roosting on beaches or on drifting logs or seaweed.

The majority of Terns feed almost entirely on small fish which they obtain when they are near the surface by plunging down from the air. When flying over the sea they constantly scan the surface and the bill is usually pointed downwards at right angles to the body. When a school of small fish is sighted they hover over it in the air and at a favourable moment close the wings and drop swiftly head first. After a brief immersion they reappear and immediately take flight again. Small cuttlefish, crustacea and pelagic molluscs form part of the food of marine species, while those which frequent marshes feed largely on dragon-flies and other large insects. Unlike Gulls, Terns do not feed on dead fish or floating refuse.

Many species suffered severely until recent times owing to the demand for their plumage for trimming ladies' hats, but fortunately public sentiment in most civilised countries has now brought about legislation prohibiting this trade, and the numbers of these most graceful and elegant sea-birds are increasing.

A few species of Terns are mainly black, and the majority have the top of the head black, at least in the breeding season. Otherwise their plumage is mainly a harmony of pale grey and white, sometimes with a beautiful roseate tinge. In winter most species lose much of their black colouring and in this plu-mage the identification of species seen on the wing is very difficult or impossible. The sexes are alike in all species. The bills and feet of Terns are frequently black, but are often bright red, orange or yellow, especially in the breeding season. A number of the larger species have the feathers on the back of the head elongated to form a crest, and the Inca Tern has remarkable moustache-like tufts on the cheeks. Young Terns usually resemble their parents in winter plumage but have the upper parts mottled with brown.

In size Terns may be divided into three groups: "large" species with wings over 11.5 inches long, "medium-sized" species with the wing from 9 to 11.5 inches long and "small" species with the wing less than 9 inches long.

In the following pages they are arranged according to size and their colouring in the breeding season in nine groups:

   I. Large, with grey mantle, white or pale grey underparts and black crown (Species 1–10).

  II. Medium-sized, with grey mantle, white or pale grey underparts and black crown (Species 11–22).

 III. Medium-sized, with grey mantle, dark abdomen and black crown (Species 23–24).

 IV. Medium-sized, with dusky upperparts and white underparts (Species 25–27).

  V. Medium-sized, with grey mantle and underparts and white head (Species 28).

 VI. Medium-sized, with dusky plumage (Species 29–30).

VII. Small, with plumage mainly dusky (Species 31–34).

VIII. Small, with grey mantle, white or pale grey underparts and black crown (Species 35–39).

 IX. Small, with pale grey or white plumage (Species 40–42).

As an aid to their identification the Terns are here grouped according to the colours of their bills and feet. (The adults of some species in winter plumage revert to the colours characteristic of the young, so that the colours given for the young sometimes apply also to winter adults.)

I. TERNS WITH BILL AND FEET RED OR ORANGE OR REDDISH BROWN

(10) South American, (11) Forster's, (12) Black-fronted, (13) Kerguelen, (14) Swallow-tailed, (15) Common, (16) Arctic, (17) White-cheeked, (24) Whiskered, (29) Inca and (34) White-winged Black Terns (adult); and (9) Gull-billed Tern (young).

II. TERNS WITH BILL ORANGE AND FEET YELLOW

(35) Little Tern (adult).

III. TERNS WITH BILL RED OR ORANGE AND FEET BLACK

(1) Caspian, (2) Royal, (3) Elegant and (5) Lesser Crested Terns (adult).

IV. TERNS WITH BILL YELLOW AND FEET RED OR ORANGE

(18) Indian River, (23) Black-bellied and (28) Trudeau's Terns (adult).

V. TERNS WITH BILL AND FEET YELLOW OR GREENISH

(19) Large-billed, (36) Amazon and (38) Fairy Terns (adult); (2) Royal, (5) Lesser Crested, (12) Black-fronted, (13) Kerguelen, (22) Aleutian and (40) Black-naped Terns (young).

VI. TERNS WITH BILL YELLOW AND FEET BLACK OR DUSKY

(4) Cayenne, (6) Chinese Crested, (7) Crested, and (37) Chilean Terns (adult).

VII. TERNS WITH BILL BLACK AND FEET RED OR ORANGE OR REDDISH BROWN

(20) Roseate, (21) White-fronted and (42) Marquesan White Terns (adult); (11) Forster's and (34) White-winged Black Terns (young).

VIII. TERNS WITH BILL BLACK OR DUSKY AND FEET YELLOW

(39) Damara Tern (adult); (4) Cayenne, (10) South American, (17) White-cheeked, (28) Trudeau's and (35) Little Terns (young).

IX. TERNS WITH BILL AND FEET BLACK OR DUSKY

(8) Sandwich, (9) Gull-billed, (22) Aleutian, (25) Sooty, (26) Brown-winged, (27) Spectacled, (30) Common Noddy, (31) Lesser Noddy, (32) White-capped Noddy, (33) Black, (40) Black-naped, (41) Blue-grey Noddy and (42) White Terns (adult); (3) Elegant, (15) Common, (16) Arctic, (20) Roseate and (21) White-fronted Terns (young).

X. TERNS WITH BILL BLACK AND FEET BLUE

(42) White Tern (adult).

I. LARGE TERNS WITH GREY MANTLE, WHITE OR PALE GREY UNDERPARTS AND BLACK CROWN IN BREEDING SEASON

1. **Caspian Tern** (*Hydroprogne tschegrava = H. caspia*). (*Plates 37 and 38*)

Adult.—Top of head and nape black, streaked with white in winter; mantle ash-grey; tail slightly forked, greyish-white; inner webs of primaries slate-grey; under-parts and upper tail-coverts white; bill very stout, red; feet black; length 18–22 ins.; wing 15.7–17.3; tail 4.5–6; bill 2.4–3; tarsus 1.5–1.8. *Young.*—Similar, but top of head streaked with black and white; upper parts spotted with dusky; bill dull orange; feet blackish-brown.

Range.—North America, Europe, Asia, Africa, Australia and New Zealand, but rather local in north temperate regions. Breeds on coasts and inland lakes in various parts of North America, Europe, Africa and central and southern Asia (*H. t. tschegrava*) and coasts of Australia, Tasmania and New Zealand (*H. t. strenua*). *Egg-dates:* Throughout the year (in tropical localities); April-July, (north temperate regions); Nov.–Jan. (south temperate regions).

Notes.—Distinguished by its very large size, large, stout, red bill, and entirely black forehead and crown.

2. Royal Tern (*Thalasseus maximus*). (*Plates 39 and 41*)

Adult.—Crown and nape black, the feathers elongated; forehead sometimes also black, frequently white; in winter crown also streaked with white; mantle pale grey; outer web of outermost primary darker grey; inner webs of primaries with a broad dark grey streak next the shaft; tail deeply forked, greyish-white; neck, underparts, rump and edge of wing white; bill orange-red; feet black; length 19 ins.; wing 14–15.5; tail 5.1–7.7; bill 2.2–2.8; tarsus 1.1–1.4. *Young.*—Similar, but crown almost white, fore-head with black stripes; upperparts spotted with dusky; tail feathers dusky towards the tip; bill and feet dull yellow.

Range.—Coasts of America from California and Massa-chusetts, south in winter to Peru and Argentina and the north-west coast of Africa from the Straits of Gibraltar to Angola. Breeds on the Pacific coast of Mexico, the south-ern coasts of the United States from Texas to Virginia and in the West Indies (*T. m. maximus*). *Egg-dates:* April–June.

Notes.—Resembles the Caspian Tern but decidedly smaller with a longer forked tail, bill more slender, and forehead usually white. The form found on the coast of Africa has been named *T. m. albidorsalis* but its breeding-place is not known.

3. Elegant Tern (*Thalasseus elegans*). (*Plates 39 and 41*)

Adult.—Similar to the Royal Tern but decidedly smaller and with a longer and more slender bill, the mantle slightly darker and the tail whiter; bill orange-red; feet black; length 16.5 ins.; wing 11.5–12.6; tail 4.5–6.5; bill 2.2–2.8; tarsus 1.1–1.2. *Young.*—Similar to the young Royal Tern but the bill blackish, much shorter than in the adult.

Range.—Pacific coast of America from California to Chile, occasionally to Texas. Breeds in Lower California. *Egg-dates:* April–May.

Notes.—Hardly distinguishable from the Royal Tern in life.

4. Cayenne Tern (*Thalasseus eurygnatha*)

Adult.—Similar to the Royal Tern but smaller; bill lemon yellow; feet black, back of leg dull yellow; length 17.5 ins.; wing 11.8–12.6; tail 6.5; bill 2.7; tarsus 1.1. *Young.*—Similar to the young Royal Tern but bill blackish, greenish at base; feet ochre-yellow.

Range.—Atlantic coast of South America from northern Colombia and the Lesser Antilles to Port Desire, Patagonia. Breeds on the coasts of Venezuela and Brazil.

Note.—Distin from other large South American Terns by its p bill.

5. Lesser Cres (*Thalasseus bengalensis* = *S. media*)

Adult.—Similar to the Royal Tern but smaller, the mantle rather darker grey, and the tail the same tint; bill waxy yellow or orange, shorter and straighter; feet black; length 13.5–17 ins; wing 11.5–12.5; tail 6–6.7; bill 2.2–2.5; tarsus 1–1.2. *Young.*—Similar to the young Royal Tern but smaller.

both coasts of Africa to the Cape of Good Hope, the Red Sea, Persian Gulf, Arabian Sea and Bay of Bengal. Breeds on the coasts of the United States and Mexico southwards from North Carolina (*T. s. acuflavidus*), and on the western and southern coasts of Europe from the British Is. to the Black Sea (*T. s. sandvicensis*). *Egg-dates:* April–June.

Notes.—Distinguished from the other large Terns, except the Gull-billed Tern, by its black bill, and from the latter by its more slender bill with yellow tip, the crest on the back of its head and its more forked white tail. The American form is usually called "Cabot's Tern."

9. **Gull-billed Tern** (*Gelochelidon nilotica = G. anglica*).
   (*Plate* 37)

Adult.—Top and sides of head black, in winter white with black streaks; upperparts and tail pearl-grey or very pale grey; outer-webs of outermost primaries slate grey, inner web with a white wedge on the upper part; underparts, including under surface of wings, white; bill short and stout, black; feet black with a reddish tinge; tail short and moderately forked; length 14.5–16.2 ins.; wing 10.8–14.5; tail 4.1–6; bill 1.3–2; tarsus 1.1–1.5. *Young.*—Similar, but head dull white with dusky streaks; back and scapulars buff spotted with brown; wing-coverts and primaries ash-grey; bill and feet reddish brown.

Range.—Eastern North America and both coasts of Central and South America, temperate Europe, North Africa, temperate and tropical Asia, the Malay Archipelago and Australia. A summer visitor in the northern parts of its range. Breeds in the south-eastern United States, the Bahamas, Cuba and Mexico (*G. n. aranea*), Salton Sea, California (*G. n. vanrossemi*), Brazil and Argentina (*G. n. gronvoldi*), north-west Africa, Europe and Asia from Denmark and Spain to Mongolia and the Punjab (*G. n. nilotica*) China (*G. n. addenda*) and Australia (*G. n. macrotarsa*). *Egg-dates:* April–July (northern hemisphere), Nov.–Dec. (southern hemisphere).

Notes.—Distinguished from other large terns by its stout, black bill and less forked, pale grey tail. Chiefly frequents lakes and estuaries and obtains its food from the surface like a gull, not by diving.

10. South American Tern (*Sterna hirundinacea*)

Adult.—Top of head black, in winter forehead and crown white, mottled with black; a white streak on the sides of the head below the black area; neck, mantle, throat and breast pale pearl-grey, the underparts nearly white in winter; rump, abdomen and deeply-forked tail white, the tail-feathers with a grey tinge on the outer webs; bill and feet vermilion; length 16–16.5 ins.; wing 10.7–11.8; tail 7; bill 1.7; tarsus 0.8 *Young.*—Similar, but crown white, mottled with black; mantle barred with blackish-brown and white, a conspicuous brownish bar along the upper wing-coverts; bill blackish; feet reddish-yellow.

Range.—South America from Peru and Bahia to the Falkland Is. and Tierra del Fuego. Breeds throughout its range. *Egg-dates:* June–July, Nov.–Jan.

Notes.—Very similar to the Swallow-tailed and Arctic Terns, but decidedly larger and with a longer, somewhat curved, bill.

II. MEDIUM-SIZED TERNS WITH GREY MANTLE, WHITE OR PALE GREY UNDERPARTS AND BLACK CROWN IN BREEDING SEASON

11. Forster's Tern (*Sterna forsteri*)

Adult.—Top of head black, in winter greyish-white with black streaks and black patches before and behind the eye; mantle pearl-grey; primaries dark grey, inner border of inner web of outermost white; rump and underparts white; tail pale pearl-grey, the inner web of the outer feathers darker towards the end and the outer web whitish; bill rather stout, dull orange, blackish towards tip; in winter mostly black; feet orange, in winter brownish; length 14–15 ins.; wing 9.5–10.5; tail 5.5–8.6; bill 1.5–1.7; tarsus 0.8–1. *Young.*—Similar to adult in winter but mantle mottled with brownish; tail much shorter.

Range.—North America, south in winter to Central America and occasionally to Brazil. Breeds, chiefly on inland lakes, in western Canada and in the United States. *Egg-dates:* April–July.

Notes.—Very similar to the Common Tern, but in breeding plumage distinguished by its slightly larger size, white underparts, longer tail and orange and black bill; in winter or immature plumage by the black band on each side of the head. Its note is distinctive, being a harsh, grating, nasal sound in a low key and it feeds largely on insects in the breeding season.

12. Black-fronted Tern (*Sterna albistriata = S. antarctica*)

Adult.—Top of head black, in winter probably ash-grey mottled with black; a broad streak of white on each side of the head; mantle dark pearl-grey; outer primaries with pale grey margins to the inner webs and white shafts; rump white; tail dark pearl-grey, the outer feathers nearly white above; breast and abdomen pearl-grey; under tail-coverts greyish-white; bill orange; feet red; length 12 ins.; wing 9.5–10; tail 4.5–5; bill 1.2; tarsus 0.6–0.7. *Young.*—Similar, but head white mottled with black; wing-coverts and tail-feathers marked with brown; bill yellow with blackish tip; feet dull yellow.

Range.—New Zealand, occasionally to Norfolk I. Breeds on rivers in the South Island. *Egg-dates:* Oct.–Nov.

Notes.—Though formerly abundant, this Tern is now scarce and nearly confined to the South Island of New Zealand. Its name indicates one of its chief differences from the White-fronted Tern, from which it is also distinguished by its smaller size, darker colour and orange or yellow bill.

13. Kerguelen Tern (*Sterna virgata*)

Adult.—Similar to the Black-fronted Tern but the underparts darker, so that the white moustachial streak between the black cap and grey throat is conspicuous; primaries, especially the outermost, darker, shafts greyish; outer web of outer tail-feathers distinctly grey; bill blood-red; feet orange-red; in winter bill and feet yellowish; length 13 ins.; wing 10; tail 6.2; bill 1.2; tarsus 0.6. *Young.*—Similar, but forehead brownish-grey; crown and nape mottled with black; upperparts mottled with brownish black; underparts greyish, flecked with brown.

Range.—Islands of the South Indian Ocean. Breeds at Marion I., the Crozet Is., Kerguelen and Heard I. *Egg-dates:* Oct.–Feb.

Notes.—Distinguished from the Swallow-tailed Tern by its smaller size, darker colouring and shorter tail.

14. Swallow-tailed, or Wreathed, Tern (*Sterna vittata*). (*Plate 42*)

Adult.—Similar to the Kerguelen Tern but larger and paler with a longer and more deeply forked tail; tail nearly white, the outer webs of the feathers very pale grey; shafts of the primaries white; bill vermilion; feet orange-red; length 16 ins.; wing 10.5; tail 7.5–8; bill 1.4; tarsus 0.7. *Young.*—Similar to the young Kerguelen Tern but paler; upperparts barred with pale buff and black; abdomen white; bill and feet dull blackish-red.

Range.—Southern Oceans and Antarctic Seas. Breeds at Tristan da Cunha, Gough I., Kerguelen, St. Paul and Amsterdam Is. (*S. v. vittata*), South Georgia (*S. v. georgiae*) and the South Orkneys, and the subantarctic islands of New Zealand (*S. v. bethunei*). *Egg-dates:* Nov.–Jan.

Notes.—Very similar to the Arctic and Kerguelen Terns and in life probably indistinguishable. From the Arctic Tern it may be distinguished by the greater breadth of the grey line on the primaries inside the shaft, and from the Kerguelen Tern by the features mentioned in the description above.

15. Common Tern (*Sterna hirundo* = *S. fluviatilis*). (*Plate 43*)

Adult.—Top of head black, in winter forehead and crown streaked and mottled with white; mantle dark pearl-grey; outermost primaries with outer web black, inner web broadly grey next the shaft and white on the margin, except at the tip; inner primaries paler grey with dark grey margins to the inner web; tail grey, the inner webs of the feathers white; throat, rump, under surface of wings and under tail-coverts white; breast and abdomen pale vinaceous grey, white in winter; bill coral-red with black tip or entirely black, in winter chiefly black; feet coral-red, duller in winter; length 12.5–15 ins.; wing 9.5–10.7; tail 4.5–7.1; bill 1.3–1.7; tarsus 0.7–1. *Young.*— Similar to the adult in winter plumage but mantle mottled with ash-brown; a dark grey band on the upper wing-coverts; outer webs of tail-feathers dark grey; bill brownish; feet flesh-coloured.

Range.—Eastern North America and temperate Europe and Asia, south in winter to Ecuador, Patagonia, South Africa, India, Ceylon, Malacca, New Guinea and Australia, visiting the Pacific coast of the United States on migration. Breeds on coasts, lakes and rivers in North America, the Bahamas, West Indies and Venezuela, in the Azores, Canary Islands, and Madeira, in Tunisia, and across Europe and Asia from the British Is. to the Yenisei, Caspian Sea and Persia (*S. h. hirundo*), central Asia and Mongolia (*S. h. minussensis*), also Turkestan, Tibet (*S. h. tibetana*), and in north-eastern Asia (*S. h. longipennis*). *Egg-dates:* May–July.

Notes.—Very similar to the Arctic Tern and Forster's Tern. Distinguished from both by its shorter outer tail-feathers, from the former by its black-tipped bill and from the latter by its pale grey breast.

16. **Arctic Tern** (*Sterna paradisea* = S. *macrura* = S. *arctica* = S. *antistropha*). (*Plates* 35 *and* 36)

Adult.—Similar to the Common Tern but throat, breast and abdomen French-grey with no vinaceous tint; a white streak on the sides of the head below the black cap; outermost primaries with inner web narrowly grey next the shaft; secondaries broadly margined with white; outside tail-feathers very long with dark grey outer webs; bill blood-red; feet coral-red; length 13–15 ins.; wing 9.4–11;

tail 5.3–8; bill 1.1–1.6; tarsus 0.5–0.7. *Young.*—Similar to young Common Tern, but bill yellow with blackish tip; feet yellow. In intermediate plumage the bill and feet become black.

Range.—Arctic regions south in winter to Chile, Argentina, South Africa and Antarctica. Breeds from Arctic coasts of Alaska, Canada, Greenland, Europe and Siberia south to British Columbia, Massachusetts, the British Is., Holland, the Commander Is. and Aleutian Is. *Egg-dates:* May–July.

Notes.—Performs the most extensive migration of any bird as it breeds to within 8° of the North Pole and in the northern winter is found on the coasts of the Antarctic Continent. On migration it appears to keep to the oceans and is not found in southern Asia and the Indian and western Pacific Oceans. From the Common Tern it is distinguished by its longer outer tail-feathers, entirely red bill and other features mentioned above, from Forster's Tern by its red bill and grey underparts, from the Swallow-tailed Tern by the narrow grey line on the inner web of the outermost primaries, and from the South American Tern by its smaller size.

17. White-cheeked Tern (*Sterna repressa* = *S. albigena*)

Adult.—Similar to the Arctic Tern, but mantle much darker grey; secondaries smoky-grey; rump grey; outer webs of outer tail-feathers dark grey; underparts vinaceous grey, much darker than in the Common Tern; under wing-coverts and under tail-coverts pale grey; bill slender, coral-red with dusky tip; feet red; length 12.5–14.5 ins.; wing 9.7–9.9; tail 4.1–6.5; bill 1.4–1.6; tarsus 0.7. *Young.*—Similar, but forehead and crown greyish; a dark band on the upper wing-coverts; underparts white; bill nearly black; feet yellowish-brown.

Range.—Red Sea and Indian Ocean from the east coast of Africa to the west coast of India. Breeds on the coasts of British East Africa, Somaliland and southern Arabia, in the Persian Gulf and at the Laccadive Is. *Egg-dates:* May–Aug.

TERNS OR SEA SWALLOWS AND NODDIES

Notes.—A darker bird than the Common Tern, which visits the same region in winter.

18. Indian River Tern (*Sterna aurantia* = *S. seena*)

Adult.—Top of head and circle round eye greenish-black in summer, in winter forehead white, crown grey; mantle, tail-coverts and tail dark pearl-grey, outermost tail-feathers greyish-white; inner webs of outer primaries light brown edged with dusky; throat, under wing-coverts and under tail-coverts white; breast and abdomen pearly greyish white; tail very long and deeply forked; bill stout, orange-yellow, with a dusky tip in winter; feet orange-red; length 15–17 ins.; wing 11–11.5; tail 7–9.5; bill 1.5–1.8; tarsus 0.6–1. *Young.*—Similar, but forehead and crown buffish-white with dusky flecks; a white streak over the eye; upperparts barred with ash-brown and buffy-white; bill dull yellow.

Range.—Tropical Asia from Persia and Baluchistan throughout India to Ceylon, and from Assam and western Yunnan through Burma to Malacca and Singapore. Breeds on inland lakes and rivers. *Egg-dates:* Feb.–Aug.

Notes.—Chiefly an inland bird, but sometimes visits estuaries and coasts. Distinguished by its stout orange-yellow bill and very long, deeply forked tail.

19. Large-billed Tern (*Phaetusa simplex* = *P. magnirostris*)

Adult.—Top of head glossy black; a narrow white line above bill; mantle and tail slate-grey; upper wing-coverts and most of secondaries white; primaries dark brown; underparts white; tail short, nearly square, the outer feathers broad; bill very stout, chrome-yellow; feet olive with yellow webs; length 14.7 ins.; wing 10.5–12.3; tail 3.8–5.1; bill 2.2–2.8; tarsus 0.9–1. *Young.*—Upperparts grey mottled with brownish-black; underparts white.

Range.—Tropical South America from Colombia and Trinidad south to Peru and Argentina, chiefly on the great rivers and estuaries; occasionally to Cuba. Breeds on sandbanks in rivers in northern and north-eastern South America (*P. s. simplex*), and from Bolivia and southern Brazil to Argentina (*P. s. chloropoda*). *Egg-dates:* Sept.–Oct.

Notes.—This river Tern is readily distinguished by its stout yellow bill and square tail.

20. Roseate Tern (*Sterna dougalli*)

Adult.—Top of head black, in winter the forehead spotted with white; mantle pale pearl-grey; primaries rather darker grey: their inner webs edged with white to the tip; outer web of outermost primaries greyish-black; rump and tail white or very pale grey; underparts white with a rosy tinge, less marked in winter; bill black, vermilion-red at base in summer; feet vermilion-red in summer, orange in winter; length 14–15.5 ins.; wing 8.5–9.5; tail 5.4–8.4; bill 1.4–1.9; tarsus 0.7–0.8. *Young.*—Similar, but head buffy with black streaks; upperparts mottled with ash-brown; a dark grey band along the upper wing-coverts; underparts white; bill and feet dusky.

Range.—Coasts of Atlantic Ocean from Maine and Scotland south in winter to Brazil and the Cape of Good Hope, Mediterranean Sea, Indian Ocean and western Pacific from China to northern Australia and the Tuamotu Is. Breeds on coasts of the eastern United States, Bahamas, Venezuela, Lesser Antilles, Azores, Madeira, British Is., western and southern Europe and northern Africa (*S. d. dougalli*), the Seychelles (*S. d. arideensis*), Malacca and the Liu Kiu Is. (*S. d. bangsi*) Ceylon and the Andaman Is. (*S. d. korustes*), the Moluccas, northern Australia and New Caledonia (*S. d. gracilis*). *Egg-dates:* April–Aug. (North Atlantic), throughout the year (in the tropics).

Notes.—Distinguished by its white underparts with rosy tinge, very long outer tail-feathers and mainly black bill and on its breeding grounds by its loud harsh alarm-note, a single "cack." At other times it utters a distinctive short, rather mellow, plover-like note.

21. White-fronted Tern (*Sterna striata = S. frontalis*).
(*Plate 44*)

Adult.—Forehead white, crown and nape black, in winter crown white spotted with black; mantle, rump and tail pale grey; outer web of outermost primary blackish; inner webs of primaries edged with white to the tips; underparts, including under surface of wings, white, sometimes with a pink tinge in summer; bill black; feet reddish-brown; length 16–17.8 ins.; wing 10.7–11.2; tail 7–7.3; bill 1.6–2.2; tarsus 0.8. *Young.*—Head and back streaked with black and white and spotted with brownish; wing-coverts barred with grey, black and brown; a broad band of dark brown on the upper wing-coverts; primaries ash-grey; rump, upper tail-coverts and outer webs of tail-feathers grey; underparts white; bill dark horn-colour.

Range.—East coast of Australia, Tasmania, New Zealand, Auckland, Campbell and Chatham Is. Breeds in the Auckland Is., Chatham Is. and New Zealand. *Egg-dates:* Nov.–Dec.

Notes.—Distinguished from the Black-fronted and Roseate Terns by its white forehead.

22. Aleutian Tern (*Sterna aleutica*)

Adult.—Forehead white; crown, nape and a line from the bill to the eye black; mantle slate grey; primaries darker grey, the outer web of the outermost blackish, inner webs mostly white but with a broad stripe of dark grey next the shaft and a narrow grey edge, shafts white; rump and tail white; chin, under wing-coverts, and under tail-coverts white; fore-neck, breast and abdomen pale grey; bill and feet black; length 13.5 ins.; wing 9.9–11; tail 4.1–7.6; bill 1.2–1.6; tarsus 0.6–0.7. *Young.*—Head and mantle greyish-brown, streaked and spotted with black and buff; wing-quills dark grey; rump and tail pale grey, outer webs of outermost tail-feathers white; underparts white with some smoky-brown on sides of neck and breast; bill dusky yellow; feet reddish-yellow.

Range.—Bering Sea south to Japan. Breeds on coasts of eastern Siberia and Alaska. *Egg-dates:* June.

Notes.—Differs from the Arctic and Common Terns in the breeding season by its white forehead and darker grey colour, especially on the underparts, which contrast conspicuously with the white under surface of the wings when it is flying.

III. MEDIUM-SIZED TERNS WITH GREY MANTLE, DARK ABDOMEN AND BLACK CROWN IN THE BREEDING SEASON

23. **Black-bellied Tern** (*Sterna melanogastra* = S. *javanica*)

Adult.—Top of head black, in winter forehead and crown grey streaked with black and a black patch round eye; mantle grey; outer primaries pale pearl-grey on outer web, nearly white on inner web; tail pearl-grey, outer webs of outermost feathers white; throat and under surface of wings white; fore-neck and breast pearl-grey; abdomen and under tail-coverts brownish-black, in winter greyish-white; bill orange-yellow, tipped with dusky in winter; feet vermilion; length 12–12.8 ins.; wing 8.7–9.3; tail 6–6.2; bill 1.4–1.6; tarsus 0.5–1. *Young.*—Similar to adult in winter but upperparts variegated grey and buff with black streaks; wing-quills and tail-feathers with white margins.

Range.—Tropical Asia from southern Afghanistan through India to Ceylon, Burma and Cochin China, occasionally to Reunion. Breeds on rivers and marshes throughout its range. *Egg-dates:* March–April.

Notes.—An inland species rarely visiting coasts, often associating with the Indian River Tern from which it is distinguished by its smaller size, more slender bill and, except in winter plumage, its black abdomen.

24. **Whiskered Tern** (*Chlidonias hybrida* = C. *leucopareia*)

Adult.—Top of head deep black, in winter forehead white, crown and nape white streaked with black; a conspicuous white streak from the bill along the sides of the head below the black cap; mantle slate-grey; primaries darker grey, with white areas on the inner webs of the outermost; upper tail-coverts and tail grey, the outermost tail-feathers with white outer webs; tail short, slightly forked, outer feathers rounded; throat grey, darkening to slate-grey on the breast and to black on the abdomen; in winter underparts white; under wing-coverts and under tail-coverts white; bill blood-red; feet vermilion; length 13 ins.; wing 8.5–9.8; tail 3.1–4.5; bill 1–1.5; tarsus 0.7–0.9. *Young.*—Similar to adult in winter plumage but crown and nape blackish-brown; mantle and tail mottled with brown.

Range.—Warmer parts of the eastern hemisphere, occasionally north to northern Russia, Germany and the British Is., accidentally to Barbados. Breeds in South Europe and North Africa (*C. h. hybrida*), India (*C. h. indica*), South China (*C. h. swinhoei*), Malay Peninsula, Java and Celebes (*C. h. javanica*), Moluccas, New Guinea and Australia (*C. h. fluviatilis*), Nyasaland and South Africa (*C. h. sclateri*). *Egg-dates:* May–Dec.

Notes.—Frequents swamps and lagoons inland, feeding mainly on insects, and rarely visits coasts. The short, slightly-forked tail and red bill distinguish it from the Black-bellied Tern.

IV. MEDIUM-SIZED TERNS WITH DUSKY UPPER-PARTS AND WHITE UNDERPARTS

25. **Sooty Tern** (*Sterna fuscata* = *S. fuliginosa*). (*Plates 37 and 42*)

Adult.—A broad, white band on the forehead ending above the eyes; crown, nape and a stripe from bill to eye black; upperparts dark brownish-black; outer web of very long outer tail-feathers white; throat and breast white; abdomen and under tail-coverts greyish-white; bill and feet black, with a slight reddish tinge; length 17 ins.; wing 11–11.7; tail 7–7.2; bill 1.5–2.1; tarsus 0.9–1. *Young*

—Upperparts sooty-brown, feathers of the mantle with white tips; underparts brown, lighter on the abdomen.

Range.—Tropical and sub-tropical seas; sometimes wanders to Maine, the British Is. and western Europe. Breeds on islets off southern coasts of the United States, the Bahamas, West Indies, Fernando Noronha, Ascension and St. Helena (*S. f. fuscata*), Mait I., Gulf of Aden (*S. f. somaliensis*), the Seychelles, the Laccadive Is., Paracels Is. and Cocos Keeling Is. (*S. f. nubilosa*), coasts of northern Australia and New Caledonia (*S. f. serrata*), the Kermadec Is. (*S. f. kermadeci*), Hawaiian Is. and southward through Oceania (*S. f. oahuensis*), Galápagos Is., Clipperton I. and Revillagigedo Is. (*S. f. crissalis*). *Egg-dates:* Throughout the year in different localities.

Notes.—Breeds in immense colonies, whose perpetual screaming day and night has earned the bird the name of "Wideawake." The eggs are often collected by fishermen and islanders to whom the Sooty Tern is the "Egg-bird." Small parties are frequently seen far from land in the warmer parts of the ocean.

26. **Brown-winged Tern** (*Sterna anaethetus* = *S. panayensis*). (*Plate 37*)

Adult.—Similar to the Sooty Tern, but smaller; white band on forehead narrower and extending back beyond the eyes; upperparts dark greyish-brown; bill and feet black; length 14–15 ins.; wing 9.6–10.8; tail 5.8–7.5; bill 1.4–1.8; tarsus 0.7–0.9. *Young.*—Similar to adult, but head mottled with brownish; feathers of upperparts with pale tips; underparts greyish-white.

Range.—Tropical and sub-tropical seas. Breeds on islets off coast of Honduras, West Indies and Bahamas (*S. a. melanoptera*), in the Red Sea and Persian Gulf (*S. a. fuligula*), the Seychelles, Mauritius, Laccadive Is. and Cocos Keeling Is. (*S. a. antarctica*), the Philippine Is. and Formosa (*S. a. anaethetus*), Western Australia (*S. a. rogersi*), Queensland (*S. a. novaehollandiae*), the Pacific coast of Mexico and Central America (*S. a. nelsoni*) and throughout Oceania. *Egg-dates:* April–July (northern hemisphere), Oct.–Dec. (southern hemisphere).

Notes.—An oceanic species often seen far from land, the adult is smaller and lighter coloured than the Sooty Tern, with a white superciliary stripe extending behind the eye. It breeds in crevices of cliffs or under shrubs. The young differs from the young Sooty Tern in its whitish underparts.

27. Spectacled Tern (*Sterna lunata*)

Adult.—Similar to the Brown-winged Tern, but upperparts dark grey; outer tail-feathers white, the inner webs grey towards the tip; underparts white; bill and feet black; length 13.5–15 ins.; wing 9.5–10.5; tail 5–6.7; bill 1.7–1.9; tarsus 0.8–0.9. *Young.*—Head mottled with black and white; mantle brownish-grey, the feathers with white tips; underparts white; bill and feet brown.

Range.—Tropical Pacific Ocean from the Molucca Is. and Fiji Is. to the Hawaiian Is. and Tuamotu Is. Breeds throughout Oceania. *Egg-dates:* May–July.

Notes.—Very similar to the Brown-winged Tern, but greyer above and whiter below in all plumages.

V. MEDIUM-SIZED TERNS WITH GREY MANTLE AND UNDERPARTS AND WHITE HEAD

28. Trudeau's Tern (*Sterna trudeaui*)

Adult.—Head white, with a black patch in front of the eye and a black streak behind it; upperparts pearl grey, almost white on rump and outer tail-feathers; secondaries with broad white edges; outer primaries with dark grey edges to the inner webs; chin and under surface of wings white; breast and abdomen grey; bill yellow with a broad subterminal black band; feet orange; length 14 ins.; wing 9.8–10.9; tail 4.5–5.7; bill 1.5–1.8; tarsus 0.9–1. *Young.*—Similar but the crown is greyish-white; mantle mottled with brown; tail-feathers dark ash-grey with white margins; bill dusky with the base yellowish-brown; feet yellow.

Range.—Temperate South America, on the east coast from Rio de Janeiro to northern Patagonia, and on the coast of Chile north to Arica. Breeds inland in Argentina. *Egg-dates:* Oct.–Jan.

Notes.—The white head with black stripes through the eyes distinguishes this bird from other South American Terns in summer plumage, but it closely resembles Forster's Tern in winter and immature plumage.

VI. MEDIUM-SIZED TERNS WITH DUSKY PLUMAGE

29. **Inca Tern** (*Larosterna inca = Naenia inca*)

Adult.—Dark bluish slate-colour, lighter on the throat and under wing-coverts; primaries and outer tail-feathers brownish-black; the four outermost primaries edged with white; secondaries mostly broadly tipped with white; a white moustachial streak from the bill below the eye ending in long curling white feathers on the cheeks; tail moderately forked; bill strong, somewhat curved, blood-red; fleshy wattles at sides of mouth bright yellow; feet crimson; length 16 ins.; wing 11.2; tail 5.8; bill 1.9; tarsus 0.9. *Young.*—Similar to the adult, but browner and the head paler; moustachial streak greyish; bill and feet reddish-brown.

Range.—Coasts of Peru and Chile, where it breeds. *Egg-dates:* Throughout the year.

Notes.—A very distinct species peculiar to the Humboldt Current. It breeds in burrows and crevices among rocks.

30. **Common Noddy** (*Anous stolidus*). (*Plates 37 and 41*)

Adult.—Top of head lavender-grey, almost white on the forehead; a black band from bill to eye; upperparts dark brown; primaries and tail nearly black; underparts dark brown, under surface of wings paler, throat greyer; bill black; feet brownish-black, with yellowish webs; tail not forked; length 14.5–16 ins.; wing 10.2–11.5; tail 5.9–7; bill 1.6–2.1; tarsus 1. *Young.*—Similar to adult but lighter and browner; top of head greyish-brown; a narrow white line above the eye.

Range.—Tropical and sub-tropical seas, except the west coast of South America; occasionally to Bermuda and the British Is. Breeds on islands in the Caribbean Sea, Gulf of Mexico and tropical Atlantic south to Tristan da Cunha (*A. s. stolidus*), in the Red Sea (*A. s. plumbeigularis*) off the coast of Madagascar, Mauritius, the Seychelles, Laccadive Is., Cocos Keeling Is., Christmas I., off Western Australia, in the Philippine Is., Paracels Is. and Liu Kiu Is., off Queensland, in the Pacific from New Caledonia to the Hawaiian and Tuamotu Is. (*A. s. pileatus*), the Galápagos Is. (*A. s. galapagensis*), and islands off the west coast of Mexico and Central America (*A. s. ridgwayi*). *Egg-dates:* Throughout the year in different localities.

Notes.—Decidedly larger than the Lesser, White-capped and Hawaiian Noddies with stouter bill and greyer crown, but not easily distinguished from its smaller relatives in life unless two species are seen together.

VII. SMALL TERNS WITH PLUMAGE MAINLY DUSKY EITHER THROUGHOUT THE YEAR OR IN BREEDING PLUMAGE

31. **Lesser Noddy** (*Anous tenuirostris*)

Adult.—Top of head greyish-white; a black band from the bill through the eye; mantle and tail brownish-grey; primaries blackish; underparts sooty-brown, almost black on the throat; bill black; feet blackish-brown; length 12–13 ins,; wing 8.3–8.7; tail 4.5–5; bill 1.8–2.5; tarsus 0.8–0.9. *Young.*—Similar to adult but browner.

Range.—Indian Ocean. Breeds in the Seychelle Is. (*A. t. tenuirostris*) and Houtmann's Abrolhos Is., Western Australia (*A. t. melanops*). *Egg-dates:* Sept.–Dec.

Notes.—A rare species distinguished from the Common Noddy by its smaller size, longer bill and almost white cap.

32. White-capped Noddy (*Anous minutus* = *Micranous leucocapillus*). (*Plate 45*)

Adult.—Similar to the Lesser Noddy but top of head whiter; rest of plumage darker, almost black; bill black; feet dark brown; length 13–14 ins.; wing 8.3–9.7; tail 4–5.2; bill 1.5–2.1; tarsus 0.7–0.9. *Young.*—Forehead and crown white; neck sooty black; mantle, tail and underparts brown; primaries blackish.

Range.—Tropical Atlantic and Pacific Oceans. Breeds on islands in the Caribbean Sea off the coast of Honduras (*A. m. americanus*), in the tropical Atlantic (*A. m. atlanticus*), in the Philippine Is. (*A. m. worcesteri*), in the Pelew Is., Marianne Is. and Marcus I. (*A. m. marcusi*), in the South Pacific from the coasts of New Guinea and Queensland to the Tuamotu Is. (*A. m. minutus*), in the Hawaiian Is. (*A. m. melanogenys*), and on Clipperton and Cocos Is. off the Pacific coast of Central America (*A. m. diamesus*). *Egg-dates:* Throughout the year in different localities.

Notes.—Distinguished from the Common Noddy by its smaller size and whiter cap, and from the Lesser Noddy by its blacker plumage. It nests in trees, sometimes at a considerable height.

33. Black Tern (*Chlidonias nigra* = *Hydrochelidon nigra*). (*Plates 37 and 44*)

Adult.—Head and neck black, in winter white mottled with dark grey on crown and nape; mantle and tail slate-grey, the wings whitish on the edge; breast and abdomen dark lead colour, in winter white; under surface of wings light grey; under tail-coverts white; bill black; feet purplish-brown; tail slightly forked, the outer feathers rounded; length 9.6–10 ins.; wing 7.5–8.5; tail 2.9–4; bill 1–1.2; tarsus 0.6–0.7. *Young.*—Similar to adult in winter, but back of head browner; mantle mottled with brown; sides greyish.

Range.—North America and Europe, south in winter to Chile, Guiana, Loango, Tanganyika, the Persian Gulf and northwest India. Breeds on lakes and swamps in the interior of Canada and the United States (*C. n. surinamensis*) and in Europe south of the Baltic (*C. n. nigra*). *Egg-dates:* May–Aug.

Notes.—This little Tern is chiefly found on fresh water inland and feeds largely on insects; on migration in spring and autumn it occurs on coasts or well out to sea, and obtains its food from the surface, not by plunging. In breeding plumage it is unmistakable, its grey tail distinguishing it from the White-winged Black Tern. In winter plumage its slate-grey mantle and slightly-forked grey tail are distinctive and there is a conspicuous black patch on each side of the head behind the eye.

34. White-winged Black Tern (*Chlidonias leucoptera = Hydrochelidon leucoptera*). (*Plate 37*)

Adult.—Head, neck and upper back black, in winter white mottled with black on the crown and nape; lesser wing-coverts and edge of wing white; mantle grey; primaries greyish-black; upper tail-coverts and tail white; underparts, including under surface of wings, black, in winter white; under tail-coverts white, bill red, in winter black; feet orange-red; tail slightly forked; length 8.5–9.5 ins.; wing 7.7–8.6; tail 2.5–3.1; bill 0.9–1.2; tarsus 0.6–0.8. *Young.*—Similar to adult in winter, but upperparts mottled with brown; upper tail-coverts white; tail grey.

Range.—Central and southern Europe and central Asia to China, south in winter to South Africa, southern Asia and Australia, occasionally to British Is. and northern Europe, accidentally to the United States, Barbados and New Zealand. Breeds on lakes and swamps in southern Europe, Algeria and temperate Asia. *Egg-dates:* May–June.

Notes.—An inhabitant of swamps feeding largely on insects, only occasionally visiting sea coasts. Distinguished from the Black Tern in breeding plumage by its black under wing-coverts and white tail, and in immature and winter plumage by its white upper tail-coverts.

VIII. SMALL TERNS WITH GREY MANTLE, WHITE OR PALE GREY UNDERPARTS AND BLACK CROWN

35. **Little (Lesser or Least) Tern** (*Sterna albifrons = S. minuta*). (*Plates 36 and 37*)

Adult.—Crown, nape and a band from bill to eye black; forehead white; mantle and rump pearl grey; outer web of outer primary and a broad line on the inner web next the shaft dark grey; edges of inner webs of primaries white; tail white or pale grey; underparts white; bill yellow or orange, tipped with black; feet orange-yellow; tail deeply forked; length 8–11 ins.; wing 6.1–7.4; tail 2.4–5.7; bill 0.9–1.4; tarsus 0.6–0.7. *Young*—Similar to adult, but crown buffy-white with black streaks, upperparts grey mottled with buffy-brown; bill dark brown; feet dull yellow.

Range.—North America from California and Labrador, south in winter to Peru and Brazil; Europe, Africa, Asia and northern and eastern Australia; a summer visitor in the northern parts of its range. Breeds on the coast of California (*S. a. browni*), Atlantic coast of United States south from Massachusetts, in the Mississippi Valley, on coasts of Gulf of Mexico and Caribbean Sea to Venezuela and in the Bahamas and West Indies (*S. a. antillarum*), on coasts and rivers of Europe from British Is. and Baltic to Mediterranean, North Africa, Madeira, the Canary Is., western Siberia and N. W. India (*S. a. albifrons*), on coasts and rivers of tropical W. Africa (*S. a. guineae*), coasts of Red Sea, East Africa, Madagascar, Mascarene and Seychelle Is., Persian Gulf, Mekran coast and Sind (*S. a. saundersi*), rivers of northern India and Burma, Java and Sumatra (*S. a. pusilla*), coasts of Japan, China,

Liu Kiu Is., Formosa, Ceylon, Bay of Bengal, Malaysia, northern and eastern Australia (*S. a. sinensis*). *Egg-dates:* March–June (northern hemisphere), May–Aug. (in the tropics), Nov. (southern hemisphere).

Notes.—Distinguished by its small size, white forehead and orange bill and feet.

36. Amazon Tern (*Sterna superciliaris*)

Adult.—Similar to the Little Tern but larger with shorter tail and stouter bill; mantle and tail darker grey; four outer primaries chiefly dusky black; bill greenish-yellow; feet dull yellow; length 9 ins.; wing 7.2; tail 3.2; bill 1.5; tarsus 0.6. *Young.*—Similar to young Little Tern but much darker; bill and feet dull yellow.

Range.—Estuaries and rivers of eastern South America from the Orinoco to the La Plata. Breeds on sandbanks in rivers. *Egg-dates:* July–Sept.

Notes.—A fresh-water Tern inhabiting the great South American rivers and extending far inland up the Amazon, Parana and Paraguay.

37. Chilean Tern (*Sterna lorata*)

Adult.—Similar to the Little Tern, but darker and larger; mantle, rump and tail slate-grey, the outer tail-feathers paler; outer web of outermost primary black; throat and under wing-coverts white; breast and abdomen pale grey; bill slender, greenish-yellow with blackish tip; feet brownish; length 9.6 ins.; wing 7.3; tail 4.1; bill 1.4; tarsus 0.6. *Young.*—Not described.

Range.—West coast of South America from Ecuador to northern Chile, breeding on coast of Peru. *Egg-dates:* Jan.

Notes.—In the northern summer this is the only little Tern on the west coast of South America. From the Little Tern which sometimes visits Peru in winter it can hardly be distinguished in life.

38. Fairy Tern (*Sterna nereis*)

Adult.—Forehead white; a spot before the eye, a narrow ring round the eye, crown and nape black; mantle very pale pearl grey; outer primaries slightly darker; tail and underparts white; bill yellow; feet dull yellow; length 10 ins.; wing 7.2; tail 4; bill 1.5; tarsus 0.6. *Young.*—Similar, but crown and nape greyish, mottled with brownish-black; mantle spotted with dull white.

Range.—Western and southern coasts of Australia (from Broome to Melbourne), Tasmania, New Caledonia and New Zealand. Breeds in S. W. Australia (*S. n. horni*), S. E. Australia and Tasmania (*S. n. nereis*), New Caledonia (*S. n. exsul*) and New Zealand (*S. n. davisae*). *Egg-dates:* Nov.–Dec.

Notes.—Larger than the Little Tern and much paler above, with less black before the eye and a bright yellow bill.

39. Damara Tern (*Sterna balaenarum*)

Adult.—Top of head black, in winter forehead and crown mottled with white; mantle and rump pale lavender-grey; outer webs of two outer primaries and line next the shaft on inner webs, dark grey; tail grey, the outer feathers whitish; underparts white, slightly grey on breast; bill slender, black; feet yellowish; length 8.5–9 ins.; wing 6.7; tail 2.6–3; bill 1.1–1.3; tarsus 0.6. *Young.*—Similar to adult but upper wing-coverts somewhat darker; bill pale at base.

Range.—Coasts of south-west Africa from Loango to Table Bay. Breeds throughout its range.

Notes.—Distinguished from the Little Tern by its black forehead and slender black bill.

IX. SMALL TERNS WITH PALE GREY OR WHITE PLUMAGE

40. Black-naped Tern (*Sterna sumatrana* = *S. melanauchen*). (*Plate* 37)

Adult.—Head and neck white, with a triangular, black spot before the eye and a black band on the nape; mantle and rump pale pearl-grey; outer web of first primary blackish-grey; tail long, deeply forked, white, the central feathers greyish; underparts white with a rosy tinge; bill black with a yellowish tip; feet black; length 13.5–14.5 ins.; wing 8.5–8.6; tail 6; bill 1.6–2.1; tarsus 0.7. *Young.* —Top of head buffy-white with blackish streaks and a black patch on the nape; upperparts grey, the feathers barred with ash-brown and tipped with buff; primaries grey with white inner margins; bill yellowish; feet yellowish-brown.

Range.—Tropical Indian and Pacific Oceans. Breeds on coral islands from Madagascar and the Seychelle Is. to the Chagos Is. (*S. s. matheosi*) and in the Andaman Is., the Malay Archipelago and northern Australia, southern China, the Philippine Is., Liu Kiu Is. and Samoan Is. (*S. s. sumatrana*). *Egg-dates:* May–Dec.

Notes.—Distinguished by its light colouring, very long forked tail and the black crescent on the nape.

41. Blue-grey Noddy (*Procelsterna cerulea* = *P. cinerea*)

Adult.—Forehead and throat pale grey; crown and nape grey; a narrow black ring round the eye; upperparts smoke-grey; secondaries margined with white at tips; underparts grey under wing-coverts white in some races; tail forked in centre; bill black; feet black with lemon-yellow webs; length 9.7–11 ins.; wing 7.4–8.5; tail 4–4.5; bill 1.2–1.3. Tarsus 0.9–1. *Young.*—Slate-grey with blackish primaries.

Range.—Tropical Pacific Ocean. Breeds in the Hawaiian Is. (*P. c. saxatilis*), Christmas I. (*P. c. cerulea*), Phoenix, Ellice and Samoan Is. (*P. c. nebouxi*), Society, Marquesas and Tuamotu Is. (*P. c. teretirostris*), Lord Howe, Norfolk, Kermadec and Friendly Is. (*P. c. albivitta*), Henderson I. and Easter I. (*P. c. skottsbergi*) and St. Ambrose I., Chile (*P. c. imitatrix*). *Egg-dates:* May–Jan.

Notes.—An entirely grey bird, except for the white tips of the secondaries and, in some races, white under wing-coverts.

42. **White Tern** (*Gygis alba = G. crawfordi*). (*Plate 46*)

Adult.—White; ring round eye black; shafts of primaries and tail-feathers sometimes dusky; tail long, forked in centre; bill black, blue at base; feet black or pale blue, with yellow or white webs; length 10.4–13 ins.; wing 8.6–10.2; tail 3.2–5.1; bill 1.5–1.8; tarsus 0.4–0.6. *Young.* —Similar, but with a black spot behind the eye and black shafts to the wing-quills and tail-feathers.

Range.—Tropical Oceans. Breeds at Fernando Noronha, South Trinidad and Ascension (*G. a. alba*), at Madagascar, and the Mascarene, Seychelle and Chagos Is. (*G. a. monte*), the Caroline Is., Marianne Is., Marcus I., Christmas I., Hawaiian Is., Revillagigedo Is., Cocos I. and Galápagos Is. (*G. a. candida*), Kermadec Is. (*G. a. royana*), Marquesas Is. (*G. a. microrhyncha*) and islands throughout the South Pacific (*G. a. pacifica*). *Egg-dates:* May–Jan.

Notes.—The White Tern, or "Love Tern," cannot be mistaken for any other species. Its single egg is placed on a rock, or more frequently on the branch of a tree, sometimes at a considerable height.

CHAPTER VII

Skimmers or Scissor-Bills

(Order *Charadriiformes*: Family *Rynchopidae*)

THE MEMBERS OF this small family are very long-winged sea-birds, resembling large Terns with black or dark brown upper parts and white foreheads and underparts. Their legs are short, their feet small and webbed and their tails moderately forked. Their bills are quite unlike those of any other birds. The lower mandible is much longer than the upper one, and both its edges are compressed to a knife-like thinness; the end of the upper mandible is grooved beneath to received the very sharp lower mandible when the bill is closed. The name of "Scissor-bill" is thus not quite appropriate as the blades of the scissors do not pass one another. The name "Skimmer" has been bestowed upon them from their unique method of feeding. When seeking food they fly rapidly just over the water with the bill open and the long lower mandible cutting the surface, so that they may be said literally to "plough the main." Their food consists of aquatic weeds and small fish or other animals which may be captured in this manner. Sometimes they fish in such shallow water that the bill catches the bottom. Their "skimming" is usually done during the early hours of the morning or late in the evening and also on moonlight nights. During the daytime they commonly rest on sandbanks.

Skimmers are sociable birds, and breed in colonies on sand-banks, their nests being mere hollows scooped in the sand by the simple process of turning round. The eggs are large, three to five in number, whitish or buffy in ground colour, with spots or blotches of brown, chocolate or purplish. The young chicks are covered with sandy-coloured down, and when danger threatens remain motionless, so that they are very hard to discover owing to their protective colouration. The parents are exceedingly noisy and bold when their breeding grounds are invaded, repeatedly swooping at the invader and uttering a sharp, yapping cry, resembling the noise made by hounds on a trail.

Skimmers are found on the coasts, large rivers and lakes of the warmer parts of America, Africa and India, one species occurring in each continent. The females are decidedly smaller than the males, and the young birds have shorter bills and are duller in colour. Until they are fledged the bills of young birds are not too abnormal to prevent them from picking up food from the ground, but when they can fly the lower mandible rapidly elongates.

1. Black Skimmer (*Rynchops nigra*). (*Plate 47*)

Adult.—Crown, nape and mantle black, in winter with a white collar across the neck; secondaries with white borders; tail-feathers, brown with white borders, the outer ones almost entirely white; forehead and underparts white; under surface of wings and under tail-coverts white or grey; bill bright red at base, yellow towards tip and black at tip; feet orange-red; length 15–20.5 ins.; wing 13–17; tail 4–6; bill 2.5–4.5; tarsus 1.1–1.5. *Young.*—Similar but upperparts browner, streaked with greyish white; underparts more or less mottled with buff and greyish white; bill shorter, brown; feet reddish brown.

Range.—Coasts and large rivers of America from New Brunswick to Buenos Aires, and from Ecuador to southern Chile, north of Florida only in summer; in winter also to Pacific coasts of Mexico and Central America. Breeds on the coasts of the United States from New Jersey to Texas (*R. n. nigra*), on the coasts and rivers of northern and eastern South America from Columbia south to the Amazon (*R. n. cinerascens*), and on the rivers of southern Brazil, Paraguay, Uruguay and Argentina (*R. n. intercedens*). *Egg-dates:* May–July (N. America); Sept. (S. America).

Notes.—The only Skimmer found in America.

2. African Skimmer (*Rynchops flavirostris*)

Adult.—Similar to the Black Skimmer but upperparts deep brownish-grey; under wing-coverts smoky brown; bill with upper mandible vermilion or deep orange, lower mandible yellow; feet vermilion; length 14–17 inches; wing 12.5–14; tail 4–5.2; bill 1.7–3; tarsus 0.9–1.1. *Young.*—Similar but browner above, feathers of the mantle and tail with greyish tips; forehead streaked with grey; bill yellow with black tip.

Range.—Coasts, rivers and great lakes of tropical Africa from Senegal to the Orange River, and from Egypt and the Red Sea to the Zambezi. Breeds from Nubia southwards. *Egg-dates:* Apr.–Sept.

Notes.—The only Skimmer found in Africa.

3. Indian Skimmer (*Rynchops albicollis*)

Adult.—Crown, nape and mantle dark brown; back of neck, rump and tail white; primaries brownish black; secondaries broadly edged with white; forehead and underparts white; under wing-coverts pale smoky grey; bill orange with yellow tip; feet vermilion; length 16–16.5 ins.; wing 14–16; tail 4.7–5; bill 2.7–3.2; tarsus 0.9–1.1. *Young.*—Similar but upperparts paler brown, the feathers mottled with buffish-white and grey; tail feathers with brown tips; forehead streaked with brown.

Range.—Large rivers and lakes of India and Lower Burma. Breeds on sandbanks in large rivers. *Egg-dates:* March–May.

Notes.—The only Skimmer found in Asia.

CHAPTER VIII

~~~~~~~~~~~~~~~~~~

Skuas and Jaegers

(Order *Charadriiformes:* Family *Stercorariidae*)

~~~~~~~~~~~~~~~~~~

THE MEMBERS OF this family are large, dark-coloured birds, with some resemblance to immature Gulls but characterised by their stout, hooked beaks. The upper mandible is sharply curved downwards at the tip and its basal portion is covered by a separate horny plate called the cere, the front edge of which partly overhangs the nostrils. The wings are long and the legs and webbed feet rather stout. The larger species have short, almost square tails, whilst the smaller species, known as Jaegers in America, have rather long wedge-shaped tails, the two central feathers being elongated in the adult.

Skuas are mainly birds of high latitudes. Four species breed in northern or arctic regions and the Great Skua is represented in the southern hemisphere by races which breed in high southern latitudes. The three smaller species migrate to the southern hemisphere during the northern winter, whilst the Great Skua visits temperate regions in both hemispheres during winter. It thus happens that on the coasts of South America, South Africa and Australia, arctic Skuas are found in summer and antarctic Skuas in winter.

Skuas are among sea-birds analogous to the birds of prey. The Great Skua with its large size and broad

140

wings with rounded primaries, has a considerable resemblance to Eagles and Buzzards, whilst the smaller Jaegers, with their long pointed wings and great powers of flight, may be regarded as representing Falcons. They are, in fact, largely birds of prey, feeding when on land in the breeding season on small mammals and large insects as well as on the eggs and young of other birds. They also feed on carrion and any floating animal matter or refuse picked up from the surface of the water. In addition, they attack Shearwaters, Gulls and Terns and force them to give up any food they may have secured. If the victim is pursued on the wing and drops the fish it may have secured, the Skua swiftly plunges down and seizes it, in many cases before it reaches the water.

When not breeding Skuas ordinarily occur further off-shore than the majority of Gulls. Their flight is gull-like, but swifter and more powerful, recognisable from the peculiar gliding character of each stroke of the wings.

Skuas nest on the ground, often choosing a locality near a colony of Penguins, Gulls or other birds, whose eggs and young provide them with an abundant supply of food. They are not so sociable as most other sea-birds, though numerous pairs may often be found breeding on the same island or tundra. The nest is a hollow slightly lined with grass or weeds. The eggs are usually two or three in number, occasionally four, and are generally olive brown in colour with large spots of dark brown or purplish. The young when hatched are covered with down, brownish above, paler and greyer below, and are dependent on their parents for food until they are fledged. When the nests are approached the parents are extremely bold, attacking the intruder savagely by swooping down and striking with the feet. It is said that they successfully attack even Falcons in defence of their young. They are comparatively silent birds but sometimes utter a wailing cry, from which the name "Skua" is probably derived, and also have a deep note of anger several times repeated. They also scream when feeding or fighting. The name "Jaeger" is the German word for a hunter and is, of course, descriptive of their rapacious habits.

The sexes are indistinguishable in size and colouring and the young birds do not differ greatly from the adults, but are usually more mottled or barred in colouring. The immature Jaegers do not have the elongated central tail feathers characteristic of the adults. In several of the species there is a good deal of variation in colour independent of age or sex and at least two of the species have dark and light phases, though intermediate forms also occur. The variations are not yet properly understood, especially in the species of the southern oceans.

1. **Great Skua** (*Catharacta skua = Megalestris catarrhactes*). (*Plate 49*)

Adult.—Upperparts brown, varying from nearly black to light brown, the neck streaked with yellowish or whitish brown, and the back with rufous or chestnut; basal portions of inner webs of primaries white, forming a conspicuous band when the bird is flying; shafts of wing-quills and tail-feathers white; underparts greyish-brown, cinnamon or pale chestnut brown; under wing-coverts dark brown or cinnamon; bill and feet black, the latter often mottled with yellowish; tail short, slightly wedge-shaped; length 21–24 ins.; wing 15–17.2; tail 6.5–7; bill 1.5–2.5; tarsus 2.4–3.2. *Young.*—Similar but feathers of back and underparts with somewhat rufous margins.

Range.—North Atlantic and adjacent Arctic Seas, south in winter to Newfoundland, Nova Scotia, Madeira and Gibraltar; occasionally to New York and Italy, also southern oceans from Antarctica north in winter to Callao, Peru, Rio de Janeiro, Walvisch Bay, Madagascar, southern Australia, New Zealand and the Chatham Is., accidentally to Ceylon. Breeds in Iceland, the Faroe Is., Shetland Is. and Orkney Is. (*C. s. skua*), Tierra del Fuego and southern Chile (*C. s. chilensis*), Falkland Is. (*C. s. antarctica*), South Georgia, the South Orkneys, the South Shetlands, Tristan da Cunha, Gough I., Kerguelen, Marion I., the Crozets, Heard I., Bouvet I., the South Island of New Zealand and the New Zealand subantarctic islands (*C. s. lonnbergi*). *Egg-dates:* May–June (northern hemisphere), Aug.–Jan. (southern hemisphere).

Notes.—A large, broad-winged bird, with heavy flight, dark brown, with a conspicuous white bar in the wing, distinguished from other northern Skuas by its heavy build and short tail.

2. **McCormick's Skua** (*Catharacta maccormicki = Megalestris maccormicki*)

Adult.—Similar to the Great Skua, but much lighter in colour; crown brown, forehead, sides of head and underparts almost white or light brown, becoming coffee-brown on the abdomen; feathers of neck marked with straw colour; upperparts dark brown; bill short and stout, blackish; feet black; length 21 ins.; wing 15.5–15.7; tail 6.5; bill 2.3; tarsus 2.6. *Young.*—Similar but head and neck dark brown; underparts blackish-grey; feet bluish.

Range.—Antarctic Seas, occasionally north to the South Orkneys and accidentally to Ceylon, New Zealand and Japan. Breeds on the Antarctic continent and in the South Shetlands. *Egg-dates:* Nov.–Jan.

Notes.—Much lighter than the Great Skua and rarely ranging much north of the Antarctic ice. The most southerly of all birds; observed by Mawson on the Antarctic continent 125 miles from the coast.

3. **Pomarine Jaeger or Skua** (*Stercorarius pomarinus*). (*Plate 49*)

Adult.—Top of head sooty black; back, wings and tail dark greyish-brown, the bases of the primaries and their shafts whitish, forming a light band when the wing is spread; neck and breast white, sides of neck straw-yellow, hind-neck, chest and sides barred with dusky; abdomen and under wing-coverts greyish-brown (light phase); or under-

143

parts dark like the upperparts (dark phase); bill dull brown with black tip; feet blackish; tail long and wedge-shaped, the central feathers projecting with broad, rounded tips twisted vertically; length 21–22 ins.; wing 13.5–14.7; tail 5–9.6; bill 1.5–1.7; tarsus 1.9–2.2. *Young.*—Upperparts dark, greyish-brown, spotted with buff on scapulars and rump; head, neck and underparts dull buff, barred with dusky (light phase); or entirely sooty greyish-brown barred with buff on rump, sides, breast and abdomen (dark phase); central tail-feathers not elongated.

Range.—Arctic Seas, south in winter to Peru, South Africa, Ceylon, Burma and northern Australia. Breeds on tundras of northern Alaska and Canada, western Greenland, Iceland, Novaya Zemblya and northern Siberia. *Egg-dates:* May–June.

Notes.—Distinctly smaller and more graceful than the Great Skua and its southern allies, and when adult distinguished by its unique central tail-feathers. The whitish bar on the wing helps to distinguish it from the Arctic Skua, than which it is decidedly larger. The immature bird can only be distinguished in life by its size from young Arctic and Long-tailed Skuas.

4. Parasitic Jaeger or Arctic Skua (*Stercorarius parasiticus = S. crepidatus*). (*Plates 49 and 50*)

Adult.—Top of head, back, wings and tail dark ash brown, the primaries with white shafts; sides of head and neck straw yellow; chin and breast dull white; under wing-coverts, abdomen and under tail-coverts ash brown (light phase); or neck and underparts sooty-brown, only slightly lighter than upperparts, sometimes with a trace of straw yellow on sides of neck (dark phase); bill brownish; feet black; tail long and wedge-shaped, the central feathers elongated and pointed; length 17–20 ins.; wing 11.5–13.4; tail 6.5–9.3; bill 1.1–1.5; tarsus 1.5–1.8. *Young.*—Upperparts mottled with various shades of brown; upper tail-coverts barred with white aand rufous; underparts whitish barred with brown; under wing-coverts barred with buff; central tail-feathers pointed but not elongated.

Range.—Bering Sea, North Atlantic and Arctic Seas, south in winter to Chile, Argentina, South Africa, India, southern Australia and New Zealand. Breeds in the Commander and Aleutian Is., Alaska, Canada, Greenland, Iceland, Scotland, northern Europe and Siberia. *Egg-dates:* May–July.

Notes.—Larger than the Long-tailed Skua, but smaller than the other species. When adult distinguished by its projecting central tail-feathers much shorter than those of the Long-tailed Skua, but pointed and not twisted like those of the Pomarine. The white shafts of the primaries are distinctive on close view, there being no other white area on the wing. Immature birds are not certainly recognisable in life.

5. **Long-tailed Jaeger or Skua** (*Stercorarius longicaudus* = *S. buffoni*). (*Plate 49*)

Adult.—Top of head brownish-black; mantle and upper tail-coverts greyish-brown; wing-quills and tail-feathers almost black, the two outer primaries with white shafts; sides of head and neck buffish-yellow; breast white; flanks, abdomen and under wing-coverts ash-brown; bill brownish, with black tip; feet bluish-grey, the ends of toes and webs black; tail long and wedge-shaped, the two central feathers greatly elongated and pointed; length 21–23 ins.; wing 11.6–12.9; tail 9.4–14; bill 1.1–1.3; tarsus 1.5–1.7. *Young.*—Upperparts ash-brown, darkest on head, feathers of mantle and tail-coverts tipped with buff; underparts greyish-white, barred with ash-brown; central tail-feathers pointed but not elongated.

Range.—Arctic seas, south in winter to Chile, Argentina, Gibraltar and Japan. Breeds north of the Arctic circle in Alaska, Canada, Greenland, Russia and Siberia. *Egg-dates:* June–July.

Notes.—The smallest of the Skuas, readily distinguished when adult by its long central tail-feathers, but not recognisable in life in immature plumage. The dark phase of this species appears to be very rare, and adults in this plumage have never been collected.

145

CHAPTER IX

Penguins

(Order *Sphenisciformes:* Family *Spheniscidae =
Aptenodytidae*)

THIS FAMILY IS composed of flightless sea-birds inhabiting the southern hemisphere, which differ from all other birds in having no specially developed quill-feathers on the wings. The flippers, as the wings of Penguins are usually termed, are covered all over with small scale-like feathers and are used only for swimming. Penguins are stout-bodied, short-necked birds of moderate or large size with short, flat, webbed feet, set very far back, so that when on land they stand upright. Their bills are stout and covered with several separate horny plates, somewhat as in Albatrosses, instead of a single sheath on each mandible as in most birds. Their tails are usually very short, composed of from 12 to 20 feathers, according to the species, often entirely hidden by the upper tail-coverts.

The name "Penguin" was originally applied to the Great Auk or Garefowl of the North Atlantic. On the discovery of similar flightless birds in the southern hemisphere the name was very naturally applied to them also, and, with the extinction of the northern bird, has now become theirs alone.

Penguins are essentially adapted for life in the

sea, and are the most completely marine of all birds, rivalling seals and porpoises in their speed. Beneath the water the flippers are the sole means of propulsion, the feet being stretched out behind and used to assist in steering. They travel for considerable distances below the surface with brief periods of emergence for breathing, and when at the surface swim very low in the water so that only the head, or the head and back, are above it. Some species when travelling swiftly progress by alternate leaps and dives. The leaps carry them clear of the water, they make a short curve in the air, and then take a header back into the water. Most species can also leap out of the water to a height of three or four feet to land on an ice-floe or rock.

Penguins are sociable birds both when at sea and when breeding. For the latter purpose they come ashore on islands or desolate coasts and hop, run, waddle or scramble over rocks, and even up steep hillsides to their breeding grounds or "rookeries," to which their constant passage has often worn smooth tracks over the rocks. Most of the species construct a slight nest of bits of grass or weeds in cavities between rocks, caves, hollows scraped out beneath tussock-grass or bushes, or deserted burrows of petrels; but some of the larger species merely utilise a slight hollow in the open and line it with stones. Penguins lay one, two, or occasionally three, eggs, which are usually nearly spherical or broadly pear-shaped with a white, chalky shell. The King and Emperor Penguins, which only lay a single egg, incubate it while standing upright, the egg being placed on their feet and covered with a flap of loose skin which forms a sort of pouch between the legs. The most remarkable fact connected with this habit is that the Emperor Penguin chooses the perpetual darkness of the antarctic winter as the period, and the ice-barrier as the scene of the operation. Other species of Penguin brood their eggs in the ordinary fashion. The eggs of the

147

Jackass Penguin are collected under Government regulation on the South African coast for sale in the towns, and both this species and the Humboldt Penguin are of some importance as producers of guano.

Young Penguins when hatched are densely covered with down, which is replaced by feathers resembling those of the adult before they venture into the sea. They feed by reaching into the gullets of their parents for half-digested crustacea. Adult Penguins come ashore to moult. This process takes place very rapidly, the whole of the old feathers being replaced simultaneously by a new set in a few days or weeks. Some species moult before the breeding season and on the completion of the moult return to the sea for a few weeks before beginning to breed. Other species moult after breeding.

Penguins feed almost entirely on fish, cuttlefish and crustacea obtained by diving. Their voices are loud and are often heard at night on the water. When congregated in rookeries on land they are generally very noisy, and some species utter a regular bray which has earned them the name of "Jackass."

Penguins are found on the coasts of the Antarctic continent and on all the subantarctic islands in the South Atlantic and Indian Oceans from Cape Horn to New Zealand. On the coasts of Australia, South Africa and eastern South America they range north nearly to the tropic of Capricorn, whilst on the west coast of South America one species extends into the tropics (breeding to 6° S. lat.) and another inhabits the Galápagos Islands on the equator.

The species may be divided for purposes of identification into three size groups: "large" species having a total length of over 3 feet; "medium-sized" species measuring from 2 feet to 2 feet 6 inches in total length; and "small" species 20 inches long or less. In colouring all the species are bluish grey or blackish above and white below, but they differ in the arrangement of black and white on the face and throat and some have a loose crest of long feathers on the crown of the head. Their bills are either black, reddish brown or red, and their feet black, red or whitish. The dark and light pattern of the flippers also varies according to the species. They may be arranged in four groups:

  I. Large, with orange or yellow patches on the sides of the upper neck (Species 1–2).
 II. Medium-sized, crested, with orange or yellow lines on each side of the crown above the eyes (Species 3–8).
III. Medium-sized, with no crest or yellow colour on the head, but usually with stripes of white or black on the head or breast (Species 9–14).
 IV. Small, without crest or yellow colouring on heads (Species 15–17).

I. LARGE PENGUINS WITH ORANGE OR YELLOW PATCHES ON THE SIDES OF THE UPPER NECK

1. Emperor Penguin (*Aptenodytes forsteri*). (*Plates 51 and 57*)

Adult.—Upperparts and upper surface of flipper bluish-grey; top of head, cheeks, chin and throat black; a broad semicircular patch on each side of the upper neck orange yellow, fading into the white foreneck; a wide blackish band bordering the shoulder and ending in an obtuse point on the side of the lower neck; underparts and under surface of flipper white; tail short, of 20 feathers; bill long, curved downwards towards tip, bluish-black with a lilac patch at the base of the lower mandible, along which the feathers extend for some distance; length 48 ins.; flipper 12.6–12.9; tail 3.6; bill 4.7. *Young.*—Similar but semicircular patch on sides of neck white or slightly yellow.

Range.—Antarctic Seas, north to the South Orkneys and Kerguelen. Breeds during winter on the ice-barrier on the coast of Antarctica. *Egg-dates:* July–Sept.

Notes.—The largest Penguin and the species with the most southerly range. Distinguished from the King Penguin by its size and the colouring of its neck and throat, and by having the base of the lower mandible feathered. The egg and chick are kept on the feet covered by a fold of loose skin between the legs. On land it walks with the body upright.

2. **King Penguin** (*Aptenodytes patagonica*). (Plates 51, 52 and 53)

Adult.—Similar to the Emperor Penguin but smaller; the black of the throat ending in a point on the foreneck, margined on each side by orange yellow bands which connect the orange patches on the sides of the head with a patch of this colour on the foreneck; a narrow black line on each side of the breast; bill black with the base of the lower mandible red but not feathered; feet black; length 36–38 ins.; flipper 11–13.4; tail 3.2–3.5; bill 3.5–5.4; tarsus 2. *Young.*—Similar but the patches on sides of head and neck yellow, not orange; bill entirely blackish.

Range.—Southern Oceans from Tierra del Fuego to Macquarie I.; occasionally north to the Falkland Is., Tasmania and New Zealand. Breeds at Staten I., South Sandwich Is., South Georgia, Marion I., the Crozet Is., Kerguelen, Heard I. and Macquarie Is. *Egg-dates:* Oct.–March.

Notes.—More northerly in its range than the Emperor Penguin from which it is distinguished by its smaller size and the colouring of the head and neck, and by the absence of feathers at the base of the lower mandible. It runs with the body held perfectly upright and does not hop. The egg is held in a fold of skin between the legs.

II. MEDIUM-SIZED CRESTED PENGUINS WITH ORANGE OR YELLOW LINES ON EACH SIDE OF THE CROWN ABOVE THE EYES

3. **Rock-hopper Penguin** (*Eudyptes crestatus* = *E. chrysocome* = *E. serresianus*). (*Plates 51 and 54*)

Adult.—Upper parts bluish-grey; head, sides of face, chin and throat slaty-black; feathers of crown somewhat elongated, on each side a line of pale yellow plumes running from behind the nostrils to above the eye, the hinder plumes considerably elongated; under-parts white; flipper slaty-black, with a patch on the under-surface and both margins white; tail of 16 feathers; bill short and very stout, orange, red or pink; feet whitish or reddish with darker webs; length 25 ins.; flipper 5.1–7; tail 3.4–4.4; bill 1.5–1.9; tarsus 1. *Young.*—Similar but duller in colour; no elongated feathers on the head; the stripes on the side of the crown whitish yellow; chin greyish; lower throat white.

Range.—Southern Oceans from Patagonia to the subantarctic islands of New Zealand, north in winter to Buenos Aires, Cape Colony, southern Australia and New Zealand. Breeds at Tierra del Fuego and adjacent islands, the Falkland Is., Tristan da Cunha and Gough I. (*E. c. crestatus*), Prince Edward I., Marion I., the Crozet Is., Heard I., Kerguelen, St. Paul I., Amsterdam I., Campbell I., Auckland Is., Antipodes I. and Macquarie Is. (*E. c. filholi*). *Eggdates*: Aug.–Dec.

Notes.—Distinguished by the yellow lines at the sides of the crest, which do not meet on the forehead, and end in long plumes posteriorly. On land it hops with both feet placed together.

4. **Victoria Penguin** (*Eudyptes pachyrhynchus*)

Adult.—Similar to the Rock-hopper Penguin, but feathers of crown not much elongated and posterior feathers of yellow lateral stripe not drooping; flipper with a very narrow margin of white on inner edge of upper surface, ·

consisting of a single row of white feathers; sides of throat often with a whitish patch; tail of 16 feathers; bill with sides of upper plate (culminicorn) diverging beyond the nostrils, red; feet white; length 19.7–28 ins.; flipper 5.8–8.5; tail 4; bill 1.7–2.7; tarsus 1.2–1.5. *Young.*—Similar but chin and throat greyish-white; a line of pale lemon-yellow feathers on each side of the crown behind the level of the eye; bill black with a reddish tip.

Range.—New Zealand seas, ranging in winter to the Chatham Is., Tasmania and southern Australia. Breeds on the coasts of New Zealand, and at Stewart I. and the Snares Is. *Egg-dates:* Sept.–Dec.

Notes.—Distinguished from the Rock-hopper by its shorter crest and from both Rock-hopper and Big-crested Penguins by the narrow white inner margin of the flipper and the form of the bill. It swims with the whole body submerged. On shore it walks or hops rather clumsily.

5. Big-crested Penguin (*Eudyptes sclateri*)

Adult.—Similar to the Victoria Penguin but larger; a broader white stripe on the inner margin of the flipper, consisting of two rows of feathers; upper tail-coverts sometimes white; tail of 16 feathers; bill with sides of upper plate (culminicorn) almost parallel beyond the nostrils, brownish-red; feet flesh colour; length 28–29 ins.; flipper 7.9–8.4; tail 3.5–4.8; bill 2.1–2.4; tarsus 1.3. *Young.*—Similar but chin and throat mostly white; stripes on side of crown very pale yellowish.

Range.—Southern Ocean south of New Zealand, occasionally north to Victoria, New Zealand and the Chatham Is. Breeds at the Auckland Is., Antipodes I. and Bounty Is. *Egg-dates:* Sept.

Notes.—Distinguished from the Victoria Penguin by the features mentioned above, and from the Rock-hopper by its larger size and shorter plumes in the crest.

6. Macaroni Penguin (*Eudyptes chrysolophus*). (*Plate 51*)

Adult.—Upperparts dark bluish-grey; head, chin and throat blackish; feathers in a line across the forehead and along the sides of crown golden-orange at base with long pointed black tips, the longest plumes above and behind the eye orange throughout; sometimes a white patch on upper tail-coverts; flipper bluish-grey above with the inner margin edged with white, white below with the outer margin and a patch at the base of the inner margin black; underparts white; tail of 14 feathers; bill with the upper plate (culminicorn) expanding beyond the nostrils, black with a reddish tip and a pink naked space at base; length 26–30 ins.; flipper 6.9–8.1; tail 3.5–3.9; bill 2.1–2.5; tarsus 1.5. *Young.*—Similar but line of feathers above the eye yellow.

Range.—Southern Atlantic and Indian Oceans. Breeds at the South Shetlands, South Orkneys, South Sandwich Is., South Georgia, Falkland Is, Bouvet I., Prince Edward I., Marion I., Kerguelen and Heard I. *Egg-dates:* Nov.–Jan.

Notes.—Distinguished from the Rock-hopper, Victoria and Big-crested Penguins by the colouring of the lines on the sides of the crown which meet on the forehead, and from the Royal Penguin by its dark throat.

7. Royal Penguin (*Eudyptes schlegeli*)

Adult.—Upperparts slate-grey; sides of head and neck, chin, throat and underparts white; upper tail-coverts often mostly white; a broad orange band across the forehead and along the sides of the crown; tail of 14 feathers; bill with the upper plate (culminicorn) expanding beyond the nostrils, reddish-brown; length 26.5–30 ins.; flipper 6.5–9; tail 3–5; bill 2.4–3.2; tarsus 1–1.5. *Young.*—Similar but sides of head and neck, and throat, greyish-brown; feathers of band round crown yellow, not orange.

Range.—Southern Ocean south of New Zealand, occasionally north to New Zealand and Tasmania. Breeds at Macquarie I. *Egg-dates:* Sept.–Nov.

Notes.—The adult differs from other crested Penguins in having white cheeks and throat. The yellow or orange

153

stripes on the head meet in front as in the Macaroni Penguin.

8. Grand or Yellow-eyed Penguin (*Megadyptes antipodes*)

Adult.—Upperparts slate-grey; head blackish; feathers of forehead and back of head somewhat elongated, a pale yellow band from behind the eyes round the back of the head of slightly elongated feathers; throat brown; foreneck and underparts white; flipper dark slate-grey above, margined with white on both edges, the band on the inner edge broad, composed of two rows of feathers, white below; a patch of whitish on upper tail-coverts; bill long, laterally compressed, brownish orange; feet dark brown; length 30–32 ins.; flipper 7.5–8.2; tail 2.3–3; bill 2–2.5; tarsus 1.5. *Young.*—Similar but yellow band only on sides of head.

Range.—New Zealand Seas. Breeds on the coast of the South Island of New Zealand and at Stewart I., the Auckland Is. and Campbell I. *Egg-dates:* Sept–Nov.

Notes.—Distinguished from the Macaroni and Royal Penguins by the pale yellow area on the head which is very broad on the forehead and does not end in elongated feathers.

III. MEDIUM-SIZED PENGUINS WITH NO CREST OR YELLOW COLOUR ON THE HEAD, BUT USUALLY WITH STRIPES OF WHITE OR BLACK ON THE HEAD, NECK OR BREAST

9. Gentoo Penguin (*Pygoscelis papua*). (*Plates 51, 54 and 55*)

Adult.—Upperparts slaty-grey; head, throat and neck brownish-black, with a white band across the back of the head from one eye to the other; flipper greyish-brown above, edged on both sides with white, white below with a black patch at the tip; underparts white; tail long, of 14, 16 or 18 feathers; bill rather long, red or orange with the upper edge of the upper mandible black; feet orange;

length 30 ins.; flipper 9–9.5; tail 4.3–6; bill 2.8–3.3; tarsus 1. *Young.*—Similar but chin and throat mottled with greyish black.

Range.—Southern Oceans from Antarctica occasionally north to New Zealand, and Tasmania. Breeds on islands adjacent to the Antarctic continent and at the South Shetlands, South Orkneys, South Georgia, Staten I., the Falkland Is., Marion I., the Crozet Is., Kerguelen, Heard I. and Macquarie I. *Egg-dates:* Sept.–Jan.

Notes.—Easily distinguished by the white band across the back of its head. In the water it swims with body horizontal and head and back above the surface and never leaps clear of the water. The name "Rock-hopper" is frequently applied to this species though it does not hop when on land but runs. Except at the Falkland Islands it is usually known as the "Johnny."

10. Bearded Penguin (*Pygoscelis antarctica*). (*Plate 51*)

Adult.—Upperparts bluish-grey; top of head blackish; throat, sides of head and neck, and underparts white; a black transverse line across the throat from one ear to the other; upper surface of flipper blue-grey with white inner margin, under surface white with a terminal patch and the outer margin black; tail rather long, of 12 feathers; bill short, black; feet orange or yellowish; length 30 ins.; flipper 4.7–7.5; tail 4.4–5; bill 2.6. *Young.*—Similar but tail of 14 feathers.

Range.—Southern Atlantic Ocean and adjacent Antarctic Seas, north in winter to the Falkland Is. and east to 106° E. Breeds on islands off the Antarctic continent and at the South Shetlands, South Orkneys, South Sandwich Is., South Georgia and Bouvet I. *Egg-dates:* Oct.–Feb.

Notes.—Often called the "Ringed or Chin-strap Penguin." Distinguished by its white chin and cheeks and the narrow black line across the throat.

11. Adelie Penguin (*Pygoscelis adeliae*). (*Plates 51 and 57*)

Adult.—Upperparts bluish-black; top of head, cheeks and throat black, this colour ending in a point on the foreneck; eyelids white; underparts white; upper surface of flipper blue-black with white inner margin, under surface white with a terminal patch and the outer margin black; tail very long, of 14 feathers; bill short, brick-red; feet rosy-white above, black below; length 30 ins.; flipper 7; tail 6.3–7; bill 2.2. *Young.*—Similar but throat white like underparts; eyelids black; bill blackish.

Range.—Antarctic Seas. Breeds on coasts of Antarctica and outlying islands, also at the South Shetlands, South Orkneys and South Sandwich Is. *Egg-dates:* Oct.–Jan.

Notes.—The adult is readily distinguished from the Bearded Penguin by its entirely black head and throat. The young bird has the throat white but the chin and cheeks are black. The Adelie Penguin stands very upright, walks slowly with a waddling gait and on snow or ice often travels on its breast using flippers and feet for propulsion. When swimming its back is submerged.

12. Jackass Penguin (*Spheniscus demersus*). (*Plate 51*)

Centre of forehead and crown, sides of face and throat, and upperparts black; underparts white, with a narrow black horseshoe shaped band across the breast and along the sides to the flanks; a white band from the base of the bill along the sides of the crown and neck to the flanks above the black band; a rounded white spot on the tail; flippers black above with narrow white margins on both edges, white below; tail very short, of 20 feathers; bill rather long and stout, black with a transverse grey bar; naked skin about eye grey, at base of bill pink or bluish; feet black, mottled with grey; length 24.5–27 ins.; flipper 6.7–8.4; tail 1.5–1.6; bill 2.3–2.5. *Young.*—Upperparts black; underparts white.

Range.—Coasts of South Africa, occasionally north to Angola and Natal. Breeds on islands off the coast from Angra Pequena to Algoa Bay. *Egg-dates:* Throughout the year, chiefly May–June.

Notes.—The only Penguin common on the coasts of South Africa, with a striking black and white pattern. It swims very low in the water and dives quietly without jump or splash. On land it runs or waddles, but does not hop. It is of some commercial importance as a producer of guano and its eggs are collected for sale under Government regulation.

13. Humboldt Penguin (*Spheniscus humboldti*). (*Plate 51*)

Adult.—Upperparts slaty-grey or brownish-grey; throat and sides of head blackish; chin and a narrow band from bill along sides of crown and neck white; front of neck and underparts white, with a narrow horseshoe-shaped black band across the breast and along the sides to the tail; tail very short, of 20 feathers; bill stout, blackish with the base flesh-coloured; length 27 ins.; flipper 6.9–8.4; tail 1.4; bill 2.6–3. *Young.*—Similar but with no pectoral band and the pattern on the throat, neck and sides of the head reversed; chin, throat and sides of head pale grey; sides and front of neck dark smoky brown.

Range.—West coast of South America from Corral, Chile, north to Paita, Peru. Breeds on islands off the coast from Valparaiso to Paita. *Egg-dates:* Throughout the year.

Notes.—The only Penguin on the coast of Peru and northern Chile, formerly of considerable importance as a producer of guano. In central Chile it meets the Magellan Penguin from which the adult differs in having the front and sides of the neck white.

14. Magellan Penguin (*Spheniscus magellanicus*). (*Plates 31, 51 and 56*)

Adult.—Similar to the Humboldt Penguin but with an additional black band on the foreneck between the black of the throat and the black horse-shoe-shaped band on the breast; tail of 20 feathers; bill blackish; feet black, mottled with white; length 28 ins.; flipper 7.5–9; tail 1.4; bill 2–2.8. *Young.*—Similar but throat and a broad band on the foreneck dark grey.

Range.—Coasts of southern South America, north to Coquimbo, Chile, and to Rio de Janeiro, Brazil. Breeds in Tierra del Fuego, Staten I., the Falkland Is., on the southern coasts of Patagonia and Chile and at Juan Fernandez. *Egg-dates:* Oct.–Dec.

Notes.—Can only be confused with the Humboldt Penguin which it meets in central Chile, and from which it differs as described above. The "Jackass Penguin" of the Falkland Islands, its braying note being like that of the true Jackass Penguin of the Cape of Good Hope.

IV. SMALL PENGUINS WITHOUT CREST OR YELLOW COLOURING ON HEAD

15. Galápagos Penguin (*Spheniscus mendiculus*)

Adult.—Similar to the Magellan Penguin but decidedly smaller; chin and upper part of throat white, connected by a narrow stripe with a narow band of white along the sides of the crown and neck; flipper blackish-slate above, black below with a broad white band down the middle and a whitish patch on the inner margin; tail of 18 feathers; bill with upper mandible black, lower mandible yellow with black tip; length 20 ins.; flipper 5.9–6.3; tail 0.8–1.1; bill 2.1–2.4.

Range.—Coasts of the Galápagos Is., where it undoubtedly breeds, though it has not been found nesting.

Notes.—The only Penguin confined to the tropics. Its range extends to islands just north of the Equator. Its restricted habitat prevents confusion, as no other species ranges so far north. On land it uses both flippers and feet to scramble over the rocks.

16. Little Penguin (*Eudyptula minor = E. undina*). (Plate 51)

Adult.—Upperparts bluish-grey; sides of face and sides of breast ashy; chin and underparts white; flipper dark blue-grey above, with the inner margin white, the band consisting of two rows of feathers, white below; tail of 16 very narow, short, white feathers, hidden by the upper tail-coverts; bill short and stout, upper mandible brownish-black, lower mandible pinkish-white; feet pinkish-white;

length 15.7–16 ins.; flipper 4.4–4.7; tail 1.1–1.3; bill 1.4–1.5; tarsus 0.9–1.1. *Young.*—Similar.

Range.—Coasts of southern Australia (north to Swan River, Western Australia, and Moreton Bay, Queensland), Tasmania, New Zealand and the Chatham Is. Breeds on islands off the coast of Australia from Rockingham, Western Australia, to the Solitary Is., New South Wales, and on coasts of Tasmania (*E. m. novaehollandiae*) and in New Zealand, Stewart I. and the Chatham Is. (*E. m. minor*). *Egg-dates:* July–Jan.

Notes.—The only Penguin common on Australian coasts distinguished by its small size and plain colouring. On land it shuffles along with the body bent forwards with a curious undulating motion.

17. White-flippered Penguin (*Eudyptula albosignata*)

Adult.—Similar to the Little Penguin but rather larger; upperparts lighter greyish-blue; upper tail-coverts usually white; both margins of flipper widely bordered with white and a more or less distinct white patch near the middle of the inner margin; length 16.5 ins.; flipper 5.6; tail 1.2; bill 1.6 *Young.*—Similar.

Range.—East coast of South Island, New Zealand. Breeds on Banks Peninsula. *Egg-dates:* Sept.–Jan.

Notes.—Cannot be distinguished from the Little Penguin when seen in the water, but on land the broad white margins on both edges of the flipper are easily distinguished.

CHAPTER X

~~~~~~~~~~~~~~~~~~~~~~~~~~~~~~~~~~~~

Auks, Guillemots and Puffins

(Order *Charadriiformes:* Family *Alcidae*)

~~~~~~~~~~~~~~~~~~~~~~~~~~~~~~~~~~~~

THE MEMBERS OF this family are rather small, or very small sea-birds with comparatively short necks, with small, narrow wings and with very short tails of 12 to 18 feathers. Their legs are short and are placed very far back near the tail, and they have only three toes, which are connected by webs. The various species differ remarkably in the form of their bills. In some they are fairly long and slender, but in most species they are comparatively short and considerably compressed, and in a few they are much enlarged in the breeding season.

In colouring Auks are usually dark above and white below, but a few species are entirely dark and several are dark with white patches in the wings. Immature birds and adults in winter plumage are frequently much whiter than in breeding plumage. Some species are adorned during the breeding season with tufts of long plumes on the head. The bills and feet of some species are bright red, yellow, blue, or whitish, though in the majority they are black or dusky.

Auks are peculiar to the seas of the colder parts of the northern hemisphere, being most numerous in Bering Sea and the adjacent parts of the North Pacific Ocean. A number of species are also found in arctic seas and in the North Atlantic Ocean. During the winter months they spend their time at sea in small flocks or larger parties, usually not occurring very many miles from land. On the water they float high like Gulls and thus appear very different from Penguins. This character helps to distinguish them from the Loons or Divers. They obtain their food, which consists mainly of fish and crustacea, by diving, using their wings when under water. Thus they fill the place in the northern seas which is occupied by the Penguins and Diving-Petrels in the southern oceans. The largest living species of Auk is, however, only about the same size as the smallest species of Penguin.

The best known member of the family is probably the Great Auk or Garefowl, which was at one time plentiful on islands round the North Atlantic Ocean. This was the bird to which the name Penguin was originally applied, though the name has now been transferred to birds of the southern hemisphere which resemble it superficially. The Great Auk, like the Penguins, was flightless and had very small wings, though these were furnished with quill-feathers. It was killed in great numbers in the seventeenth and eighteenth centuries by sealers and fishermen for food or bait, and for its feathers and oil. By 1800 it had become very scarce and the few remaining individuals were sought as rarities for collections. The last was killed in 1844, and about eighty skins and nearly eighty of its eggs are preserved in museums.

The surviving members of the family can all fly, but their flight, while rapid and strong, is direct and not buoyant. The small wings are flapped very rapidly and the birds never seem to travel very far in the air. Often they fly one behind the other in a string a few feet above the waves. When alarmed Auks generally endeavour to escape by diving, and if pursued they frequently splash along the surface of the water as if unable to fly, diving through the crests of the waves.

Auks congregate for breeding on islands and cliffs.

The breeding colonies often consist of many thousands of birds and sometimes contain several species intermingled. Most Auks breed in crevices among fallen rocks or in cliffs, or in holes in the ground, but a few of the larger species nest on the ledges of precipitous cliffs or the summits of rock-stacks, and Kittlitz's Murrelet breeds in the open high up in the mountains. Most species make no nests, but deposit one, two or three eggs on the bare rock or soil, but the Puffins, which breed in holes, make a rude nest of grass and feathers. The oval or pear-shaped eggs are very large in proportion to the size of the birds and are either white or variously coloured. Eggs of the Common and Brunnich's Murres (or Guillemots) are specially remarkable for their variability, no two being quite alike. They are white, buff, pale blue or green, mottled, blotched, streaked or scrawled with black, brown, purple, or red markings. Several of the smaller Auks which breed in holes are nocturnal during the breeding season, flying in from the sea at night and leaving before dawn.

The young when hatched are covered with black, dark grey, or brown down, and are dependent on their parents for food until they are fledged. At sea Auks rarely or never make any sound, but in their breeding colonies they utter curious growling, moaning and yelping notes. The name Murre, applied to two of the species in America, is said to be derived from one of their calls. The young birds make shrill, yelping or whistling cries when waiting to be fed either on the cliffs or in the water.

When on land Auks commonly stand upright owing to the posterior position of their feet. Some species stand on the feet only, but others rest on the feet and tarsi. The species which breed on the ledges of cliffs may frequently be seen bowing to one another and indulging in curious amatory antics, and probably those which breed in holes go through similar performances.

When flying up to the cliffs or when about to settle on the water the feet are often spread out at each side of the tail to act as brakes or to assist in steering, and they are also used for steering when the birds are progressing under water by means of their wings. Whether they are used for propulsion under water is doubtful.

Whilst it is easy to recognise a bird as a member of this family by its squat body and small, narrow wings, it is usually difficult to ascertain the species of those seen at sea except under specially favourable circumstances, as they are mostly small and few have characteristic markings visible at a distance.

They fall naturally into four groups—very small, small, medium-sized and large—and are here further subdivided according to their colouration in the breeding season. "Very small" Auks are those under 8 inches long, with wings under 4.5 inches long; "small" species are those from 8 to 11 inches long, with wings from 4.5 to 6 inches long; "medium-sized" species are those from 12 to 15 inches long, with wings from 6 to 7 inches long; whilst "large" species are from 16 to 19 inches in total length, with wings over 7 inches long. In the following pages the Auks are arranged in seven groups:—

I. Large, with plumage almost entirely dark (Species 1.)

II. Large, with upperparts dark and underparts mainly or entirely white (Species 2–4).

III. Medium-sized, with upperparts dark and underparts mainly or entirely white (Species 5–7).

IV. Medium-sized, with plumage entirely dark in breeding season, or with white patches on the wings—sometimes mainly white both above and below in winter (Species 8-10).

V. Small, with plumage entirely dark in breeding season, or with underparts somewhat whiter (Species 11–12).

163

VI. Small, with upperparts dark and under parts white, or with white abdomen sharply contrasting with dark throat or breast (Species 13–20).

VII. Very small, with upperparts dark and underparts partly dusky becoming white on abdomen (Species 21–22).

I. LARGE AUKS WITH PLUMAGE ALMOST ENTIRELY DARK

1. Tufted Puffin (*Lunda cirrhata*). (*Plate 59*)

Adult.—Upperparts sooty-black; chin, cheeks, throat and foreneck sooty-brown; under wing-coverts deep brownish-grey; underparts deep greyish-brown; in breeding season forehead and region about eyes white and elongated, yellow tufts on sides of head; bill very large, salmon-red at tip, olive-green at base, skin about gape vermilion; feet bright salmon-red; length 16 ins.; wing 7–8.1; tail 2.2–2.6; bill 2.1–2.6; tarsus 1.1–1.4. *Young.*—Similar to adult in winter, but bill smaller.

Range.—Bering Sea and adjacent parts of Arctic Sea and North Pacific Ocean, south in winter to Lower California. Breeds from Koliutschin I., eastern Siberia and Cape Lisburne, Alaska to Commander, Kurile, Aleutian and Pribilof Is., and down the American coast to Sta. Barbara Is., California. *Egg-dates:* April–July.

Notes.—A very distinct bird, whose large size, dark colouring, large, brightly coloured bill and yellow tufts in breeding season render it unmistakable. It flies more strongly than most Auks, sometimes at some height above the water, though it finds difficulty in starting. It breeds in burrows or crevices among rocks.

II. LARGE AUKS WITH UPPERPARTS DARK AND UNDERPARTS MAINLY OR ENTIRELY WHITE

2. **Razor-billed Auk** (*Alca torda*). (*Plates 59 and 60*)

Adult.—Head, neck and upperparts black, with a narrow, white line from bill to eye, in winter cheeks, throat and foreneck white; secondaries tipped with white; underparts, including axillaries and under wing-coverts, white; tail wedge-shaped, of 12 feathers; bill deep and very narrow, black, crossed by a white band, inside of mouth yellow; feet black; length 16.5 ins.; wing 7.4–7.9; tail 2.8–3.5; bill 1.2–1.4; tarsus 1.2–1.4. *Young.*—Similar to adult in winter, but bill smaller and without white bar.

Range.—North Atlantic Ocean and adjacent parts of Arctic Sea north to Spitzbergen, south in winter to Long I., Azores and Gibraltar, occasionally to North Carolina, Canary Is., Italy and Algeria. Breeds in Bay of Fundy, Gulf of St. Lawrence, southern Greenland, Norway and North Russia (*A. t. pica*), Iceland, Faëro Is., British Is. and Brittany (*A. t. islandica*) and on islands in the Baltic (*A. t. torda*). *Egg-dates:* March–June.

Notes.—Breeds on cliffs. Distinguished from Common and Brunnich's Murres by its deep, compressed bill. When swimming, its pointed tail is carried raised.

3. **Common Murre or Guillemot** (*Uria aalge* = *U. troille* = *U. ringvia*). (*Plates 59 and 61*)

Adult.—Head, neck and upperparts sooty-brown, in winter throat, cheeks and foreneck whitish with a dark line behind the eye; tips of secondaries, breast and abdomen white; some individuals of the North Atlantic race have a white ring round the eye and a white stripe behind it; tail rounded, of 12 feathers; bill long, straight, pointed, black, inside of mouth yellow; feet dusky; length 16–18 ins.; wing 7.2–8.8; tail 1.5–2.1; bill 1.4–2.3; tarsus 1.2–1.6. *Young.*—Similar to adult, but underparts dirty white, bill shorter and feet paler.

Range.—North Pacific and North Atlantic Oceans and adjacent parts of Arctic Sea, south in winter to northern Japan, southern California, Maine, Spain and the western Mediterranean. Breeds in Kamchatka, the Commander, Aleutian and Pribilof Is. and from Alaska south to Washington (*U. a inornata*), California (*U. a. californica*), from Bay of Fundy to southern Greenland, Spitzbergen, Iceland, Norway, Shetland and Orkney Is. and Scotland (*U. a. aalge*), Faroe Is. (*U. a. spiloptera*), Bear I. (*U. a. hyperborea*), islands in the Baltic (*U. a. intermedia*) and Ireland, England, Heligoland, France and Portugal (*U. a. albionis*). *Egg-dates:* May–Aug.

Notes.—Breeds on cliffs. Rather larger than Razor-billed Auk, browner in colour and with long, straight bill. More slender, entirely black bill, and in winter white face with black line through eye, distinguish it from Brunnich's Murre.

4. Brunnich's Murre or Guillemot (*Uria lomvia*). (*Plates 58, 59 and 61*)

Adult.—Head, neck and upperparts greyish-black, in winter throat and foreneck white; tips of secondaries, breast and abdomen white; bill long, stout, pointed, black, base of upper mandible greenish or bluish grey; feet yellowish in front, black behind; length 16.5–19 ins.; wing 7.8–9.1; tail 1.6–2.4; bill 1.2–1.8; tarsus 1.2–1.6. *Young.*—Similar to adults in winter, but browner and with smaller bill.

Range.—Bering Sea, Arctic Sea and adjacent parts of North Atlantic Ocean, in winter south to northern Japan, Maine and Norway, occasionally to South Carolina and British Is. Breeds from Koliutschin I., Wrangel I., Herald I. and Point Barrow south to Kodiak I., Aleutian Is. and Commander Is. (*U. l. arra*), also from Gulf of St. Lawrence, Labrador and Hudson's Bay to north Greenland, Novaya Zemblya, Jan Mayen Land, Iceland, Spitzbergen, Franz Josef Land and the Taimyr Peninsula (*U. l. lomvia*). *Egg-dates:* June.

Notes.—Distinguished from the Common Murre, which it resembles in habits, by its stouter bill with a pale line on upper mandible, and in winter also by having the sides of the face to below the eye dark.

III. MEDIUM-SIZED AUKS WITH UPPERPARTS DARK AND UNDERPARTS MAINLY OR ENTIRELY WHITE

5. **Horned Puffin** (*Fratercula corniculata*). (*Plate 59*)

Adult.—Crown greyish-brown; neck and upperparts black; chin brownish-grey; cheeks white in summer, grey in winter; under wing-coverts brownish-grey; underparts white; bill very large, brownish-red, light yellow at base, inside mouth orange; feet deep vermilion; length 13.5–16.6 ins.; wing 6.6–7.5; tail 2.4–2.7; bill 1.8–2.2; tarsus 1–1.2. *Young.*—Similar to adult in winter, but bill much smaller and brownish in colour.

Range.—Bering Sea and adjacent parts of Arctic Sea and North Pacific Ocean, in winter south to Kurile Is. and Queen Charlotte I., British Columbia, occasionally to Monterey Bay, California. Breeds from Koliutschin Is., Arctic coast of eastern Siberia and Cape Lisburne, Alaska, southward to northern Kurile Is., Aleutian Is., and south-eastern Alaska. *Egg-dates:* June–Sept.

Notes.—Distinguished from the Common and Brunnich's Murres by its large, triangular bill and white cheeks; from the Tufted Puffin by its white underparts, white cheeks and absence of plumes on the head. It breeds in burrows or crevices in the ground. Its name is derived from a peculiar excrescent growth on the eyelid, which projects upwards, only present during the breeding season.

6. **Atlantic Puffin** (*Fratercula arctica*). (*Plate 62*)

Adult.—Upperparts and foreneck blackish; nape with a narrow, greyish collar; cheeks and throat white or greyish, in winter blackish; under wing-coverts light brownish-grey; underparts white; bill very large, greyish-blue at base, vermilion at tip, crossed with bars of yellow, inside mouth yellow; feet vermilion; length 11.5–14 ins.; wing

5.7–7.4; tail 1.6–2.1; bill 1.7–2.3; tarsus 0.9–1.2. *Young.*—Similar but bill much smaller and brownish in colour.

Range.—North Atlantic Ocean and adjacent Arctic Seas, south in winter to Massachusetts, the Azores, Canary Is. and Mediterranean. Breeds in northern Greenland, Spitzbergen, Novaya Zemblya and Jan Mayen (*F. a. naumanni*), from Maine to Labrador, southern Greenland, Iceland and northern Norway (*F. a. arctica*), and in southern Norway, Sweden, the British Is. and Brittany (*F. a. grabae*). *Egg-dates:* May–July.

Notes.—Distinguished from all other Atlantic Auks by its large, triangular, brightly-coloured beak. It breeds in holes and is sometimes called the "Sea Parrot."

7. Rhinoceros Auklet (*Cerorhinca monocerata*). (*Plate 59*)

Adult.—Upperparts sooty-blackish; underparts white, more or less clouded with brownish-grey on chin, throat, chest, sides and flanks; axillaries and under wing-coverts brownish-grey; a line of straight, elongated, white plumes extending from eye across cheeks and another from bill below eye; tail of 16 or 18 feathers; bill rather long, orange-yellow, with a blackish, horny projection at base of upper mandible in summer; feet yellowish; length 14 ins.; wing 6.7–7.2; tail 1.6–2.4; bill 1.3–1.5; tarsus 1.1–1.2. *Young.*—Similar to adult in winter but without white head plumes; bill smaller and darker.

Range.—Coasts of North Pacific Ocean, south in winter to south-eastern Siberia, Japan and Lower California. Breeds on the Kurile Is. and the coast of Kamchatka, also from Sitka, Alaska, south on the American coast to Washington. *Egg-dates:* April–July.

Notes.—Distinguished from all other fair-sized Auks in the breeding season by the blunt horn on the base of the beak, from which its name is derived. The little Whiskered Auklet has a somewhat similar but smaller knob. It breeds in burrows and is nocturnal in its habits when on land. In the water it floats low with the head drawn back level with the back.

IV. MEDIUM-SIZED AUKS WITH PLUMAGE IN BREEDING SEASON EITHER ENTIRELY DARK OR DARK WITH WHITE PATCHES IN THE WINGS—SOMETIMES MAINLY WHITE BOTH ABOVE AND BELOW IN WINTER

8. **Black Guillemot** (*Cepphus grylle*). (*Plates 63 and 65*)

Adult.—In summer sooty-black; a large patch on the wing-coverts, the axillaries and the under wing-coverts white; in winter white, the upperparts mottled with black, the wings black with a large white patch and the tail black; tail of 12 feathers; bill straight, pointed, black, inside the mouth vermilion; feet vermilion; length 12–14 ins.; wing 5.9–6.9; tail 1.6–2.2; bill 1.1–1.3; tarsus 1.1–1.4. *Young.*—Similar to adults in winter but white patch on wing-coverts and underparts mottled with black.

Range.—North Atlantic Ocean and adjacent parts of Arctic Sea, south in winter to New Jersey and northern France. Breeds from Maine, Gulf of St. Lawrence, and southern Labrador to Iceland, the British Is., the Baltic, Norway and the White Sea (*C. g. grylle*), in northern Labrador and southern Greenland (*C. g. arcticus*), and on arctic coasts and islands of Canada, Europe and Siberia (*C. g. mandtii*). *Egg-dates:* May–Aug.

Notes.—The "Sea Pigeon," as this bird is sometimes called, breeds in crevices among rocks. In summer its black plumage, with large white patch in the wing, distinguishes it from all other Atlantic Auks and in winter its mottled white and black plumage is almost equally distinctive. Birds with the wings entirely black occasionally occur and have been thought to be a distinct species and named *C. motzfeldi*.

9. **Pigeon Guillemot** (*Cepphus columba*). (*Plate 59*)

Adult.—Similar to the Black Guillemot but the white area on the wing divided by transverse bars of black into two or three patches, wings sometimes entirely black in winter; axillaries and under wing-coverts brownish-grey;

tail of 14 feathers; bill black, inside mouth vermilion; feet vermilion; length 14.5 ins.; wing 6.3–7.1; tail 1.7–2; bill 1.1–1.4; tarsus 1.2–1.4. *Young.*—Similar to young Black Guillemot.

Range.—Bering Sea and adjacent parts of Arctic Sea and North Pacific Ocean, south in winter to Japan and Lower California. Breeds from the Sta. Barbara Is., California, north along the American coast to the Aleutian Is. and from the Commander Is. along the Kamchatkan and Siberian coasts to Wrangel I. and Herald I. (*C. c. columba*), also on the coasts of southern Kamchatka and the Kurile Is. (*C. c. snowi*). *Egg-dates:* May–July.

Notes.—The Pacific representative of the Black Guillemot, which it resembles in habits. Darker than the Spectacled Guillemot and usually with white in the wing.

10. Spectacled Guillemot (*Cepphus carbo*).

Adult.—In summer slaty-black, shoulders, under wing-coverts and axillaries brownish, white round eyes; in winter chin, throat and underparts white; tail of 14 feathers; bill black; feet red; length 14.5 ins.; wing 7–7.6; tail 1.8–2.1; bill 1.6; tarsus 1.4–1.5. *Young.*—Similar to adult in winter, but foreneck greyish.

Range.—Okhotsk and Japan Seas ranging to the Commander Is. Breeds on the coasts of Kamchatka, the Okhotsk Sea, the Kurile Is., northern Japan and Korea.

Notes.—Distinguished from the Pigeon Guillemot by its greyer colour and the white patch round the eye in summer, and by the absence of white in the wing.

V. SMALL AUKS, WITH PLUMAGE ENTIRELY DARK IN BREEDING SEASON, OR WITH UNDERPARTS SOMEWHAT WHITER

11. Crested Auklet (*Aethia cristatella*).

Adult.—Upperparts slate-blackish; a blackish crest on forehead curving forwards; elongated white plumes behind the eye bending downwards across the cheeks; forehead and underparts brownish-grey; bill short, orange-red with a whitish tip; feet pale violet-grey; length 10.5 ins.; wing 4.9–5.6; tail 1.2–1.5; bill 0.4–0.5; tarsus 0.9–1.1. *Young.*—Similar to adult but without crest on forehead and plumes on cheeks; bill smaller and dull brown in colour.

Range.—Bering Sea and adjacent parts of Arctic Sea and North Pacific Ocean, south in winter to Amurland, northern Japan and Kodiak I. Breeds on the Pribilof, Aleutian, Commander and Kurile Is. *Egg-dates:* June–Aug.

Notes.—Distinguished by its entirely dark underparts, small size and the curious plumes on the head. It is a noisy species, which breeds in deep burrows and crevices between rocks. They usually fly in small compact flocks close above the surface of the water.

12. Marbled Murrelet (*Brachyramphus marmoratus*)

Adult.—Underparts dark sooty-brown, the back, rump and upper tail-coverts barred in summer with rusty or buff, in winter with grey; a white band across the nape and a white ring round the eye in winter; scapulars mostly white; underparts white, much blotched with fuscous in summer; axillaries and under wing-coverts fuscous; tail of 14 feathers; bill slender, black; feet flesh-coloured; length 9.5–10 ins.; wing 4.4–5.6; tail 1.1–1.4; bill 0.5–0.9; tarsus 0.6–0.7. *Young.*—Upperparts dusky with some white on nape and scapulars; underparts white, mottled with dusky.

Range.—Sea of Okhotsk and North Pacific Ocean, south in winter to the Liu Kiu Is. and San Diego, California. Breeds in Kamchatka, the Kurile Is. and Yezo (*B. m. perdix*) and on the American coast from Unalaska to Vancouver Is. (*B. m. marmoratus*). *Egg-dates:* April–June.

Notes.—The commonest small Auk on the coasts of southeastern Alaska and British Columbia. Though a few eggs have been obtained, the breeding habits are not properly known. It probably lays its eggs on the ground high up in the mountains. When on the water, it carries its bill and tail cocked up. It may also be distinguished by the white band on each side of the back above the wings.

In summer plumage, when seen flying, at a short distance it looks uniformly dark.

VI. SMALL AUKS, WITH UPPERPARTS DARK AND UNDERPARTS WHITE, OR WITH WHITE ABDOMEN SHARPLY CONTRASTING WITH DARK THROAT OR BREAST

13. Dovekie or Little Auk (*Plautus alle*). (*Plates 59 and 64*)

Adult.—Head, neck, upperparts and upper breast black, in winter throat whitish and nape sometimes grey; a short white streak above eye; secondaries tipped and scapulars streaked with white; lower breast and abdomen white; bill short and thick, black, light yellow inside mouth; feet flesh-coloured; length 8 ins.; wing 4.2–4.8; tail 1.2–1.6; bill 0.5–0.6; tarsus 0.7–0.8. *Young.*—Resembles adult in winter but browner and without white over eye and on scapulars.

Range.—North Atlantic Ocean and adjacent portions of Arctic Sea, south in winter regularly to New Jersey and the North Sea; occasionally to South Carolina, Bermuda, Azores and Canary Is. Breeds in arctic Canada, Greenland, Iceland, Novaya Zemblya, Spitzbergen (*P. a. alle*) and Franz Josef Land (*P. a. polaris*). *Egg-dates:* June.

Notes.—Much smaller than other Atlantic Auks. Breeds among boulders or in crevices of cliffs. Swims very low in the water and very much down by the stern. Distinguished also by its short, stout bill.

14. Cassin's Auklet (*Ptychoramphus aleuticus*)

Adult.—Upperparts greyish dusky; chin, throat and foreneck brownish-grey; small white spots above and below the eye; sides and flanks grey; under wing-coverts brownish-grey; underparts white; bill rather long, conical, black, pale at base of mandible; feet dusky bluish; length 9 ins.; wing 4.3–5.1; tail 1–1.4; bill 0.7–0.8; tarsus 0.9–1. *Young.*—Similar.

Range.—Pacific coast of North America from Aleutian Is. to Lower California. Breeds throughout its range. *Egg-dates:* March–July.

Notes.—Distinguished by its small size, dusky colouration above and conical bill. It breeds in burrows and crevices, and is nocturnal in the breeding season.

15. Paroquet Auklet (*Cyclorrhynchus psittacula*). (*Plates 59 and 65*)

Adult.—Upperparts dull slate-blackish; in summer elongated white plumes behind the eye extending downwards across the cheeks; chin, throat, foreneck, sides and flanks greyish-fuscous in summer, white in winter; under surface of wings greyish-brown; underparts white; bill short and deep, orange-red, the lower mandible curved upwards; feet pale bluish-grey; length 10.5 ins.; wing 5.5–6; tail 1.5–1.7; bill 0.5–0.7; tarsus 1–1.2. *Young.*—Similar to adult in winter, but bill smaller and brownish-red in colour.

Range.—Bering Sea and adjacent parts of North Pacific Ocean, south in winter to Okhotsk Sea, northern Japan and California. Breeds from north-eastern Siberia and north-western Alaska to Kurile, Commander, Aleutian and Shumagin Is. *Egg-dates:* June–Aug.

Notes.—Distinguished from other Auklets by its larger size, white breast, blackish upperparts, small red bill and the white plumes on the cheeks in the breeding season. It breeds among or under rocks, and its flight is strong and usually higher above the water than in most other species.

16. Ancient Murrelet (*Synthliboramphus antiquus*). (*Plate 59*)

Adult.—Head, hind-neck, face and throat black; a broken stripe of white on each side of the crown; sides of neck and underparts white; in winter cheeks and throat white and chin greyish; upperparts slaty-blue; darker on wings and tail; sides and flanks sooty-black; under wing-coverts white; bill short and stout, bluish-

173

white; feet greyish-white; length 10.5 ins.; wing 5.1–5.5; tail 1.3–1.5; bill 0.5–0.6; tarsus 1–1.1. *Young.*—Similar to adult in winter.

Range.—North Pacific Ocean and adjacent portion of Bering Sea, south in winter to Japan and southern California. Breeds on the Kurile, Commander, Aleutian and Pribilof Is., southern coasts of Alaska and Queen Charlotte Is. *Egg-dates:* April–July.

Notes.—Distinguished by the uniform, bluish upperparts and sharply defined black and white colouring on the head. It breeds in burrows.

17. Crested Murrelet (*Synthliboramphus wumizusume*)

Adult.—Crown, sides of neck, sides and flanks black; front of crown in summer with a loose crest of long feathers curving backwards and on each side broad white stripes, which meet at the back of the head; cheeks, throat and upperparts slate-grey; underparts white; short, stout, bill and feet yellowish; length 10.5 ins.; wing 4.8–5; tail 1.3–1.5; bill 0.5–0.6; tarsus 0.9–1. *Young.*—Similar to adults in winter but head and upperparts brownish-grey.

Range.—Coasts of Japan, where it breeds.

Notes.—Distinguished by its uniform blue-grey upperparts and in summer plumage the black crested head with broad white stripes on each side, meeting behind.

18. Kittlitz's Murrelet (*Brachyramphus brevirostris*)

Adult.—In summer upperparts dusky, streaked with light buff; tail edged and tipped with white; cheeks, chin and neck light buff; underparts white with U-shaped black bars on chest and sides; axillaries and under wing-coverts deep brownish-grey; in winter upperparts slate-grey with white spots; a white collar on nape; sides of head, foreneck and underparts white, with a grey crescent in front of eye and grey bars on sides of breast; bill black; feet pale brownish; length 9.5 ins.; wing 5–5.5; tail 1.1–1.3; bill 0.4; tarsus 0.6–0.7.

Range.—Arctic coasts of Siberia and Alaska, and Bering Sea, south in winter to northern Japan. Breeds from Cape

Yakan, Siberia, to Kamchatka, the Kurile Is., the Aleutian Is. and Alaska east to Sitka. *Egg-dates:* May–June.

Notes.—Distinguished from the Marbled Murrelet by its lighter upperparts. The single egg is laid on the bare ground above snow-line high up in the mountains.

19. Xantus' Murrelet (*Brachyramphus hypoleucus*)

Adult.—Upperparts and flanks slate-grey, darker on wings; underparts, including under wing-coverts, white; tail of 14 feathers; bill small and slender, black, pale bluish at base of mandible; feet pale blue above, dusky below; length 8.5 ins.; wing 4.5–5; tail 1.2–1.3; bill 0.6–0.9; tarsus 0.9–1. *Young.*—Similar but bill smaller.

Range.—Coasts of southern California and Lower California from Monterey Bay to Cape San Lucas. Breeds on Sta. Barbara Is. and Los Coronados Is. *Egg-dates:* March–July.

Notes.—Distinguished from the Ancient Murrelet by the absence of black on the head, and from Craveri's Murrelet by its white under wing-coverts.

20. Craveri's Murrelet (*Brachyramphus craveri*)

Adult.—Upperparts blackish slate-colour; underparts white; flanks and under wing-coverts brownish slate-grey; tail of 14 feathers; bill small and slender, black; length 8.5 ins; wing 4.6; tail 1.4; bill 0.8; tarsus 0.8–0.9. *Young.*—Similar but breast and sides spotted with blackish.

Range.—Southern Lower California, north on west coast to latitude 28° N. and on east coast to latitude 24° N. Breeds on Isla Raza, Gulf of California. *Egg-dates:* Feb.–April.

Notes.—Distinguished from Xantus' Murrelet by its darker upperparts and dark under wing-coverts. The most southerly Auk, the only species which reaches the tropics. Some authorities consider it a southern race of Xantus' Murrelet.

VII. VERY SMALL AUKS, WITH UPPERPARTS DARK AND UNDERPARTS PARTLY DUSKY BECOMING WHITE ON ABDOMEN

21. Whiskered Auklet (*Aethia pygmaea*)

Adult.—Head, neck and upperparts dusky grey; a blackish crest on forehead curving forwards, tufts of white elongated plumes in front of the eye, one passing upwards and bending forwards, the other passing downwards and backwards, a tuft of elongated white plumes behind the eye bending downwards across the cheeks; chest dull grey; under wing-coverts greyish-brown; lower abdomen and under tail-coverts white; bill short, bright red with a whitish tip, with a blunt knob at the base in summer; feet bluish-grey; length 7.5 ins.; wing 4.1–4.6; tail 1.1–1.3; bill 0.3–0.4; tarsus 0.7–0.9. *Young.*—Similar to adult in winter but bill smaller and dusky in colour and without the ornamental plumes.

Range.—Southern Bering Sea and Kurile Is. south in winter to northern Japan. Breeds on the Aleutian Is. from Unalaska westward, the Commander Is. and Kurile Is. *Egg-dates:* May.

Notes.—Distinguished from the Crested Auklet by having a whitish patch under the tail, by the arrangement of the crests and plumes on the head, and in the breeding season by the knob on the bill. The rarest and least known of the Auklets, smaller than any other except the Least Auklet which is whiter below.

22. Least Auklet (*Aethia pusilla*)

Adult.—Upperparts slate-blackish, scapulars partly white, secondaries more or less tipped with white; in summer with white-pointed feathers on forehead; a row of white elongated plumes behind the eye extending downwards across the cheeks and another row from the corner of the mouth; axillaries and under wing-coverts white and pale grey; cheeks and chin dark slate-colour; underparts mostly white, more or less blotched with blackish, in summer frequently forming a dark band across the foreneck; bill small, conical, dusky, with dark reddish tip; feet brownish; length 6.5 ins.; wing 3.5–3.9; tail 0.9–1.1; bill 0.3–0.4; tarsus 0.6–0.8. *Young.*—Similar to adults in winter but bill smaller.

Range.—Bering Sea and adjacent parts of North Pacific Ocean, south in winter to Okhotsk Sea, the Liu Kiu Is. and Washington. Breeds on islands in Bering Sea and the Aleutian Is. *Egg-dates:* June–Aug.

Notes.—Smaller than any other Auk; to be confused only with the slightly larger Whiskered Auklet; distinguished by its black upperparts with white marks on scapulars and wings, small dusky bill and the white feathers and plumes on the head. It breeds in crevices among rocks.

CHAPTER XI

Frigate-Birds or Man-o'-War Hawks

(Order *Pelecaniformes*: Family *Fregatidae*)

THE LARGE TROPICAL sea-birds which constitute this family are the most completely aerial of water-birds and perhaps of all birds except Swifts. They have very long wings, long forked tails and very short legs. They never settle on the water or on a level coast and are probably incapable of rising from such situations. Throughout the hours of daylight they remain in the air, floating over the water or their island home without the slightest effort on motionless wing, plunging down to the surface of the sea to pick up some floating object, or pursuing other sea-birds to make them disgorge their booty. At dusk they retire in companies to some favourite clump of trees near the coast to roost. In some of the Pacific Islands Frigate-birds are domesticated and used like Pigeons for sending messages from one island to another.

In plumage adult Frigate-birds are either entirely black, or black above with white areas below, whilst the young have white heads. They have long, slender bills with a sharp hook at the end and a patch of naked skin between the edges of the lower mandible on the chin. In the males this forms a bright red pouch which can be inflated to a very large size and is the bird's chief ornament in the breeding season.

The feet are small and at their bases the toes are united by a web which extends also to the hind toe.

Frigate-birds are perhaps the most easily recognised of all sea-birds, but in ordinary sailing flight the tail is not spread, so that its forked nature is not always apparent. When the birds are playing or fighting in the air they frequently open and close the tail. Usually Frigate-birds are quite silent, but fighting males utter harsh grating cries and at other times they sometimes make a croaking call. Their food consists of fish, molluscs, jelly-fish and other creatures, picked up from the surface of the water by a swift movement of the bill when they are in flight, and they also pursue Boobies, Pelicans, Cormorants, Gulls, or Terns and force them to disgorge fish which they have caught. Other sea-birds have little chance of escaping from these swift-flying marauders and if they are overtaken before they have dropped their food the Frigate-bird delivers a fierce peck with its long hooked beak which may dislocate a wing. Usually before this happens the victim surrenders its meal, on which the Frigate-bird pounces before it reaches the water. The names "Frigate-bird" and "Man-o'-War Hawk," by which they are known, were bestowed on them in the days of sailing ships in reference to this habit.

Frigate-birds breed in colonies on tropical islands. Their nests are large structures clumsily constructed of sticks and are placed in trees, on bushes or sometimes on rocks. During the breeding season one or other of the parents is almost always at the nest, for, if it is left unguarded, neighbouring Frigate-birds will at once begin to steal the sticks of which it is composed. After the chick is hatched the parents' vigilance becomes even more necessary, as the neighbouring birds do not hesitate to appropriate it for a meal if opportunity offers.

The Man-o'-War Hawk lays a single white oval egg and the chick is entirely naked when hatched. Later it acquires a covering of white down which is soon replaced by feathers. When the nest is approached the chick utters a squealing call and rattles its bill.

Young birds can always be distinguished by their white heads and it is probably at least two years before the adult plumage is attained. Adult females are decidedly larger than the males and except in the Ascension Frigate-bird the sexes are differently coloured. Until recently only two species were recognised, but it is now known that there are at least five. Two of these are only known from very restricted areas in the neighbourhood of Ascension I. in the Atlantic, and Christmas I. in the Indian Ocean, where they respectively breed. The other three species are widely distributed.

1. Great Frigate-Bird (*Fregata minor*). (*Plates 67 and 68*)

Adult Male.—Plumage generally black, with blue-green sheen on head, green gloss on back and brownish tinge on underparts; a brown band on wings across the median wing-coverts and innermost secondaries; bill black, brown or grey-blue; a large red, distensible pouch on the throat; feet black, brown or pink; length 34–40 ins.; wing 21.7–25, span about 7 feet; tail 14.4–17; bill 3.8–5.9; tarsus 0.7. *Adult Female.*—Head, neck, upperparts, flanks and abdomen black with a brown collar on the back of the neck; a light brown band on wings; throat and foreneck greyish-white; lower neck, breast and sides white; bill horn-colour, rose, violet or light blue; feet red, rose, violet, bluish-white, bronze or black. *Young.*—Upperparts brownish black; head, neck and underparts white more or less tinged with rusty; bill and feet bluish.

Range.—Tropical Indian and Pacific Oceans and South Atlantic off coast of Brazil, occasionally south to Kerguelen, southern Australia and New Zealand. Breeds at South Trinidad I., off Brazil (*F. m. nicolli*), the Seychelle Is. and Aldabra (*F. m. aldabrensis*), Christmas I. and Cocos Keeling Is., near Java and Paracels Reefs, South China Sea (*F. m. minor*), Raine I., Queensland (*F. m. peninsulae*), islands in Central and South Pacific (*F. m. palmerstoni*),

Hawaiian Is. (*F. m. strumosa*), and Galápagos Is. (*F. m. ridgwayi*). *Egg-dates:* Throughout the year.

Notes.—The male can be distinguished by the light bar on the wing from the male Magnificent Frigate-bird and adult Ascension Frigate-birds. The female is the only Frigate-bird with white underparts and whitish throat. The young may be distinguished by the rusty colouring of the white parts.

2. **Magnificent Frigate-Bird** (*Fregata magnificens*). (*Plates 66 and 67*)

Adult Male.—Similar to male Great Frigate-bird but wings entirely black, without brown band; head and back with metallic purple sheen; bill lead blue; pouch red; feet black; length 37.5–41 ins.; wing 24.8–26; tail 15–20; bill 4.4–5.8; tarsus 0.9–1. *Adult Female.*—Similar to female Great Frigate-bird but head and back with purplish sheen, with a whitish collar on the back of the neck; throat and foreneck black; bill horn-colour; feet red. *Young.*—Similar to young Great Frigate-bird but white parts without rusty tinge.

Range.—Tropical Atlantic Ocean from Florida and the Bahamas to Brazil and Gambia, Gulf of Mexico, Caribbean Sea and Pacific coast of America from southern California to northern Peru, occasionally north to Bermuda and Nova Scotia. Breeds at the Galápagos Is. (*F. m. magnificens*), on coasts of tropical America, West Indies and Bahamas (*F. m. rothschildi*) and at the Cape Verde Is. (*F. m. lowei*). *Egg-dates:* Throughout the year.

Notes.—The male cannot be distinguished on the wing from adults of the Ascension Frigate-bird, but only in the south tropical Atlantic does its range coincide with that of the latter. The female differs from the female Great Frigate-bird in having the throat black, and the young is without the rusty colouring characteristic of the young of that species.

3. Ascension Frigate-Bird (*Fregata aquila*)

Adult Male.—Plumage entirely black, with metallic green sheen on the back; pouch red; feet red; wing 22–23.5 ins.; tail 15–16; bill 3.6–4.9; tarsus 0.9–1. *Adult Female.*—Plumage mainly black; upper breast brownish. *Young.*—Head white; rest of plumage brownish-black.

Range.—South Tropical Atlantic. Breeds at Boatswainbird I., near Ascension. *Egg-dates:* Throughout the year.

Notes.—Adults cannot be distinguished on the wing from male Magnificent Frigate-birds, but this is the only species in which the female is entirely black. The young is the only Frigate-bird with dark underparts and white head.

4. Christmas Frigate-Bird (*Fregata andrewsi*). (*Plate 67*)

Adult Male.—Upperparts black with oil-green iridescence; throat, foreneck and breast black with purplish sheen; abdomen white; bill black; pouch red; feet black with yellow soles; length 35–40 ins.; wing 24–25.5; tail 15.3–16.5; bill 5–6.1; tarsus 0.8. *Adult Female.*—Head, neck and upperparts black, with greenish sheen on the back; breast and abdomen white; bill rose; feet white. *Young.*—Upperparts brownish-black with a pale bar on the wing; head and neck rufous; a blackish bar across the chest; abdomen white.

Range.—Eastern Indian Ocean. Breeds at Christmas I. (near Java) and probably in the Anamba Is. *Egg-dates:* April–June.

Notes.—The male is the only Frigate-bird with black plumage and white abdomen. The female can be distinguished from the female Great Frigate-bird by its black throat. The young of these two species are indistinguishable.

5. Lesser Frigate-Bird (*Fregata ariel*)

Adult Male.—Plumage generally black with deep blue, purplish or greenish sheen on the back; underparts browner with a white patch on each side of the abdomen; bill grey; pouch red; feet black or reddish-brown; length 31.5 ins.;

wing 21.1–22.2; tail 10.6–13.2; bill 3.1–4.2; tarsus 0.9.
Adult Female.—Plumage mainly black with purplish sheen
on the back; a chestnut collar on the hind-neck; a brownish patch on the wing-coverts; breast buffy white; a white
patch on each side of the abdomen; bill bluish; skin of
throat red; feet red. *Young.*—Upperparts brownish-black;
head, neck, breast and abdomen white, streaked with rusty,
the head sometimes brown.

Range.—South Atlantic and Indian Oceans and western
Pacific, occasionally north to Japan and Manchuria and
south to New Zealand. Breeds at South Trinidad I., off
Brazil (*F. a. trinitatis*), Aldabra I., near Madagascar (*F. a.
iredalei*), Cocos Keeling Is., islands off northern Australia
and New Caledonia and in the South Pacific (*F. a. ariel*).
Egg-dates: Throughout the year.

Notes.—Adults are distinguished from all other species
by the conspicuous white patch on the side under the
wing. This is the common species on Australian coasts but
elsewhere seems to be rare.

CHAPTER XII

~~~~~~~~~~~~~~~~~~~~~~~~~~~~~~

Pelicans

(Order *Pelecaniformes:* Family *Pelecanidae*)

~~~~~~~~~~~~~~~~~~~~~~~~~~~~~~

PELICANS ARE VERY large water-birds with heavy bodies, broad rounded wings and fairly long necks. Their bills are extremely large and a great distensible pouch is suspended from the lower mandible. Their legs are short and their feet large, with all the four toes connected by a web. Their tails are rather short and rounded and are usually composed of 22 feathers, but some species have 20 or 24.

Pelicans are distributed throughout the tropical and temperate regions of both hemispheres, though they are not found in temperate eastern South America, New Zealand and Oceania. The majority of the species frequent large freshwater lakes, lagoons and estuaries, also visiting sea-coasts. These species are mainly white or grey in colour. On the coasts of the warmer parts of the American continent two species occur which are mainly brown in colouring and are entirely marine in their habits.

Pelicans are sociable birds, often seen flying in flocks, or feeding together in shallow water. When flying with a favourable breeze they travel high before it; with a head wind they skim low over the water. The usual flock formation is a diagonal single file, and the birds progress by alternations of flapping and sailing in unison. Sometimes they rise high into the air and soar round in circles on motionless wings. They are such large, heavy birds that much flapping is necessary to enable them to rise from the water, but once fairly launched their flight is buoyant and strong. In flight their heads are carried well back on the shoulders so that the large bill rests on the front of the neck.

When on the water they float high and usually carry the neck well up with the bill resting against it in front. Their food consists largely of fish, which is chiefly obtained in shallow water. Frequently they form in line a short distance from the shore and by flapping their wings drive shoals of small fish into the shallows, where they are scooped up into their capacious pouches.

The Brown and Chilean Pelicans obtain their food by diving. Like Gannets, birds of these species circle round, and flap to and fro, at some height above the water, until they observe fish swimming near the surface. Then the wings are almost closed, and they plunge downwards with such force that the spray dashes high about them, and the resulting splash may be heard half a mile away. A flock of these great birds fishing is one of the most noteworthy sights to be seen at sea. Sometimes after its plunge the bird remains under water for several seconds and it usually reappears tail first, the bill with the fish secure in the pouch appearing last.

Pelicans nest in colonies, usually on islands, either in lakes or on the sea-coast. The nests are sometimes mere hollows with a ring of sticks and sand scraped up round them by the sitting bird; more often they are roughly constructed of sticks and weed-stalks, and may be placed on the ground, on a low bush or on a mangrove or other tree. This variation in habit does not depend on the species, for most species vary the form and position of their nests according to the situation of the colony. The eggs are large, two to four in number, bluish-white with a chalky coating when first laid, but they soon become discoloured. The young are born naked and with quite short bills, but they soon become covered with white down and their bills enlarge rapidly. They are fed on partly digested fish, which they obtain by thrusting their bill, and often also their whole head and neck, into the capacious pouch of the parent. The ancient legend that young pelicans were fed on the blood of their parents, which inflicted wounds on their breast for the purpose, is of course wholly imaginary.

If reared in a nest placed on a bush or tree the young Pelicans remain there till they are fledged, but if the nest is on the ground they leave it when partly grown and wander about the vicinity. The young birds are very noisy and the commotion in a large colony when the young are hatched is very great, but adult Pelicans are almost silent birds, occasionally making grunting sounds.

Pelicans probably take several years to reach maturity, and, at least in the species inhabiting the tropics, only a small proportion seem to breed in any one season. Their numbers appear to be much the same at all times of the year in localities far away from their breeding grounds. This is perhaps most noticeable in the Grey Pelican, which is numerous throughout India at all seasons, though it is not known to breed in that country.

According to their colouration Pelicans fall into three groups:—

I. With plumage mainly white and primaries black. (Species 1–5).

II. With plumage mainly grey and without black in the wings (Species 6).

III. With plumage mainly brown and primaries black (Species 7–8).

I. PELICANS WITH PLUMAGE MAINLY WHITE AND PRIMARIES BLACK

1. American White Pelican (*Pelecanus erythrorhynchus*). (*Plates 69 and 72*)

Adult.—Plumage mostly white, with patches of pale yellow on the breast and wing-coverts; primaries and some of the secondaries black; a crest of elongated feathers on the back of the head in early summer white or pale yellow, succeeded in later summer by a grey patch; a horny prominence on the bill in summer; tail of 24 feathers; bill and pouch reddish in summer, yellow in winter; naked skin of face orange in summer, yellow in winter; feet orange red in summer, yellow in winter; length 54–70 ins.; wing 20–25; span of wings 8 to 10 feet; tail 6–7.1; bill 11–15; tarsus 4.5–4.7. *Young.*—Similar to adult in winter but without yellow on breast and wing-coverts.

Range.—North America, south in winter to the West Indies and Panama. Breeds on lakes in Western Canada and the United States. *Egg-dates:* May–June.

Notes.—Easily distinguished from the other American Pelicans by its white plumage and large size.

2. Eastern White Pelican (*Pelecanus onocrotalus*)

Adult.—Plumage mostly white, tinged with rose colour, with a tuft of yellowish feathers on the breast; primaries and some of the secondaries black; a slight crest on the back of the head; feathers of the forehead ending in a point above the bill; tail of 22 or 24 feathers; bill grey with pink or red edges; pouch yellow; skin of face purplish white or yellow; feet pink; length 54–73 ins.; wing 25–29.5; tail 7–8.7; bill 10.8–18; tarsus 4.5–5.6. *Young.*—Pale buffish brown above, somewhat mottled; primaries brown; underparts white with no rosy tinge.

Range.—Southern Europe, Africa and Central Asia east to China, in winter south to India, the Malay Peninsula and the Philippine Is. Breeds on lakes and inland seas of

187

S. E. Europe, tropical Africa and western Asia (*P. o. onocrotalus*), in China and on islands in the Persian Gulf (*P. o. roseus*). *Egg-dates:* Jan.–July.

Notes.—Distinguished from the Pink-backed and Dalmatian Pelicans most easily by its pink feet. The shape of the line bordering the feathers on the forehead is also characteristic.

3. Pink-backed Pelican (*Pelecanus rufescens*)

Adult.—Plumage mainly white, tinged with pink in summer on the back, rump, flanks and under tail-coverts; primaries and some of the secondaries and wing-coverts black; tail greyish, the feathers with dark brown shafts; in winter wings and tail brown; a crest of elongated feathers on the back of the head, and a tuft of elongated feathers on the chest; tail of 20 feathers; bill yellowish-white, orange at the tip; pouch flesh-coloured; feet yellowish-white; length 56–58 ins.; wing 22.5–25; tail 7.5–7.8; bill 13.5–14.5; tarsus 3.2–3.5. *Young.*—Similar to adult in winter.

Range.—Africa from the Cape of Good Hope to Gambia and Abyssinia, Madagascar and southern Arabia. Breeds in tropical Africa. *Egg-dates:* Feb.

Notes.—Distinguished from the Eastern White Pelican by its yellowish feet and grey or brown tail. It has also a greater amount of dark colouring in the wings.

4. Dalmatian Pelican (*Pelecanus crispus*)

Adult.—Plumage mainly white, more or less tinged with grey, with a large pale yellow patch on the lower throat; wing-quills blackish; scapulars and greater wing-coverts with blackish shafts; a crest on the back of the head; feathers of the forehead ending in a concave curved line above the bill; bill grey with red edges; pouch yellow; skin of face pink; feet deep grey; length 60–72 ins.; wing 26.3–28; tail 7.5–9; bill 14.3–16.5; tarsus 4.7–4.8. *Young.*—Upperparts brownish-grey; underparts white; pouch greyish.

Range.—From S. E. Europe through western and central Asia to China, south in winter to Egypt, Baluchistan, northern India and S. China; occasionally to Japan. Breeds on lakes and inland seas of S. E. Europe, Asia Minor, Persia, northern China and south-eastern Mongolia. *Egg-dates:* Feb.–May.

Notes.—Most readily distinguished by its dark grey feet. The form of the line bounding the feathers of the forehead is also characteristic.

5. Australian Pelican (*Pelecanus conspicillatus*)

Adult.—Plumage mostly white; wing-quills, tail-feathers, scapulars and some of the upper wing-coverts and tail-coverts black; a crest on the back of the head of greyish-brown feathers; feathers of foreneck elongated; naked skin round eye separated from the bill by feathers; bill flesh-coloured, sides slate-blue; pouch pale flesh-colour; feet light slate-colour; length 60–64 ins.; wing 24–25.7; tail 7–7.5; bill 17–18.3; tarsus 5. *Young.*—Similar but dark parts of wing and tail brown not black.

Range.—Australia and New Guinea; accidentally to New Zealand. Breeds on inland lagoons in Australia, also on islands off the coast and in Bass Strait. *Egg-dates:* July–Nov.

Notes.—The only species of Pelican in Australia and New Guinea. It has more black in the plumage than the other white species and the feathering of the face is distinctive.

II. PELICANS WITH PLUMAGE MAINLY GREY, WITHOUT BLACK IN THE WINGS

6. Grey Pelican (*Pelecanus philippensis*)

Adult.—Head, neck and upperparts grey; underparts greyish white, the under tail-coverts mottled with brown; under wing-coverts and under tail-coverts tinged with vinaceous in summer; lower back, rump and flanks tinged with vinaceous in winter; a crest on the back of the head, composed of elongated brown feathers tipped with white; bill flesh-coloured with blue spots on the upper mandible; pouch dull purple with bluish black markings; feet dark brown; length 51–62 ins.; wing 22–25.5; tail 8–9.5; bill 12.5–14.5; tarsus 2.9–3.8.

Range.—Southern Asia from Persia to southern China and the Philippine Is. and south to Ceylon and the Malay Peninsula. Breeds on islands in the Persian Gulf and on lagoons in Ceylon and Burma. *Egg-dates:* Nov.–March.

Notes.—The grey colouring, which includes the wings and tail, at once distinguishes this species.

III. PELICANS WITH PLUMAGE MAINLY BROWN AND PRIMARIES BLACK

7. **Brown Pelican** (*Pelecanus occidentalis = P. fuscus*). (Plates 1, 70 and 71)

Adult.—Head chiefly white, yellowish on crown, the white continued in a line down each side of the neck; back of head and neck and foreneck dark chestnut brown in summer, yellowish white in winter; back dusky brown; wing-coverts and tail grey; primaries black; underparts dark greyish-brown streaked with white on flanks, under wing-coverts and under tail-coverts; a small crest on the back of the head; a tuft of elongated chestnut, yellow and blackish feathers on the lower foreneck; bill mottled; pouch dusky; skin of face bluish; feet slaty-black; length 40–54 ins.; wing 18.5–22; span of wings 6 to 7 feet; tail 5.5–7; bill 9.4–14.5; tarsus 2.5–3. *Young.*—Head, neck and upperparts brownish; abdomen white.

Range.—Coasts of tropical America and the United States, from Peru and Brazil to Washington and South Carolina, occasionally north to Nova Scotia. Breeds in the West Indies (*P. o. occidentalis*), on the Atlantic coasts of tropical America from S. Carolina to the Orinoco (*P. o. carolinensis*), on the Pacific coast of N. America from Mexico to California (*P. o. californicus*), on the Pacific coast of Colombia and Ecuador (*P. o. murphyi*) and in the Galápagos Is. (*P. o. urinator*). *Egg-dates:* Throughout the year.

Notes.—The smallest species of Pelican, distinguished by its dark brown colour and by its habit of diving.

8. Chilean Pelican (*Pelecanus thagus*). (*Plate 72*)

Adult.—Similar to the adult Brown Pelican but larger; pale straw-coloured crest much more developed; brownish-black underparts streaked with white; face with warty carunculations; bill yellow, sides and tip red; pouch black with blue stripes; feet slate-colour; length 60 ins.; wing 22.7–24.5; tail 6.5; bill 14–16.2; tarsus 3.4–3.6. *Young.*—Similar to young Brown Pelican but larger.

Range.—Coasts of Peru and Chile from C. Blanco to Chiloe I. Breeds on islands off the coast of Peru. *Egg-dates:* Throughout the year.

Notes.—A species peculiar to the Humboldt current, of much importance as a producer of guano. Much larger than the Brown Pelican, of which it is sometimes regarded as a racial form, and like it obtains fish by diving.

CHAPTER XIII

~~~~~~~~

Gannets and Boobies

(Order *Pelecaniformes*: Family *Sulidae*)

~~~~~~~~

THE MEMBERS OF this family are large, long-winged sea-birds with stout conical pointed beaks, fairly short necks, stout bodies and long wedge-shaped tails. Their legs are short and all their toes are connected by webs. On the throat they have a small pouch of naked skin and there are also unfeathered areas of naked skin on the face.

The majority of the species are found in the tropics and are generally known as Boobies, a term applied to them by seamen from their apparent stupidity when settled. If they alight on a ship, or when settled on the shore, they will often allow themselves to be captured without an attempt to fly away, though they may use their sharp beaks to defend themselves. The term Gannet is applied by naturalists to birds of this family generally, and more particularly to the three species found in temperate seas. In origin "Gannet" is the same word as "Gander," the name for a male goose, and the North Atlantic species is also frequently called the "Solan Goose," "Solan" or "Sula" being the Scandinavian name for the species. It is rather remarkable that the breeding-places of temperate Gannets are all in parts of the British Empire, except that the Solan Goose also breeds in Iceland

and the Faroe Islands. Every self-governing country in the Empire has one or more colonies of Gannets, as they breed on islands off the coasts of Great Britain, Ireland, the Channel Islands, Canada, Newfoundland, South Africa, Australia and New Zealand.

Gannets and Boobies feed on fish, which they obtain by diving from the air and then pursuing them under water. They commonly dive from a height of about 60 feet, sometimes from as much as 100 feet, above the surface and have been caught in fishermen's nets at a depth of 90 feet. This habit of diving is in itself almost sufficient to distinguish a bird as a Gannet, as the only other sea-birds which dive from the air are the Brown and Chilean Pelicans, which can be recognised by their great bills; the Terns, which are all much smaller than Gannets; and the Tropic-birds, which have long tail-feathers.

Gannets are sociable birds and are usually seen in small parties or large flocks. They usually fly with direct, steady flight rather close to the surface of the water, and often form into long lines one behind the other. Occasionally a Booby will fly round a ship or follow it for some time ready to pounce upon any fish which may be disturbed by its passage.

Gannets breed in colonies on oceanic islands or precipitous crags. The nests of some species are merely hollows in the ground or mounds of guano with a hollow at the top; others build rough nests of weeds or sticks either on the ground or on the ledge of a cliff, or on a bush or tree, sometimes at a considerable height from the ground. The Gannets of temperate regions lay only one egg, but the tropical Boobies usually lay two, sometimes only one, and occasionally three. The eggs are ovate, rather small in proportion to the size of the bird, with a pale blue shell usually completely hidden by a white chalky surface layer, which can readily be scratched off. They soon become discoloured. The chick when first hatched is naked, but soon becomes covered with white down. It is fed on partly digested fish, to obtain which it thrusts its head and bill into the throat of the parent.

Though almost silent birds at sea, Gannets and Boobies are noisy when breeding, uttering loud quacks, grunts and whistles. They are also quarrelsome, pecking at neighbours who come too near their nest.

The first plumage of most of the species is brown and it is probably two or three years before the young acquire the mature plumage, which in most species is largely white. The Red-footed Booby often breeds in brown plumage, but it is not certain whether this is an immature plumage or whether it is a brown phase of the species. In many of its breeding colonies brown individuals are much more numerous than white ones.

In colouring adult Gannets fall into four groups:—

I. With head pale yellow, body white and primaries black (Species 1–3).
II. With head and body white and primaries black (Species 4–5).
III. With head, neck and underparts white, and lower back chequered with black and white (Species 6–7).
IV. With head, back and wings brown and abdomen white (Species 8–9).

I. GANNETS WITH HEAD PALE YELLOW, BODY WHITE AND PRIMARIES BLACK

1. **Northern Gannet** (*Moris bassanus*). (*Plates 74 and 75*)

Adult.—Plumage mainly white; head and neck pale straw-yellow; primaries blackish-brown; bill horny white; naked skin of throat bluish-black; feet black; length 33–40.5 ins.; wing 17–21; tail 8.7–10; bill 3.8–4.3; tarsus 2–2.7. *Young.*—Upperparts dark greyish-brown, with small white spots; underparts white, the feathers edged with greyish-brown.

Range.—North Atlantic Ocean, south in winter to the Gulf of Mexico, Madeira, the Canary Is. and the coast of North Africa. Breeds on islands in the Gulf of St. Lawrence and off the coasts of Newfoundland, Labrador, Iceland, the Faroe Is., the British Is. and the Channel Is. *Egg-dates:* May–July.

Notes.—Often called the "Solan Goose." Cannot be confused with any other sea-bird in the North Atlantic. In the southern part of its winter range it may be distinguished from the Blue-faced and Red-footed Boobies by its yellowish head and white tail.

2. Cape Gannet (*Moris capensis*). (*Plate 75*)

Adult.—Similar to the Northern Gannet but with secondaries, primary-coverts and tail-feathers blackish-brown; bill pale bluish; naked skin of face and throat black; feet black; length 31–35 ins.; wing 18–18.7; tail 7.5–8; bill 3.5–3.7; tarsus 2.1–2.3. *Young.*—Similar to young Northern Gannet. In intermediate plumage the underparts are barred with white and brown.

Range.—Coasts of South Africa and adjacent seas north to Loango and Zanzibar. Breeds on the coasts of Cape Colony. *Egg-dates:* Sept.–Oct.

Notes.—Commonly known as the "Malagash." In the northern part of its range, where it may meet the Blue-faced Booby, its yellow head is its chief distinguishing character.

3. Australian Gannet (*Moris serrator*). (*Plates 73 and 75*)

Adult.—Similar to the Cape Gannet but outer tail-feathers white and four central feathers greyish-brown; bill slate-colour; naked skin of throat slate blue; feet greenish-black; length 32–38.6 ins.; wing 18–19; tail 8–10; bill 3.4–5.5; tarsus 2–2.4. *Young.*—Upperparts greyish-brown with white spots; underparts white mottled with brown on the throat and flanks.

Range.—Coasts of Australia, south of Fremantle and Brisbane, Tasmania and New Zealand and adjacent seas.

Breeds on islands in Bass Strait and off Tasmania and New Zealand. *Egg-dates:* July–Jan.

Notes.—Its range is apparently quite distinct from that of the tropical Boobies. Its yellow head is the chief feature distinguishing it from the Blue-faced Booby.

II. GANNETS WITH HEAD AND BODY WHITE AND PRIMARIES BLACK

4. **Red-footed Booby** (*Sula sula* = *S. piscatrix* = *S. coryi*). (*Plates 74 and 75*)

Adult.—Plumage mainly white, tinged with buff; primaries blackish-brown; tail pale greyish brown; under wing-coverts mostly grey; bill light blue with brown tip and red base; naked skin of face blue, of throat black; feet red; length 26–29.5 ins.; wing 13.8–15.5; tail 8–9.1; bill 3.2–3.5; tarsus 1.4–1.6. *Young.*—Plumage generally dull brown. In intermediate plumage, in which the birds often breed, the head and underparts are lighter brown than the back and wings, whilst the rump, tail and upper and under tail-coverts are white.

Range.—Tropical Seas. Breeds on islands in the Caribbean Sea and on South Trinidad in the Atlantic (*S. s. sula*), on many islands in the Indian Ocean and western and central Pacific (*S. s. rubripes*), and on the Galápagos Is. (*S. s. websteri*). *Egg-dates:* Throughout the year.

Notes.—In adult plumage distinguished from the Blue-faced Booby by its smaller size and bright red feet, also by having the dark area of the wing confined to the primaries. The intermediate or brown-phase bird, with its brown colouring and white tail, is unlike any other Booby and as individuals in this plumage are usually numerous they serve to identify the species. In some regions, however, this brown-phase bird is apparently unknown, which has led some ornithologists to regard it as a distinct species, to which the name *Sula coryi* has been given. The Red-footed Booby nests in bushes or trees, often at a considerable height.

5. **Blue-faced Booby** (*Sula dactylatra* = *S. cyanops*). (*Plate 75*)

Adult.—Plumage mainly white; wing-quills, greater wing-coverts and tail-feathers chocolate brown; bill blue-grey, greenish-yellow, yellow, or red; naked skin of face and throat blue-black; feet yellow, orange, greenish-blue or slaty-blue; length 32.5–36 ins.; wing 16.4–17.8; tail 7–8; bill 3.9–4.4; tarsus 2.2–2.3. *Young.*—Head and neck dark brown; upperparts greyish-brown.

Range.—Tropical seas. Breeds in the Caribbean Sea, in the Bahamas and at Ascension (*S. d. dactylatra*), on Mait I., Gulf of Aden, and on Rodriguez and Farquhar Is., near Mauritius (*S. d. melanops*), on the Cocos Keeling Is., on islands off northern Australia and in the western and central Pacific (*S. d. personata*), on the Galápagos Is. and islands off the Pacific coast of tropical America (*S. d. granti*). *Egg-dates:* Throughout the year.

Notes.—Distinguished from the Red-footed Booby by its larger size and by having all the quill-feathers of the wing and the tail dark, appearing black. The feet vary in colour in different races, but are never red.

III. GANNETS WITH HEAD, NECK AND UNDER-PARTS WHITE, AND LOWER BACK CHEQUERED WITH BLACK AND WHITE

6. **Peruvian Booby** (*Sula variegata*). (*Plates 75 and 76*)

Adult.—Head, neck, upper back and underparts white; wings brownish-black; lower back, tail and flanks mottled black and white; bill bluish; feet bluish-black; length 29 ins.; wing 17.3; tail 6.5; bill 4.1; tarsus 2. *Young.*—Similar but back, sides and abdomen mottled black and white.

Range.—Coasts of Peru and Chile, ranging south to Chiloe I. Breeds on islands off the coast of Peru. *Egg-dates:* Throughout the year.

Notes.—The "Piquero" of the Peruvian coast, where it is a very important producer of guano. It is confined to the Humboldt current, where it is the most abundant sea-bird. Its white head, neck and breast and speckled lower back are distinctive.

7. Abbott's Booby (*Sula abbotti*)

Adult.—Head, neck, upper back and underparts white; wing-quills black, the inner webs largely white; scapulars, wing-coverts, lower back and flanks white with black spots; tail mottled black and white; bill fleshy white or greenish with black tip; naked skin of face greyish-black, of throat light bluish-green; feet leaden grey; length 28 ins.; wing 18; tail 8.4; bill 4.4; tarsus 2.

Range.—Tropical Indian Ocean. Breeds at Assumption I., near Madagascar and Christmas I., near Java. *Egg-dates:* May–June.

Notes.—A little known species, which nests in tall trees at some distance from the sea.

IV. GANNETS WITH HEAD, BACK AND WINGS BROWN, AND ABDOMEN WHITE

8. Blue-footed Booby (*Sula nebouxii*). (*Plate 75*)

Adult.—Head, neck and upper breast cinnamon-brown more or less mottled with white; back mottled brown and white; wings brown; tail brown, the central feathers mainly white; lower breast and abdomen white; bill olive blue; naked skin of face and throat slate-blue; feet bright blue; length 34 ins.; wing 16.1–17.3; tail 8.5; bill 4.2–4.5; tarsus 1.9–2.2. *Young.*—Similar but abdomen mottled with dusky.

Range.—West coast of tropical America from the Gulf of California to Peru, occasionally south to Chile. Breeds on islands off the coasts of Mexico, Ecuador and northern Peru and in the Galápagos Is. *Egg-dates:* Throughout the year.

Notes.—Distinguished from other Boobies in adult plumage by its mottled brown and white upperparts. This gives it considerable resemblance to the young of other species, but its bright blue feet are distinctive.

9. **Brown Booby** (*Sula leucogaster*). (*Plates 75, 76 and 77*)

Adult.—Head, neck, breast and upperparts dark chocolate-brown, in the race inhabiting western Mexico the male with a greyish-white head; primaries blackish; abdomen, under tail-coverts, axillaries and median under wing-coverts white; bill yellowish or bluish-white or blue or greenish; naked skin of face and throat greenish-yellow or blue or purplish; feet pale yellow or blue or green; length 28–30 ins.; wing 14–16.5; tail 7.2–8; bill 3.5–4; tarsus 1.6–1.9. *Young.*—Dusky brown, lighter below.

Range.—Tropical seas. Breeds on islands in the Gulf of Mexico, Caribbean Sea and tropical Atlantic (*S. l. leucogaster*), in the Indian and Pacific Oceans (*S. l. plotus*), on the Pacific coast of Mexico (*S. l. brewsteri*) and of Central America and Colombia (*S. l. etesiaca*) and on Clipperton I. (*S. l. nesiotes*). *Egg-dates:* Throughout the year.

Notes.—The commonest member of the family in most parts of the tropics. The wholly dark brown upperparts and white abdomen at once distinguish adults, but the young is difficult to distinguish from other species in immature plumage.

199

CHAPTER XIV

***

Cormorants or Shags

(Order *Pelecaniformes*: Family *Phalacrocoracidae*)

***

THE SEA-BIRDS comprising this family have long necks and rather long wings and superficially resemble Ducks. Their bills are, however, very different from those of Ducks, being slender and cylindrical with a sharp hook at the tip of the upper mandible. Their legs are very short and placed far back and their large feet have all four toes united in a web. Their tails are wedge-shaped, usually rather long and composed of 12 stiff feathers; in a few species the tail-feathers are 14 in number. A region round the eye on the sides of the face and a small pouch on the throat are usually unfeathered and often brightly coloured.

In the British Isles, where of course the English names of most birds originated, there are only two members of the family, one known as the Cormorant, the other as the Shag. Naturalists generally use the name Cormorant for all members of the family and this practice is followed in the present work. On the other hand sailors and fishermen usually call them all Shags and this is the usual vernacular name for them in Australia, New Zealand, the Falkland Is., and other parts of the world where English is spoken. Except in the British Isles therefore the names Cormorant and Shag may be regarded as interchangeable. Cormorant is a corruption of *"Corvus marinus,"* sea-crow, and is thus equivalent to their Spanish name *"cuervo de mar."* Only in its black colour does a Cormorant resemble a Crow. The origin of the name Shag is uncertain, but it may refer to the shaggy crest which the original species so named bears in the breeding season.

Cormorants occur in all parts of the world except the Central Pacific Ocean, but are specially numerous in the southern hemisphere where more than half the species are found. All the Cormorants of the northern hemisphere are black in colour but in the southern hemisphere many have white underparts, and it is a curious fact that though the Common Cormorant is black throughout Europe, Asia and Australia, the race found in tropical and southern Africa has a white breast.

Cormorants feed chiefly on fish and crustacea which they obtain by diving from the surface. They spring a few inches into the air, dive head foremost, and then pursue their prey under water, using their large feet for propulsion among rocks and seaweed and both wings and feet when in clear water over sandy bottoms. They are commonly considered to be very destructive to fish, but actual investigation in various parts of the world has shown that, in the sea at any rate, they chiefly live on rock-fish and weed-fish of little value for human food, the speedier food-fishes mostly escaping them. At the same time Cormorants are quite capable of capturing all the trout or other fresh-water fish in a small pool or artificial tank where the fish have little cover. It would seem that generally Cormorants dive for fish in likely spots without knowing beforehand whether any fish are present. The fact that they can find their prey in thick muddy water and even that a blind Cormorant has been found in good condition suggests that hearing plays a part in the matter. When the water is clear, however, Cormorants sometimes locate shoals of fish from the air, swoop down to the surface and promptly dive in pursuit. This method of fishing has been specially developed by the Guanay Cormorant which inhabits the clear water of the Humboldt current.

After capturing a fish a Cormorant has to bring it to the surface before swallowing it and this has probably led to their being trained by fishermen for the purpose of catching fish. In China and parts of India the fishermen always have a dozen or more Common Cormorants sitting, when not employed, on a cross beam in the prow of their boats. When fishing a leather collar is put round their necks to prevent the fish from being swallowed.

The plumage of Cormorants is by no means so dense and resistant to water as that of other diving-birds such as Penguins and Auks, so that when they have been diving for some time Cormorants often have some difficulty in rising from the water. After feeding they may often be seen on the beach or on rocks and stumps with their wings spread out to dry in the sun. Their long necks are constantly twisted from side to side in a fashion reminiscent of a snake, and with their black plumage this gives them a sinister appearance which doubtless accounts for Milton's description of Satan in the form of a Cormorant.

Cormorants are mostly sociable birds commonly met with in flocks, sometimes composed of several distinct species. They frequent sea-coasts, rarely going out of sight of land, but many species also occur on inland waters, lakes, rivers and estuaries. They usually fly close above the surface of the water and when starting from a post or rock generally descend close to the water before gathering momentum. This habit has led to a saying that they cannot fly without first wetting their tails. When once under way they sometimes travel at some little height, often in a line one behind the other, or in a V, with steady flapping of the wings occasionally interrupted by a short glide.

Cormorants mostly breed in colonies placing their nests on the ground on low islands, on the ledges of cliffs, or in bushes or trees growing in swamps or lakes. In the latter case the nests are composed mainly of sticks, but when by the sea they are usually of sea-weed and guano, or almost entirely of guano. Several species are of some importance as producers of guano, particularly the Cape Cormorant on the South African coast and the Guanay Cormorant on the coast of Peru, which Dr. R. C. Murphy has claimed to be the most valuable wild bird in the world.

Cormorant's eggs are usually two, three or four in number; occasionally as many as six are laid. They are rather elongate, oval, pale blue or pale green, but with this colouring more or less concealed by a white limy covering. The young when hatched are naked, but afterwards become covered with grey, brown or black down sometimes mottled with white on the breast. Immature birds are usually brownish in colour-ing, often nearly white underneath, whilst the adult plumage of nearly all Cormorants is black, with green or purple gloss, sometimes white below. Most species have certain ornaments that are only present for part of the year. These may be crests or tufts of elongated feathers on the head, white bars on the wings or patches on the flanks or back, and slender white plumes scattered thinly or thickly over various parts of the body. In the descriptions given below these ornaments are described as being worn in the nuptial plumage, but it must be understood that they are not necessarily all present at the same time even in the mating season, some may be worn for a brief period and others for over half the year. It is thus impossible to rely on them even for the identification of breeding birds though when they are present they often help to diagnose the species.

Somewhat similar to Cormorants are the Darters or Snake-birds (*Anhingidae*), but as they are almost exclusively found on fresh-water lakes and rivers they are not included in this book. There are five species, one in Africa, one in Madagascar, one in southern Asia, one in Australia, and one in tropical and sub-tropical America. The latter is commonly called the Water-Turkey. Snake-birds have longer, more slender necks than Cormorants and straight, pointed bills not hooked at the end.

The Cormorants range in size from a length of about 3 feet to a total length of 18 inches. The smallest species have long tails compared with most of their larger relatives, so that their actual body length is even less in proportion. The species under 2 feet in total length and under 18 inches without the tail are here called "Small" Cormorants. "Medium-sized" Cormorants are those from 2 feet to 2 feet 6 inches in total length and "Large" species those from 2 feet 6 inches to 3 feet; the proportionate length of their tails differs considerably, but in all of them the body without the tail is over 18 inches long. Since the plumage is either black or black above and white below in all but three species, its colouring is not very helpful in determining the species. The chief diagnostic characters are in the colouring and shape of the naked area of the face, but in life this can only be seen at close range.

The species are here arranged in five groups, viz.:—

  I. Large or medium-sized, with plumage mainly black and feet black or dusky (Species 1–14).
 II. Small, with long tail, plumage mainly dark and feet black or dusky (Species 15–17).
III. Large or medium-sized, with short tail, plumage mainly grey and feet brightly coloured (Species 18–20).
 IV. Large or medium-sized mainly black above and white below (Species 21–28).
  V. Small, with long tail, black upperparts and white underparts (Species 29).

Members of the last three groups are confined to the southern hemisphere, those of the second to the eastern hemisphere, whilst those of the first occur in all regions but are specially numerous on the coasts of the North Pacific.

I. LARGE OR MEDIUM-SIZED CORMORANTS WITH PLUMAGE MAINLY BLACK, AND FEET BLACK OR DUSKY

In addition to the fourteen species described below a black form of the Rough-faced Cormorant occurs at Stewart I., New Zealand.

1. Common Cormorant (*Phalacrocorax carbo*)

Adult.—Plumage generally glossy greenish or bluish-black; back scapulars and wing-coverts bronze-grey, the feathers edged with black; wing-quills and tail greyish-black; chin and sides of face white; in South African birds the foreneck and upper chest are also white; in nuptial plumage feathers on back of head elongated to form a slight crest, neck more or less sprinkled with lanceolate white feathers, and a large patch of white on flanks; tail of 14 feathers; feathers of throat ending in a point nearly reaching base of bill; bill and naked skin of face yellow; feet black; length 30.7–40 ins.; wing 12–15; tail 5–7.7; bill 2.3–3.1; tarsus 2.3–2.5. *Young.*—Brownish-black; underparts paler, sometimes white.

Range.—Eastern North America, Europe, Africa, Asia, Australia and New Zealand. Breeds in Nova Scotia, Labrador, Greenland, Iceland, the Faroe Is., Norway and the British Is. (*P. c. carbo*), northern Africa (*P. c. maroccanus*), north-eastern Africa (*P. c. lugubris*), tropical and southern Africa (*P. c. lucidus*), central and southern Europe to central Asia, India and China (*P. c. sinensis*), Japan (*P. c. hanedae*), Australia and Tasmania (*P. c. novaehollandiae*), New Zealand and the Chatham Is. (*P. c. steadi*). *Egg-dates:* April–July (north temperate regions), throughout the year (tropics), Aug.–Dec. (south temperate regions).

205

Notes.—The largest species of Cormorant and the most widespread. It frequents rivers, estuaries and lakes as well as the sea-coast. Its large size and the white patches on the flanks when these are present are the chief distinguishing features; the white throat patch, which is always present, is less conspicuous. The dull white underparts distinguish the young bird, and the white chest of the African form distinguishes it from other African Cormorants. It is trained to assist them in catching fish by natives of China and India.

2. **Japanese Cormorant** (*Phalacrocorax capillatus = P. filamentosus*)

Adult.—Similar to the Common Cormorant but the feathers of the throat extend forward to the lower mandible, and in nuptial plumage the head and neck are thickly covered with white filamentous plumes; tail of 14 feathers; bill yellowish; naked skin of face orange yellow; feet blackish-brown; length 33 ins.; wing 12–13; tail 5.8; bill 2.5–2.8; tarsus 2.4–2.6. *Young.*—Similar to young Common Cormorant.

Range.—Coasts of N. E. Asia, south in winter to S. China. Breeds in Ussuriland, Korea and Japan.

Notes.—Distinguished from the Common Cormorant by the characters mentioned above, and from the Red-faced Cormorant by its white chin. It is used by Japanese fishermen to assist them in catching fish.

3. **Flightless Cormorant** (*Nannopterum harrisi*)

Adult.—Plumage generally brownish-black, lighter below; scapulars and wing-coverts dark grey, the feathers with black edges; scattered white filamentous plumes on the head and neck; tail of 14 feathers; wings very small, the flight feathers reduced in number and size; a broad stiff flap of skin down the side of the tarsus; bill blackish with pale tip; naked skin of face slate-coloured, of throat flesh-coloured; feet black; length 36–39.5 ins.; wing 7–8; tail 6–7.5; bill 2.9–3.5; tarsus 2.4–3.

Range.—Albemarle and Narborough Is., Galápagos group, where it breeds. *Egg-dates:* April, Aug.

Notes.—This remarkable species is as large as the Common Cormorant, but its wings are smaller in proportion to its size than were those of the extinct Great Auk. It cannot fly and its breast-bone is without a keel. On land it waddles, or hops over obstacles, keeping the body upright.

4. Socotra Cormorant (*Phalacrocorax nigrogularis*)

Adult.—Plumage generally black with a slight gloss; wing-coverts and scapulars tinged with bronze; in nuptial plumage minute scattered white plumes on throat and hind-neck; tail of 14 feathers; bill greyish black, paler at tip, greenish at base of lower mandible; naked skin of face blackish; feet black with brownish webs; length 30.5 ins.; wing 11.5; tail 4.3; bill 3; tarsus 2.5. *Young.*—Head and upperparts brownish-black; underparts brownish-white; skin of face dull yellow; feet dusky.

Range.—Persian Gulf, Arabian Sea south to Socotra and southern Red Sea. Breeds on islands in the Persian Gulf. *Egg-dates:* Jan.–March.

Notes.—Distinguished from the Common Cormorant by its black throat, and the absence of white patches on the flanks in nuptial plumage.

5. Red-faced Cormorant (*Phalacrocorax urile = P. bicristatus*). (*Plate 80*)

Adult.—Plumage generally glossy greenish-black; in nuptial plumage with tufts of bronze feathers on crown and nape forming two crests, and a large white patch on each flank; forehead not feathered; bill bluish; naked skin of forehead and face orange, of throat blue with purplish-red corrugations posteriorly; feet black; length 28–30 ins.; wing 10.5–11; tail 5.9–6.2; bill 2.1–2.3; tarsus 2–2.1. *Young.*—Dark brown.

Range.—Bering Sea, south in winter to Japan, China and Formosa. Breeds on the coast of Kamchatka and in the

Pribilof, Aleutian, Commander and Kurile Is. *Egg-dates:* May–July.

Notes.—Distinguished by its naked forehead and the colouration of the naked skin of its face. Differs from the Common and Japanese Cormorants also in having 12 tail-feathers and a black throat, and from the Pelagic Cormorant in its larger size.

6. Pelagic Cormorant (*Phalacrocorax pelagicus*)

Adult.—Plumage generally glossy greenish-black; in nuptial plumage with tufts of bronze feathers on crown and nape forming two crests, and a large white patch on each flank; feathers of throat extending forward to the lower mandible; bill blackish-brown; naked skin of face greyish-brown with orange papillae; feet black; length 26.5–30 ins.; wing 9.4–10.8; tail 5.1–6.2; bill 1.8–2; tarsus 1.8–2.1. *Young.*—Dark brown.

Range.—Bering Sea and coasts of North Pacific from Eastern Siberia and Alaska to the Kurile Is. and Mexico, and in winter south to Japan and China, occasionally to the Hawaiian Is. Breeds in the Kurile Is., Commander Is., Aleutian Is. and on the coasts of Kamchatka, E. Siberia, Alaska and British Columbia (*P. p. pelagicus*) and on the Pacific coast of America from Washington to Mexico (*P. p. resplendens*). *Egg-dates:* April–July.

Notes.—The smallest Cormorant in the North Pacific and the commonest species on the coast of British Columbia. It is distinguished by its dark, iridescent plumage and the dark colour of the skin of the face.

7. Brandt's Cormorant (*Phalacrocorax penicillatus*). (Plate 78)

Adult.—Plumage generally glossy greenish-black; throat fawn-coloured; in nuptial plumage white hair-like plumes are scattered over the neck and upper back and there are tufts of similar feathers behind the ears; feathers of throat extending forwards to a point; bill dusky grey; naked skin of throat blue: feet black; length 30 ins.; wing 10.6–11.1;

tail 4.4–4.7; bill 2.6–3; tarsus 2.5. *Young.*—Brown, paler below.

Range.—Pacific coast of North America from southern Alaska to Lower California. Breeds throughout its range. *Egg-dates:* March–July.

Notes.—The commonest Cormorant on the Pacific coast of the United States, distinguished by the fawn-coloured patch on the throat and the shape and blue colouring of the naked skin of the throat. It is decidedly larger than the Pelagic Cormorant and about the same size as the Double-crested Cormorant.

8. Double-crested Cormorant (*Phalacrocorax auritus = P. dilophus*). (Plate 69)

Adult.—Plumage generally glossy greenish-black; back scapulars and wing-coverts bronzy-grey, the feathers with black edges; in nuptial plumage a tuft of black or black and white curly feathers on each side of the head; hinder edge of throat-pouch nearly straight; bill grey, yellow at base; naked skin of face and throat orange; feet black; length 29–35 ins.; wing 12–13; tail 5.5–7; bill 2.1–2.5; tarsus 2.3–2.5. *Young.*—Upperparts greyish-brown; rump black; breast greyish-white; abdomen blackish; naked skin of throat dull yellow.

Range.—North and Central America and the West Indies. Breeds on the Pacific coast from Alaska to Oregon (*P. a. cincinatus*) and from California to western Mexico (*P. a. albociliatus*), in the interior of Canada and the United States and on the coasts of Labrador, Newfoundland, Quebec and Maine (*P. a. auritus*), in the Bahamas, Isle of Pines, southern United States, eastern Mexico and Honduras (*P. a. floridanus*). *Egg-dates:* March–June.

Notes.—The most widespread North American Cormorant and the commonest except on the Pacific coast. It frequents rivers and lakes as well as the sea-coast and commonly occurs in flocks. Its chief distinguishing feature is the orange or yellow area on the face. The young is distinguished from the young Common Cormorant by its whitish breast and blackish abdomen, the latter having the abdomen whitish.

9. **Bigua Cormorant** (*Phalacrocorax olivaceus = P. vigua*). (Plate 79)

Adult.—Plumage generally glossy black; in nuptial plumage sides of face and throat white, a tuft of white feathers on each side of the head, and scattered white feathers on the neck; bill brownish; naked skin of throat dull yellow; feet black; length 25–30 ins.; wing 10–11.3; tail 5.8–7.2; bill 1.6–2.25 tarsus 1.8–2.1. *Young.*—Brownish; underparts more or less white.

Range.—Tropical, subtropical and south temperate America. Breeds in the Bahamas, Cuba, Louisiana, Texas, Mexico and Central America south to Nicaragua (*P. o. mexicanus*), in South America from Panama to Patagonia (*P. o. olivaceus*) and in Tierra del Fuego (*P. o. hornensis*). *Egg-dates:* Throughout the year.

Notes.—This rather small black species with a long tail, cannot be confused with any other cormorant in South America, but the northern race is difficult to distinguish from the Double-crested Cormorant, which occurs in the same region but is decidedly larger. The Bigua Cormorant is a sociable species occurring in flocks on inland waters as well as on the coast, and is plentiful on Gatun Lake in the Panama Canal. It makes a strange grunting note.

10. **Green Cormorant** (*Phalacrocorax aristotelis = P. graculus*). (Plate 79)

Adult.—Plumage generally glossy greenish-black; in nuptial plumage feathers of crown elongated into a crest curving forwards, and white hair-like plumes scattered on the neck; bill black, yellow at base; naked skin of face yellow, of throat black with yellow spots; feet black; length 26–30 ins.; wing 10.3–10.7; tail 5.3–5.6; bill 2.5–3.6; tarsus 2.3. *Young.*—Brown above, underparts whitish.

Range.—Coasts of western and southern Europe and northern Africa. Breeds from Iceland and Lapland to the

British Is. and Portugal (*P. a. aristotelis*) in the Mediterranean from the Balearic Is. to the Aegean Is. (*P. a. desmaresti*) and on the coast of Morocco (*P. a. riggenbachi*). *Egg-dates:* Feb.–June.

Notes.—The "Shag" of British writers occurs almost exclusively on rocky sea-coasts. From the Common Cormorant it may be distinguished by its smaller size, more glossy, greener plumage and yellow gape, and in nuptial plumage by its decurved crest and the absence of white on the flanks.

11. Bank Cormorant (*Phalacrocorax neglectus*)

Adult.—Plumage generally glossy black; in nuptial plumage feathers of forehead elongated to form a crest, a few white plumelets scattered on the neck, and some white feathers on the rump, sometimes forming a conspicuous patch; bill, naked skin of face and feet black; length 27–30 ins.; wing 10.5–11.7; tail 5.5; bill 2.2–2.5; tarsus 2.5. *Young.*—Brownish black.

Range.—Coasts of South Africa. Breeds on islands off the coast from Great Namaqualand to Simon's Bay. *Egg-dates:* July–Oct.

Notes.—This species derives its name from the fact that it chiefly frequents the seaweed beds on the fishing banks. It may be distinguished from the South African race of the Common Cormorant by its black breast and from the Cape Cormorant by its larger size and the dark colouring of its pouch, and when present by the white patch on the rump. When disturbed it utters a loud melancholy cry.

12. Cape Cormorant (*Phalacrocorax capensis*)

Adult.—Plumage generally black; foreneck and chest dark brown; tail of 14 feathers; bill slaty-black; naked skin of face and throat yellow; feet black; length 24–25 ins.; wing 9.9–10.7; tail 4–4.5; bill 2.2–2.5; tarsus 2–2.1. *Young.*—Brownish, foreneck and chest whitish.

Range.—Coasts of southern Africa. Breeds from the Cape of Good Hope north to the Congo and east to Durban. *Egg-dates:* Throughout the year.

Notes.—The commonest Cormorant of South African coasts, where it occurs in large flocks and is important as a producer of guano. Distinguished from the Common and Bank Cormorants by its smaller size, entirely black plumage and yellow pouch.

13. Indian Cormorant (*Phalacrocorax fuscicollis*)

Adult.—Plumage generally glossy bronze-black; cheeks pale brown; throat white; in nuptial plumage the male has a tuft of decomposed white feathers on each side of the head; bill brownish; naked skin of face pale greenish, of throat yellow; feet black; length 24–27 ins.; wing 10.6–11; tail 6–6.6; bill 2.2–2.4; tarsus 1.7–1.8. *Young.*—Upperparts black; underparts brownish-white.

Range.—India, Ceylon and Burma south to Tenasserim. Breeds throughout its range. *Egg-dates:* July–Nov.

Notes.—Frequents rivers and tanks as well as the sea-coast. Decidedly smaller than the Common Cormorant and larger than the Javanese Cormorant, also characterised by its pale cheeks.

14. Little Black Cormorant (*Phalacrocorax sulcirostris =* *P. ater*)

Adult.—Plumage generally glossy bluish-black; in nuptial plumage with small tufts of long, narrow, white plumes on each side of the head behind the ears and scattered white plumes on the cheeks; bill and naked skin of face leaden-grey; feet black; length 24–25 ins.; wing 9.4–10; tail 4.7–5.2; bill 1.6–1.9; tarsus 1.7–2. *Young.*—Brownish-black, lighter on head, foreneck and chest.

Range.—Malay Archipelago and Australasia. Breeds from southern Borneo and Java to New Guinea and northern Australia (*P. s. territori*), eastern and southern Australia, Tasmania, New Caledonia, and Norfolk I, (*P. s. sulcirostris*) and the Bay of Islands, New Zealand (*P. s. purpuragula*). *Egg-dates:* May–Dec.

Notes.—Frequents lakes, rivers and estuaries as well as the sea-coast, and is generally found in flocks. It is distinguished from the Common Cormorant by its much smaller size and dark plumage and pouch.

II. SMALL CORMORANTS WITH LONG TAILS, PLUMAGE MAINLY DARK AND FEET BLACK OR DUSKY

In addition to the three species described below the New Zealand race of the Little Pied Cormorant is usually all black except for a white chin.

15. Pigmy Cormorant (*Haliëtor pygmaeus*)

Adult.—Head and neck reddish brown; a triangular patch on the head and a line through the eyes white; scapulars and wing-coverts grey, the feathers with black margins; rest of plumage glossy greenish-black; in nuptial plumage feathers of back of head elongated, forming a short crest, and neck, underparts and upper tail-coverts marked with small elongated white spots; bill brownish; naked skin of face flesh-coloured; feet dusky; length 19–23 ins.; wing 7.8–8.5; tail 5.5–6.5; bill 1.1–1.4; tarsus 1.3–1.4. *Young.*—Upper parts blackish-grey; underparts whitish-grey, almost white on throat and abdomen; flanks and under tail-coverts black; bill yellowish.

Range.—Central and south-eastern Europe, northern Africa, south-west and central Asia. Breeds on lakes and rivers in S. E. Europe, Algeria, Asia Minor, Persia and Afghanistan. *Egg-dates:* May–June.

Notes.—Chiefly inhabits rivers and lagoons, rarely visiting sea-coasts. Its small size and reddish-brown head with white marks are distinctive.

16. Reed Cormorant (*Haliëtor africanus*)

Adult.—Plumage in summer generally glossy-black, in winter brown with dull white throat; scapulars and wing-coverts grey, the feathers with black borders; in nuptial plumage with a tuft of black feathers on the forehead and a few white plumelets scattered on face and neck; bill and naked skin of face yellow; feet black; length 22–23 ins.; wing 8–8.7; tail 5.5–6; bill 1.2; tarsus 1.4–1.5. *Young.* —Upperparts brown; underparts yellowish-white.

Range.—Africa from the Cape of Good Hope to the Gambia and Upper Egypt (*H. a. africanus*) and Madagascar (*H. a. pictilis*). Breeds throughout its range on lakes and rivers and on islands off the coast of South Africa. *Egg-dates:* June–Sept.

Notes.—Decidedly smaller than the Cape Cormorant, with short neck and long tail, rather solitary in habits and mainly frequenting rivers, lagoons and lakes. It swims very low in the water with the body almost submerged.

17. Javanese Cormorant (*Haliëtor niger = P. javanicus*)

Adult.—Plumage generally glossy black, throat white in winter; scapulars and wing-coverts grey, the feathers with black edges; in nuptial plumage the feathers on the nape somewhat elongated and with scattered white plumes on the head and neck; bill purplish-brown; naked skin of face and feet black; length 22 ins.; wing 7.5–8; tail 5.2–5.4; bill 1.1–1.2; tarsus 1.3. *Young:*—Dark brown, with whitish throat.

Range.—India, Ceylon, Indo-Burmese countries, Malay Peninsula, Java and Borneo. Breeds throughout its range. *Egg-dates:* July–March.

Notes.—Decidedly smaller than the Indian Cormorant, with short bill and long tail.

III. LARGE OR MEDIUM-SIZED, SHORT-TAILED CORMORANTS WITH PLUMAGE MAINLY GREY AND BRIGHTLY COLOURED FEET

18. Spotted Cormorant (*Phalacrocorax punctatus*)

Adult.—Head and neck black, with a white stripe down each side of the neck; upperparts grey with black spots; underparts leaden grey; tail, thighs and under tail-coverts black; in nuptial plumage feathers of forehead and crown elongated, forming two crests; bill brownish yellow; naked skin of face dark blue; feet yellow; length 29 ins.; wing 9.2–9.8; tail 3.4–3.7; bill 2.3–2.5; tarsus 2.2–2.3. *Young.* —Upperparts grey with dark spots; underparts greyish-white; naked skin of face yellowish flesh-colour; feet dull flesh-colour.

Range.—Coasts of New Zealand. Breeds on the coasts of Canterbury and Westland, and in Hauraki Gulf (*P. p. punctatus*) and at Stewart I. (*P. p. oliveri*). *Egg-dates:* July–Oct.

Notes.—Dull grey colouring and light-coloured feet distinguish this species from other New Zealand Cormorants. It frequents rocky coasts, swims low in the water and has difficulty in rising from it, making three or four leaps with the body nearly upright before it gets started in flight. It is sociable in habits, flying low over the waves in small companies.

19. Chatham Cormorant (*Phalacrocorax featherstoni*)

Adult.—Head and throat greyish-black; upperparts greenish-grey with black spots; breast and abdomen silvery grey; tail, thighs and under tail-coverts black; in nuptial plumage feathers of forehead and crown elongated, forming two crests; bill brownish; naked skin of face purple: feet orange with blackish webs; length 21–25 ins.; wing 8.6–9.4; tail 3.5–3.9; bill 1.8–2.1; tarsus 1.8–2. *Young.*—Similar but throat greyish; abdomen and under tail-coverts pale grey; feet yellow with brown webs.

Range.—Chatham Is., where it breeds. *Egg-dates:* Oct.–Nov.

Notes.—This species has a very limited range and can be readily identified by its grey underparts and orange feet.

20. Red-legged Cormorant (*Phalacrocorax gaimardi*)

Adult.—Head and neck dark grey, with an elongated white patch on each side of the neck; upperparts dark smoky-grey; scapulars and wing-coverts silvery grey, the feathers edged with brownish-black; underparts pale grey;

215

in nuptial plumage with white spots on the face and foreneck; tail of 14 feathers; bill bright yellow, orange-red at base; naked skin of face orange-red; feet coral-red; length 28 ins.; wings 9.5–9.9; tail 4–4.1; bill 2.2–2.3; tarsus 1.9. *Young.*—Plumage generally dark brown, with white patches on the sides of the neck; wing-coverts and underparts mottled with pale brownish-white.

Range.—Coasts of Peru, Chile and Patagonia. Breeds throughout its range. *Egg-dates:* Throughout the year.

Notes.—A rather solitary species, recognised by its grey plumage and bright red face and feet. It has a high-pitched chirping call.

IV. LARGE OR MEDIUM-SIZED CORMORANTS MAINLY BLACK ABOVE AND WHITE BELOW

In addition to the seven species described below the South African race of the Common Cormorant has a white chest. The young of many of the black species have whitish underparts, but their brownish upper plumage is a sign of immaturity.

21. **Guanay Cormorant** (*Phalacrocorax bougainvillei*). (*Plate 80*)

Adult.—Head, neck all round and upper parts glossy greenish-black; chin, base of neck and underparts white; in nuptial plumage the feathers of the back of the head elongated, forming a crest, a patch of white plumes above the eye and others scattered on the neck; bill horn-colour with a red wattle at the base; naked skin of face red with a green ring round the eye; feet pinkish; length 30 ins.; wing 11.4–11.8; tail 4.3–4.5; bill 2.8–2.9; tarsus 2.5–2.7. *Young.*—Similar but foreneck largely white.

Range.—Coasts of Peru and Chile from 5° S. to 40° S. Breeds on islands off the coast. *Egg-dates:* Throughout the year.

Notes.—Very abundant in the Humboldt current on the coast of Peru, and as its name implies the most important producer of guano. It occurs in immense flocks, flies high above the water, locates schools of surface fish from the air and captures them by shallow dives. Its large size, white throat and breast and red face distinguish the adult from other South American Cormorants, but the young cannot be distinguished from the Magellan Cormorant in life.

22. **Magellan Cormorant** (*Phalacrocorax magellanicus*). (*Plate 83*)

Adult.—Head and neck all round black in summer, in winter chin, throat and foreneck white, upperparts greenish-black; underparts white; flanks, thighs and under tail-coverts black; in nuptial plumage with long narrow white plumes scattered on head and neck and numerous on lower back and flanks; feathers of throat extending forward in a point almost to the base of the lower mandible; bill black; naked skin of face and throat red; feet flesh-coloured with black webs; length 26 ins; wing 9.6–10.6; tail 5.1–6; bill 1.8–2.3; tarsus 2–2.3. *Young.*—Entirely black.

Range.—Tierra del Fuego and the Straits of Magellan north to Chiloe I., Patagonia and the Falkland Is. Breeds throughout its range. *Egg-dates:* Oct.–Jan.

Notes.—Distinguished from the Blue-eyed Cormorant by its red face and the feathering of its throat, and in nuptial plumage by its entirely black neck.

23. **Blue-eyed Cormorant** (*Phalacrocorax atriceps*). (*Plates 81 and 82*)

Adult.—Top of head, back of neck and upperparts glossy black; throat, foreneck and underparts white; in nuptial plumage the head is crested, there is a thin patch of white hair-like plumes above and behind each eye, a white band across each wing and a white patch on the back; feathers of throat ending in a short point not nearly reaching bill; bill brown with yellow caruncles at base; naked skin of face blue, with orange marks below the eye; eyelids ultramarine; feet flesh-coloured with blackish webs;

217

length 27-29 ins.; wing 11.3; tail 5.2–5.3; bill 2.3–2.4; tarsus 2.5–2.6.

Range.—Southern South America, sub-antarctic islands and Antarctic coast. Breeds from islets near Cape Horn north to Concepción, Chile, and Santa Cruz, Patagonia (*P. a. atriceps*), at South Georgia (*P. a. georgianus*) and Heard I. (*P. a. nivalis*), also in the South Orkney, South Shetland and South Sandwich Is. and islands off Graham Land, Antarctica. *Egg-dates:* Oct.–Jan.

Notes.—Distinguished from the Magellan Cormorant by its blue face, nasal caruncles and unfeathered throat, and in nuptial plumage by its white foreneck, wing-bar and patch on back, though these may not all be present at the same time. From the King Cormorant it differs in having white cheeks and in the presence of a squarish white patch on the back which appears after the breeding season.

24. King Cormorant (*Phalacrocorax albiventer*)

Adult.—Similar in dimensions and plumage to the Blue-eyed Cormorant, but the purple-black plumage on the sides of the head extends on to the cheeks lower than the line of the bill and there is never a white patch on the back.

Range.—Coast of eastern South America from Cape Horn to Uruguay and neighbourhood of the Falkland, Crozet and Macquarie Is. Breeds on the coast of Patagonia south from Puerto San Julian and in the Falkland Is. (*P. a. albiventer*), Crozet Is. (*P. a melanogenis*) and Macquarie I. (*P. a purpurascens*). *Egg-dates:* Oct.–Dec.

Notes.—Closely similar to the Blue-eyed Cormorant from which it is distinguished by the features mentioned above. The ranges of the two species overlap in Patagonia.

25. Kerguelen Cormorant (*Phalacrocorax verrucosus*)

Adult.—Back of head, cheeks, hind-neck and upperparts glossy greenish-black; throat, foreneck and underparts white; in nuptial plumage with a crest on the head; feathers of throat extending forward to the base of the lower mandible; bill with well-developed yellow caruncles at the base; feet pink; length 27 ins.; wing 10.2–11; tail 4.4–5.4; bill 1.8–2.1; tarsus 2–2.3 *Young.*—Brown, paler below, white on the throat.

Range.—Kerguelen and Marion Is. Breeds at Kerguelen. *Egg-dates:* Nov.–Jan.

26. Rough-faced Cormorant (*Phalacrocorax carunculatus*)

Adult.—Top and sides of head, back and sides of neck and upperparts blue-black; line from throat along fore-neck, and underparts white, except in birds from Campbell I. where the middle of the foreneck is black, and some birds from Stewart I. in which the whole plumage is black; in nuptial plumage there may be a crest on the head, a white bar on each wing and a white patch on the back, or one or more of these ornaments; feathers of throat extend forward to the base of the lower mandible; bill dark brown frequently with yellow, orange or red caruncles at the base; naked skin of face black, purple, dark blue, crimson, orange or chocolate-brown, sometimes one of these colours with spots of another; feet flesh-coloured; length 25–30 ins.; wing 10.4–12.3; tail 4.5–5.6; bill 2–2.5; tarsus 1.7–2.8. *Young.*—Top of head, neck all round and upperparts brown; chin and underparts white, except in some birds from Stewart I. which are entirely brown.

Range.—South Island of New Zealand and outlying subantarctic islands. Breeds at White Rocks, Pelorus Sound (*P. c. carunculatus*), Stewart I. and the coast of Otago (*P. c. chalconotus = P. c. stewarti*), the Chatham Is. (*P. c. onslowi*), Campbell I. (*P. c. campbelli*), the Auckland Is. (*P. c. colensoi*), and the Bounty Is. (*P. c. ranfurlyi*). *Egg-dates:* Throughout the year.

Notes.—Each of the forms here treated as races has an isolated and limited range and differs in certain features, especially the colouring of the face, the development of caruncles and of nuptial ornaments, from each of the others. They have commonly all been treated as distinct species but it seems preferable to regard them as races of a polymorphic species. From the Pied Cormorant it differs in having the sides of the face and neck black and the chin feathered.

27. Pied Cormorant (*Phalacrocorax varius = P. hypoleucus*). (*Plate 82*)

Adult.—Top of head, hind-neck and upperparts glossy blue-black; line above eye, sides of face, front and sides of neck and underparts white; feathers of throat extending forward in a point towards the base of the lower mandible; bill dark horn colour; naked skin before eye yellow or orange, of face and throat blue; feet black; length 28–31.4 ins.; wing 11.5–12.8; tail 5.5–5.9; bill 2.5–2.8; tarsus 2.5–2.6. *Young.*—Brown above; white, mottled with brown, below.

Range.—Australia, Tasmania, Lord Howe I. and New Zealand. Breeds on the coasts, rivers and swamps of Australia (*P. v. perthi*) and New Zealand (*P. v. varius*). *Egg-dates:* March–Nov.

Notes.—The commonest Cormorant on Australian coasts and estuaries. Differs from the White-breasted and Rough-faced Cormorants in the form and colouring of the naked area of the face, which is separated from the black crown by white feathers.

28. White-breasted Cormorant (*Phalacrocorax fuscescens = P. gouldi*)

Adult.—Top of head, hind-neck, upperparts, thighs and under wing-coverts glossy blue-black; sides of face, throat, front and sides of neck and underparts white; in nuptial plumage some white plumes on back of neck and rump; feathers of chin extend forward to the lower mandible on each side; bill dark horn-colour; naked skin of face purple; feet black; length 27.6–30 ins.; wing 10.6–10.7; tail 4.2; bill 2–2.1; tarsus 2.1–2.4. *Young.*—Upperparts brown; underparts white.

Range.—Tasmania and south coast of Australia. Breeds on islands off the coast. *Egg-dates:* Nov.–Jan.

Notes.—Distinguished from the Pied Cormorant by the form and colouring of the naked area on the face, which is bordered above by the black feathers of the crown, whilst the white feathers of the chin reach the lower mandible.

V. SMALL CORMORANTS WITH LONG TAILS, BLACK UPPERPARTS AND WHITE UNDERPARTS

29. Little Pied Cormorant (*Haliëtor melanoleucus*)

Adult.—Top of head, hind-neck, upperparts, under wing-coverts and under tail-coverts black; upper wing-coverts grey, the feathers with black edges; a line over the eye, sides of head, throat, front and sides of neck and underparts white, except in the New Zealand race in which the underparts are usually black, only the sides of head, chin and throat being white; in nuptial plumage the feathers of the forehead are elongated, forming a short crest; feathers of cheeks extending forward on each side to the upper mandible, and of chin in a point to the lower mandible; bill and naked skin of face and throat yellow; feet black; length 22–24 ins.; wing 8.6–9.4; tail 5.8–6.5; bill 1.1–1.3; tarsus 1.4–1.5. *Young.*—Similar but upperparts brown, except in the New Zealand race in which the young are usually entirely black.

Range.—From Sumatra through the Malay Archipelago to New Guinea, Australia, Tasmania, New Caledonia, Lord Howe I. and New Zealand. Breeds in the Malay islands, New Guinea, Solomon Is. and northern Australia (*H. m. melvillensis*), southern Australia and Tasmania (*H. m. melanoleucus*), New Zealand (*H. m. brevirostris*) and Rennell I. (*H. m. brevicauda*). *Egg-dates:* May, Sept.–Jan.

Notes.—Much smaller than the other white-breasted Cormorants and readily distinguished by its short bill and neck and long tail. It frequents rivers and lakes as well as the sea-coast.

221

CHAPTER XV

~~~~~~

Tropic-Birds or Bo'sun Birds

(Order *Pelecaniformes*: Family *Phaethontidae*)

~~~~~~

THESE BEAUTIFUL white sea-birds are well named since they are almost exclusively confined to the tropics. They have straight heavy beaks, long wings, and short legs with all four toes webbed. Their tails are wedge-shaped and in adult birds the two central feathers are enormously elongated. They are commonly called "Bo'sun-birds" by sailors because they "carry a marlin-spike in the tail." Their white plumage is more or less marked with black bars, often crescentic in form, and frequently more or less completely suffused with rosy or salmon colour.

Tropic birds frequent the high seas flying with quick, strong beats of the wings in a fashion different from that of any other sea-bird, but somewhat resembling the flight of Pigeons. They usually fly at some height above the water and when they observe food plunge down upon it from a height of 50 feet or more. Their food consists mainly of fish and squids. They appear to have considerable curiosity and will frequently circle round a ship or travel above it for a time, occasionally uttering a shrill, rasping call.

They breed somewhat gregariously on rocky and desolate islands, laying a single egg on the bare rock or soil in a crevice of a cliff or cave or under a bush

222

or in a cavity in the trunk of a tree. The egg is ovate in form, thickly spotted with reddish-brown and with larger blotches and streaks of purplish-black, so that the yellowish or reddish ground colour is almost hidden. The young are covered thickly with whitish down. In immature plumage all the species have black bars on the upperparts and their determination when flying is difficult.

The very long central tail-feathers apparently grow in the second season and are ornaments common to both sexes. Those of the Red-tailed Tropic-bird are very narrow and bright red in colour and are used for decoration by the natives of the South Sea islands. They are obtained by merely pulling them out of the tail of the sitting bird, which suffers very little thereby. When nesting these birds are very tame and do not attempt to fly away, but when approached they make loud, indignant calls and defend themselves with their bills.

Tropic-birds do not often settle on the water, but when they do they float very high and keep their tails elevated. The family only contains three species.

1. Red-billed Tropic-bird (*Phaethon aethereus*)

Adult.—Plumage mainly white; a black band through the eye on each side of the head; upperparts finely barred with black; a black bar on the wings; tail of 14 feathers, the central pair elongated; bill coral-red or orange; legs and basal part of toes yellow or greyish-white, rest of feet black; length 24–40 ins.; wing 10.6–13; tail 7.5–26; bill 2.1–2.6; tarsus 0.9–1.2. *Young.*—Similar but with more black on head, broader black bars on back and central tail-feathers not elongated.

Range.—Tropical eastern Pacific, Caribbean Sea, Atlantic, Red Sea, Persian Gulf and Indian Ocean to the Straits of Malacca, ranging north to southern California and Bermuda and south to Chile. Breeds on Tower I. in the Galápagos Is. (*P. a. limatus*), on Daphne I. in the Galápagos group, islands off the coasts of western Mexico,

Ecuador, Panama, Venezuela and Brazil, on some of the Lesser Antilles and the Cape Verde Is. (*P. a. mesonauta*), Fernando Noronha, St. Helena and Ascension (*P. a. aethereus*), and on islands in the Persian Gulf. and Gulf of Aden (*P. a. indicus*). *Egg-dates:* Throughout the year.

Notes.—Distinguished by its red bill, black-barred back and elongated white central tail-feathers. In flight the wings are flapped steadily and constantly.

2. **White-tailed Tropic-bird** (*Phaethon lepturus* = *P. americanus*). (*Plate 84*)

Adult.—Plumage mainly white, more or less tinged with salmon or apricot colour, a black line before and over the eye; a black band on the wing; tail of 12 feathers, the central pair very long but not exceptionally narrow and the next pair also elongated; bill yellow, reddish or blackish; legs and base of toes yellowish, rest of feet black; length 15.7–32 ins.; wing 10–11.2; tail 4.1–21.5; bill 1.7–2.1; tarsus 0.7–0.9. *Young.*—Similar but with crescentic black bars on upperparts and flanks, and with central tail-feathers not greatly elongated.

Range.—Tropical Seas. Breeds in the Bermudas, Bahamas and West Indies (*P. l. catesbyi*), at Fernando Noronha and Ascension and islands in the Gulf of Guinea (*P. l. ascensionis*), in the Mascarene, Seychelle, Andaman and Cocos Keeling Is. (*P. l. lepturus*), at Christmas I., near Java (*P. l. fulvus*) and at many islands in the southwestern Pacific from the Pelew Is. and Christmas I. to New Caledonia and the Tuamotu Is. (*P. l. dorotheae*). *Egg-dates:* Throughout the year.

Notes.—The adult may be distinguished by its white back and the long white streamers in the tail; and in the Christmas I. form by the golden hue of the plumage.

3. **Red-tailed Tropic-bird** (*Phaethon rubricauda* = *P. phoenicurus*). (*Plate 85*)

Adult.—Plumage mainly silky white, sometimes with a rich roseate tinge, especially on the back; a broad black crescent before, over and behind the eye; flanks and a bar on the wings black; shafts of primaries and tail-feathers black; tail white, of 16 feathers, the two central feathers very slender, extremely elongated, deep red; bill yellow, orange or vermilion with a black streak through the nostrils; legs and base of toes pale blue, rest of feet black; length 18.5–36 ins; wing 12.3–13.7; tail 3.6–18.5; bill 2.2–3.1; tarsus 1.2–1.3. *Young.*—Silky white without roseate tinge; upperparts broadly barred with black; black of shafts of primaries expanding in a spatulate form at tips of feathers; long central tail-feathers absent; bill black; legs yellowish-white or pale blue-grey.

Range.—Tropical Indian and Pacific Oceans from Madagascar and Mauritius to the Galápagos Is. and from the Bonin and Hawaiian Is. to Australia and the Kermadec Is. Breeds at Mauritius and Aldabra (*P. r. rubricauda*), Christmas I., Cocos Keeling Is., Gunong Api in the Banda Sea, and islands off the north-west coast of Australia (*P. r. westralis*), Raine I., Torres Strait, Lord Howe and Norfolk Is. and the Kermadec Is. (*P. r. roseotincta*), the Society Is. and Palmerston I. (*P. r. melanorhynchus*) and the Bonin and Hawaiian Is. (*P. r. rothschildi*). *Egg-dates:* Throughout the year.

Notes.—The adult with long slender red streamers in its tail cannot be mistaken. It is more buoyant in flight than the Red-billed Tropic-bird, flapping its wings much more slowly and often sailing with only occasional flaps.

CHAPTER XVI

Phalaropes

(Order *Charadriiformes:* Family *Phalaropodidae*)

OCCASIONALLY the voyager far from land will come across a party of small long-necked birds or a single individual resting on the water, and in certain favoured regions within the tropics he may pass flock after flock. When disturbed they fly off over the waves with the rapid flight and appearance of Snipe or Sandpipers. These are Phalaropes, the only wading birds which habitually settle on the water, sometimes called Sea-Snipe or Swimming Plovers. All other wading birds either remain on the coasts or if they cross the sea on migration keep straight on without settling. The name Phalarope is an Anglicised form of the Latin *"Phalaropus"* and means "coot-footed," being derived from the Greek *phalaris* = a coot and *pous* = a foot.

As an adaptation to their aquatic life the toes of Phalaropes have broad fringing webs, somewhat like those of Coots and Grebes, usually lobed or scalloped. The legs (tarsi) are also very much compressed so that they offer little resistance to the water when the bird is swimming. Their under plumage is thick like that of Gulls, and they have heavy under down like Ducks.

Except during the breeding season Phalaropes appear to spend most of their time at sea. Colonel R. Meinertzhagen has shown that their winter quarters are probably definite regions of the ocean though we have not sufficient information to define them accurately at present. One of their winter homes is on the off-shore border of the Humboldt current along the coasts of Peru and Chile, where both Northern and Red Phalaropes are common in winter; another is the Guinea current off the coast of West Africa. The Northern Phalarope also winters in great numbers in the seas adjacent to Borneo and the Moluccas and along the north coast of New Guinea; it is also abundant in winter on the Mekran and Sind coasts and in the northern part of the Arabian Sea. The winter quarters of Wilson's Phalarope are generally believed to be in southern South America where occasional specimens have been found in winter, but there is no evidence that they are ever common there, and it may be that the majority spend the winter somewhere in the South Pacific.

All three species breed in the north, and in spring and autumn many pass up both coasts of North America and the coasts of western Europe and eastern Asia. Others are known to reach their northern breeding grounds across Russia and central Asia, and by way of the Mississippi Valley and the Great Lakes in America. Phalaropes breed inland, usually in the neighbourhood of pools or rivers, and in fresh water they obtain their food by spinning rapidly round in shallow water, stirring up the mud or weeds and picking out insects, molluscs and small crustacea.

The female Phalarope is larger and more brightly coloured than her mate and she does the wooing and takes the lead in selecting the nesting site. When she has laid the eggs her part is finished and the male incubates them and raises the brood. The nests of all three species are merely slight hollows in the ground, lined with a little grass or moss. The eggs are three to four to the clutch, pear-shaped, pale olive-grey or creamy-buff in colour heavily blotched with deep chocolate or lighter brown. The chicks can run as soon as they are hatched and are covered with buff-coloured down striped and mottled with black.

In spring and early summer the three species are easily distinguished by their colouring. In each the female is rather larger and much more brightly coloured than the male. In autumn and winter their gay colours are replaced by grey and white and discrimination of the species is not at all easy. On the water they float high at the shoulders and their rather long slender necks are carried very upright, giving them an outline different from that of any other bird. At sea they are generally silent birds, but on their breeding grounds they utter a chipping note when on the wing as well as a harsh grunting call.

1. **Red or Grey Phalarope** (*Phalaropus fulicarius*). (*Plates 86 and 87*)

Adult in summer.—Crown and chin dark grey (female), crown and back of neck streaked black and buff (male); cheeks white; neck and underparts reddish-brown; back buff, striped with black; wings grey, with a broad white bar; centre of rump and tail grey; sides of rump white; axillaries and under wing-coverts white; bill yellow with black tip; feet yellowish. *Adult in winter.*—Head, neck and underparts mainly white; a dusky patch before and below the eye extending back across the cheeks; back of head and hind-neck slate colour; upperparts light bluish-grey, darker on wings and tail; bar in wing and sides of rump white; bill and feet dark horn-colour. Bill rather short, broader than deep; toes webbed at the base and with scalloped lobes terminally; length 7.5–9 ins.; wing 5–5.5; tail 2–2.8; bill 0.8–1; tarsus 0.8–0.9. *Young.*—Resembles adult in winter but chest washed with buff and feathers of upperparts margined with buff.

Range.—Circumpolar regions south in winter to the coasts of Peru and Chile, the coast of West Africa and the Arabian Sea, occasionally to Patagonia, Bengal and

New Zealand. On migration on both coasts of United States, coasts of southern and western Europe, China and Japan. Breeds in Alaska, arctic Canada, Greenland, Iceland, Novaya Zemblya and northern Siberia. *Egg-dates:* June–July.

Notes.—The short bill and white bar in the wing are characteristic at all seasons. In summer the reddish underparts and white cheeks are diagnostic. In winter the forehead is whiter than in other species and the back more uniformly pale grey.

2. Northern or Red-necked Phalarope (*Lobipes lobatus*). (Plates 86, 87 and 88)

Adult in summer.—Upperparts slate grey; back striped with buff; a white bar in the wing; sides and front of neck rufous; chin, throat, spot over eye and underparts white; bill black; feet bluish-grey. *Adult in winter.*—Upperparts greyish, more or less mixed with white; a white bar in the wing; front and sides of head, neck and underparts white, more or less mottled with greyish on the breast; a blackish spot before the eye; a dusky patch below and behind the eye; bill black; feet dusky. Bill rather long, slender and pointed; toes webbed at base, with scalloped lobes terminally but small on the outer toe; length 6.4–8 ins.; wing 4–4.6; tail 2–2.5; bill 0.8–1.1; tarsus 0.8–0.9. *Young.*—Upperparts brownish-black, the feathers margined with rusty; forehead and underparts white with brownish wash on chest and flanks; feet bluish flesh-colour.

Range.—Circumpolar regions south in winter to the west coast of Africa, the Mekran coast and Arabian Sea, the seas adjacent to northern New Guinea and the Moluccas and the coast of Peru, occasionally to Patagonia and New Zealand. On migration occurs on both coasts of the United States, the coasts of western and southern Europe and of Japan, China and the Philippine Is. Breeds in Alaska, Canada, southern Greenland, Iceland, Spitzbergen, Scandinavia, the British Is., Russia, Siberia, Saghalien, the Commander Is. and the Aleutian Is. *Egg-dates:* May–July.

Notes.—The smallest species with slim neck, long slender bill and a white bar in the wing in all plumages. In summer the reddish neck contrasting with white throat and underparts are diagnostic. In winter plumage the back is darker grey than in the Red Phalarope and is striped with white; and there is less white on the forehead.

3. Wilson's Phalarope (*Steganopus tricolor*). (*Plate 86*)

Adult in summer.—Crown and middle of back bluish-grey; nape white; a black stripe through eye to side of neck, continued as a chestnut stripe down side of back; wings and lower back brownish-grey; upper tail-coverts white; tail dark grey, the outer feathers with white tips; throat and abdomen white; fore-neck and upper breast pale rufous; bill and feet black. *Adult in winter.*—Upperparts pale grey, wing-quills and tail darker grey; broad stripe over eye, upper tail-coverts, sides of back and rump, and underparts white. Bill long and slender; toes slightly webbed at base, with narrow margins of web; length 8.3–10 ins.; wing 4.6–5.5; tail 1.9–2.3; bill 1.1–1.5; tarsus 1.1–1.3. *Young.*—Similar to adult in winter but crown and back dusky, the feathers margined with buff; wing-coverts greyish-brown, the feathers margined with whitish; throat and sides buffy.

Range.—Temperate North America, south in winter to the Galápagos Is., Chile, Argentina and the Falkland Is. On migration on both coasts of the United States and Mexico. Breeds in the interior of western Canada and the United States. *Egg-dates:* May–June.

Notes.—The largest species with slim neck, long slender bill and no white bar in the wing. In summer plumage the dark stripe down each side of the neck is very distinctive. The winter quarters of this species do not seem to have been discovered and may be in the South Pacific.

CHAPTER XVII

The North Atlantic Ocean

THE SEA-BIRDS to be mentioned in this chapter are those which are found regularly in the temperate North Atlantic and which are likely to be seen on voyages across it between America and Europe, or along the coasts of either continent. Excluding occasional or purely accidental visitors about seventy of the birds described in this book are found in the North Atlantic and its subsidiary seas—the Mediterranean, Black Sea and Baltic. The Gulf of Mexico, the coasts of Florida and the Bahamas, though not actually within the tropics, are so thoroughly tropical in their sea-bird population that they are excluded from the region dealt with in this chapter. The subtropical Bermudas, Azores, Madeira, Salvage and Canary groups are included.

In the region thus defined Albatrosses, Diving-Petrels, Penguins and Frigate-birds are absent, Skimmers, Gannets and Tropic-birds are each represented by a single species, whilst Cormorants and Petrels are scarce in comparison with their numbers elsewhere. Gulls are particularly numerous, whilst Terns and Auks are well represented.

1. *The Open Ocean.*—The number of species likely to be seen out of sight of land in the North Atlantic is comparatively small, though it is perhaps larger

231

than is suspected by those who have not spent time on the look out for birds. The Petrel family is naturally the best represented. Two species, which are winter migrants from the southern hemisphere, where they breed, occur in flocks in the North Atlantic throughout the summer. These are the Sooty and Greater Shearwaters. Other members of this family, which may be seen at any time of year, are the Mediterranean (or Cory's) Shearwater, the Manx and Dusky Shearwaters (chiefly on the eastern side), Audubon's Shearwater (chiefly on the western side) and the Fulmar. The last-named breeds on northern coasts but throughout the autumn, winter and spring months is plentiful, especially on the western side of the ocean and ranges down to about 40° S. In the warm waters of the Gulf Stream the Black-capped and Bermuda Petrels should be looked for.

Five species of Storm-Petrels occur in the North Atlantic but their small size makes it easy to overlook them and difficult to identify them when they are seen. Throughout the summer Wilson's Storm-Petrel, a winter migrant from the Antarctic, is the commonest member of this family. Leach's Storm-Petrel occurs on both sides of the Atlantic, the British Storm-Petrel on the eastern side and the Madeiran and White-faced Storm-Petrels about the Azores, Madeira, Salvage and Canary Islands.

Gulls are mainly coastal birds but the Common Kittiwake is a striking exception. Except during the summer months, when it is breeding on northern coasts, it is found in great numbers throughout the North Atlantic and a flock of Kittiwakes will usually be about the steamer. Occasionally a few Herring Gulls may be seen among the Kittiwakes well away from the land, and, on the eastern side of the ocean, Lesser Black-backed Gulls occur in some numbers out of sight of land, especially during the spring and autumn months when they are migrating.

Four species of Skua occur in the North Atlantic.

All of them breed in arctic or sub-arctic regions but in autumn they travel south, the majority keeping well off shore. The Parasitic Jaeger continues its journey into the tropics or the southern hemisphere, but the Great Skua and the Pomarine and Long-tailed Jaegers may be seen in the temperate North Atlantic throughout the winter.

Flocks of Red and Northern Phalaropes may also be seen occasionally far from land, in spring and autumn, on their passage between their arctic breeding grounds and their winter quarters in the tropics.

The Northern Gannet, though chiefly found in coastal waters, may sometimes be seen far from land, whilst about Bermuda and considerably further north in the warm waters of the Gulf Stream the White-tailed Tropic-bird may be observed in summer.

2. *Northern Coasts.*—North from New England on the American coast and from France on the European coast the sea-birds frequenting the coasts of the North Atlantic and its northern extensions are almost identical. The birds seen in the Gulf of St. Lawrence are practically the same as those of the North Sea and the Baltic, whilst those of the coasts of Labrador and Greenland are mostly met with again in Scandinavia and northern Russia.

The most characteristic birds of the northern seas and coasts are the members of the Auk family, namely, the Atlantic Puffin, Common and Brunnich's Murres, Black Guillemot, Razor-bill and Dovekie (or Little Auk). On the American coast the two species with the most southerly breeding range are the Puffin and the Black Guillemot, which breed in Maine. On the European coast the Common Murre breeds in Portugal, whilst the Puffin and Razor-bill have their most southerly colonies in Brittany. These four species all breed on the coasts of Newfoundland and the British Isles, but Newfoundland has also large colonies of Brunnich's Murre, a species which on the European side of the ocean does not breed south of Iceland and Bear Island (south of Spitzbergen). The Dovekie breeds only on arctic coasts both in America and in Europe, its most southerly breeding grounds being in northern Iceland.

All six species range southward on both coasts in the winter but the extent of their southward movement depends largely on the weather. On the American coast the Common Murre is far less plentiful than Brunnich's Murre, whilst on the European coast the Common Murre (or Guillemot) is the most abundant of the Auks, and Brunnich's Murre very rare.

Several birds which breed on the northern coasts have been mentioned in the previous section, as they may be found throughout the ocean at other seasons. They include the Northern Gannet, the Fulmar, Leach's Storm-Petrel, four species of Skua and two Phalaropes. Two Terns are found breeding on northern coasts in summer, namely, the Arctic Tern from Maine and England northwards and the Common Tern north to Quebec, Newfoundland, Scotland and Norway. The Common Cormorant is another species found breeding on the northern coasts on both sides of the ocean, though in Europe it also breeds much further south. In America it now only breeds as far south as Nova Scotia and is much less common than the Double-crested Cormorant which breeds as far north as Labrador. This species does not occur on the European side where the Green Cormorant (or Shag) may be regarded as its representative and breeds north as far as Norway. It is, however, rarer than the Common Cormorant except on very rocky coasts.

The Gulls of northern coasts are numerous. The Kittiwake has been mentioned in the previous section as being of oceanic habits. It breeds in colonies, usually in company with Auks of various kinds, from the Gulf of St. Lawrence and Brittany northwards. The Herring Gull, though possibly not so numerous, is more universally distributed along the northern coasts, breeding northwards from Massachusetts and Brittany. Less common than the Herring Gull but with an almost similar breeding range is the Great Black-backed Gull. These two species range south along the American and European coasts in winter. Four other Gulls breed only in the Arctic regions but may be met with on northern coasts in winter. These are the Glaucous, Iceland, Sabine's and Ivory Gulls. The latter is rarely found far away from ice-floes. On northern European coasts three other Gulls are common, namely, the Lesser Black-backed, Mew (or Common) and Northern Black-headed Gulls. The two latter chiefly breed on lakes and swamps inland but are common on the coasts in winter. In the Baltic the Little Gull is also found breeding. The Mew Gull is represented on the American side by the Ring-billed Gull which has similar habits.

3. *The Atlantic coast of the United States.*—In the preceding section we have seen that northward from New England on the American coast the sea-birds are almost identical with those of northern Europe. From New York to the Carolinas many of these northern birds are found on the coast in winter, but in summer many of the breeding species are purely American distinct from those found in similar latitudes on the other side of the ocean.

The Laughing Gull is the only member of its family which breeds on this section of the coast, but in winter the small Bonaparte's Gull, which breeds in the interior, visits the Atlantic coast, whilst the Great Black-backed, Herring and Ring-billed Gulls come down from the north.

Terns are well represented in summer. The Common Tern breeds as far south as North Carolina, the Little (or Least) Tern from Massachusetts to the tropics, and the Royal and Sandwich (or Cabot's) Terns from Virginia southwards. The Caspian, Gull-billed and Roseate Terns breed sporadically in colonies of the other species, whilst the Black and Forster's Terns occur on the Atlantic coast on migration.

The curious Black Skimmer is found along the coast in summer, breeding southward from New Jersey.

The Double-crested Cormorant is found all along the coast in winter. As noted in the previous section it breeds in the north, but the southern race, known as the Florida Cormorant, is found breeding southwards from North Carolina. The Common Cormorant is a rare winter visitor.

The American White Pelican occasionally visits the Atlantic coast on migration and the Brown Pelican breeds southward from South Carolina.

4. *The coasts of south-western Europe, north-western Africa and the Mediterranean and Black Seas.*—On the coasts of southern Europe and northern Africa most of the northern species mentioned in section 2 above may be met with in winter. As already noted the Common Murre (or Guillemot) breeds on the coast of Portugal.

The Petrels are represented in the Mediterranean by the Mediterranean and Manx Shearwaters and the British and Leach's Storm-Petrels breed in the western parts of that sea as well as on the Atlantic coast.

The Common and Green Cormorants occur along the Atlantic coast and throughout the Mediterranean, the latter being restricted to rocky coasts. In the eastern Mediterranean and Black Sea the Pigmy Cormorant may also be met with, chiefly at the mouths of rivers. In the same region the Dalmatian and Eastern White Pelicans may be seen occasionally on migration.

Terns are numerous in summer. The Common Tern is found breeding on coasts throughout the area and, as already noted, much further north. The Little, Gull-billed and Caspian Terns breed as far north as the Baltic and the Sandwich and Roseate Terns to the British Isles. The Lesser Crested Tern breeds on the coasts of the Mediterranean, and the Whiskered,

Black and White-winged Black Terns, which breed
on inland waters, occur on the Mediterranean and
Atlantic coasts on migration. The Royal Tern is found
on the coast of northwestern Africa but is not known
to breed there.

Most of the northern Gulls listed in section 2 are
winter visitors to this region and the Yellow-legged,
Slender-billed and Mediterranean Black-headed Gulls
breed on the coasts of the Mediterranean. The rarest
of European Gulls is Audouin's Gull, which breeds
in the Mediterranean, whilst the Great Black-headed
Gull breeds by rivers and lakes inland and occurs
in winter on the coasts of the eastern Mediterranean
and Black Seas.

5. *The Sub-tropical Islands.*—In the neighbourhood
of these island groups certain sea-birds are found
which are rarely seen elsewhere in the Atlantic. To
conclude this brief account of the birds of the ocean
the species which breed in these island groups, the
Bermudas, Azores, Madeira and Canary Is. (including
the Salvage Is.) are here mentioned.

Representatives of the Petrel family are the Soft-
plumaged Petrel breeding at Madeira, Bulwer's Petrel
which breeds in Madeira and the Canaries, the Mediterranean Shearwater which breeds in the Azores,
Madeira and the Canaries, the Manx Shearwater,
which breeds in the Bermudas and Madeira, Audubon's Shearwater and the Bermuda Petrel which breed
in the Bermudas, and the Dusky Shearwater which
breeds in Madeira and the Canaries. Of these the
Mediterranean Shearwater, as already noted, ranges
widely over the ocean, but the other four species are
chiefly found near their breeding grounds.

The Storm-Petrels are represented by the Madeiran
Storm-Petrel which breeds in the Azores, Madeira and
Salvages, and by the White-faced Storm-Petrel, which
breeds only in the Salvage Is.

Several of the northern Gulls are found about the

coasts of the islands in winter, but the only breeding species is the Yellow-legged Gull which breeds in the Azores, Madeira and Canaries.

There are three breeding species of Terns, namely the Common Tern, breeding in the Azores, Madeira and the Canaries, the Roseate Tern in the Azores and Madeira, and the Little Tern in Madeira and the Canaries. Other species may occur in winter or on migration.

In winter Skuas and Jaegers may occur about the coasts and the Northern Gannet may also be seen near the islands. Phalaropes too may be met with. The only other breeding sea-bird is the White-tailed (or Yellow-billed) Tropic-bird which nests in numbers in the Bermudas.

CHAPTER XVIII

The North Pacific Ocean

THE TEMPERATE North Pacific Ocean is the home of more species of sea-birds than the temperate North Atlantic. In the following account of the birds likely to be seen on voyages across it or along its coasts the southern boundary of its area will be considered as occurring about latitude 30° N. The coasts of southern China, northern Formosa and Lower California and the Liu Kiu, Bonin and western Hawaiian Islands, though not actually in the tropics, are inhabited in the main by birds of tropical type, and their avifauna will be dealt with in the chapter dealing with the birds of the Tropical Oceans.

As thus defined the North Pacific Ocean contains representatives of all the families of birds dealt with in this book except Penguins, Diving-Petrels, Skimmers, Frigate-birds, Tropic-birds and Gannets. The absence of the latter is somewhat remarkable since Gannets are found in all other oceans. Some of the tropical species of Gannets, Frigate-birds and Tropic-birds occasionally range northwards to the coasts of Japan and California, but none of them breed within the limits of the region.

The feature of the North Pacific from the ornithological point of view is the prevalence of species of the Auk family on its coasts. Out of the 22 species included in the family 17 are found in the North Pacific, two of these are also found in the North At-

lantic where four others occur. The remaining species
is found on the coasts of Lower California. Gulls,
Terns, Cormorants and Storm-Petrels are other families which are well represented in the North Pacific.

1. *The Open Ocean.*—As in the Atlantic the majority of the North Pacific sea-birds are chiefly found near
the coasts. Birds which range freely over the ocean
and may be seen far from land include three species
of Albatross. Of these the commonest is the dark-
coloured Black-footed Albatross which with the larger,
white Short-tailed Albatross ranges north as far as
Bering Sea. The latter appears, however, to be now
almost, or quite, extinct. The Laysan Albatross pre-
fers warmer seas and does not range much north of
40° N. lat. All three species breed on the tropical or
sub-tropical islands to the south.

The only member of the Petrel family which is
known to breed in the region under consideration is
the Fulmar, which nests in vast numbers on the islands
of Bering Sea and regions to the north and in winter
ranges south throughout the ocean to about 40° N.
In summer several Petrels which breed in the Southern Hemisphere occur in the North Pacific, namely
the Sooty Shearwater, Short-tailed Shearwater, and
Peale's Petrel, which range north to Bering Sea, the
Pale-footed Shearwater which reaches Japan and California, the Pink-footed Shearwater which on the
American side ranges up to Alaska, and the Grey-
backed Shearwater which, also on the east side,
reaches California. Further information as to the move-
ments of these species and the season when they are
present in various parts of the ocean is very desirable.
Some ornithologists still believe that they will be
found breeding in the North Pacific.

The distribution and breeding localities of Storm-
Petrels in the North Pacific require much further re-
search. Leach's Storm-Petrel and the Fork-tailed
Storm-Petrel breed in numbers on the islands of Ber-

ing Sea and south to the Kurile Is. and islets off the coast of California. The Ashy Storm-Petrel also breeds off the Californian coast from which it does not appear to range far. The Black and Swinhoe's Storm-Petrels occur on both sides of the ocean, whilst the Sooty and Madeiran Storm-Petrels occur in the seas near Japan. These four species probably breed further south. Finally Wilson's Storm-Petrel, which breeds in the Antarctic regions, occurs in summer on the eastern side of the North Pacific north to California.

As in the North Atlantic the Common Kittiwake breeds in great colonies on northern coasts and ranges widely south over the ocean at other seasons. Other Gulls are mainly confined to the coasts, but the Glaucous-winged Gull is said to have followed ships from San Francisco to Honolulu.

The three species of Jaegers, which breed in the north, either pass through the North Pacific on migration or remain there for the winter, and may at times be seen far from land. The same is true of the two arctic-breeding species of Phalaropes.

2. *Northern Coasts.*—As is the case in the North Atlantic the birds of the northern coasts are largely identical on both sides of the ocean. The coasts of north-eastern Siberia, Kamchatka, Alaska and northern British Columbia, the Okhotsk and Bering Seas, and the innumerable islands which include Saghalien, the Kurile, Commander, Pribilof and Queen Charlotte groups and the great Aleutian chain, form one region. Bird life on these desolate coasts and fog-bound islands is abundant and it will be long before the distribution of the various species is completely known.

As already mentioned the Petrel family is represented by breeding colonies of Fulmars and the Storm-Petrels by the Fork-tailed and Leach's Storm-Petrels. Gulls are represented by seven species, of which the Ivory and Glaucous Gulls breed on arctic coasts and come south to Bering Sea in winter. The Common and Red-legged Kittiwakes breed in great colonies on cliffs often in association with Murres, whilst the Herring, Slaty-backed and Glaucous-winged Gulls are found in smaller numbers in more widely scattered colonies.

Terns are represented by three species, the Arctic, Common and Aleutian Terns. The first-named is a summer visitor and remains only for the breeding season, wintering in the southern hemisphere. The two others range south to the seas of Japan and China in winter. The Long-tailed and Pomarine Jaegers breed only on the arctic coasts, but the Parasitic Jaeger breeds as far south as the Aleutian Is. The Red and Northern Phalaropes also breed in the Arctic regions of Siberia and Alaska.

Cormorants are represented by the Red-faced Cormorant which breeds only in these northern regions, the Japanese Cormorant, whose breeding range extends further south on the Asiatic coasts, and the Pelagic, Brandt's and Double-crested Cormorants, whose breeding range extends further south on the American side.

Finally we come to the Auks, the characteristic birds of the region and especially of these northern seas and islands. Of these Brunnich's Murre, the Horned Puffin, Crested Auklet, Whiskered Auklet, Paroquet Auklet, Least Auklet, Ancient Murrelet and Kittlitz's Murrelet do not breed south of the Kurile and Aleutian Islands, the Marbled Murrelet breeds south to northern Japan and Vancouver Island, the Spectacled Guillemot on the Asiatic coasts to Japan, the Rhinoceros Auklet on the American coast to Washington and the Common Murre, Tufted Puffin, Pigeon Guillemot and Cassin's Auklet to California. Since almost all these species are found in Bering Sea and breed on the Aleutian Is. it will be obvious that the determination of the species in that region is a matter of difficulty.

3. *The American Coast.*—The Pacific coast of America from Vancouver I. to California is visited in winter by a large proportion of the northern species mentioned in the previous section, and also at various seasons by most of the ocean wanderers detailed in section 1 of this chapter. Besides the Petrels mentioned in those sections the Black-vented Shearwater, which breeds further south, ranges north along this coast to British Columbia. The Magnificent Frigate-bird sometimes wanders north from the tropics to the coast of southern California, and Wilson's Phalarope occurs on the coast on migration. The Brown Pelican breeds north as far as Washington and the American White Pelican occasionally visits the coast. The Pelagic, Brandt's and Double-crested Cormorants breed all along this coast as well as further north.

The only Gulls which breed on the coast are the Western Gull and the Glaucous-winged Gull, the latter only as far south as Washington. But in addition to the northern species mentioned in the last section, which travel south in winter, the California Gull, Mew (or Short-billed) Gull and Ring-billed Gull, which breed inland, occur on the coast in winter, and in smaller numbers at other seasons, whilst Franklin's and Bonaparte's Gulls may occur on migration and Heermann's Gull ranges north to Vancouver I., from its southern breeding grounds.

The Little (or Least) Tern appears to be the only member of its family which breeds on the Californian coast, but the Royal, Elegant, Forster's, Common, Arctic and Black Terns may be seen on migration.

In addition to the northern Auks which breed southwards on the American coast mentioned in the previous section, Xantus' Murrelet breeds on the coast of California.

4. *The Asiatic Coast.*—In contrast to the comparatively straight coastline on the American side, the Asiatic coast is much more complex. The Japanese

islands front the open ocean and off their eastern coast many of the ocean birds mentioned in section 1 of this chapter may be met with. Between Japan and the coasts of Manchuria and northern China are the Japan and Yellow Seas separated by the peninsula of Korea. In these seas and on the coasts of these countries many of the northern birds mentioned in section 2 occur in winter.

In addition to the Petrels mentioned in sections 1 and 2 the White-faced Shearwater is a common species and probably breeds here as well as further south.

In addition to the Glaucous, Herring and Glaucous-winged Gulls which breed further north and winter in these regions, the Slaty-backed Gull breeds as far south as northern Japan and the Japanese Gull breeds throughout this area, whilst the Yellow-legged, Mew, Little, Northern Black-headed and Chinese Black-headed Gulls, which breed on inland lakes, occur on the coasts in winter.

The Little Tern appears to be the only member of its family which breeds on the coasts of northern China and Japan, but the Common and Aleutian Terns, which breed further north, spend the winter in this region, the Crested, Lesser Crested and Roseate Terns wander up from the south, whilst the Arctic and White-winged Black Terns occur on migration.

The Crested Murrelet and Spectacled Guillemot breed on the coasts of Japan and many of the northern Auks mentioned in section 2 occur in winter.

The Common Cormorant breeds on the coasts of China and Japan and is used by Chinese fishermen to aid them in capturing fish. The Japanese Cormorant breeds in Japan and Korea as well as further north, whilst the Red-faced and Pelagic Cormorants, which breed further north, occur in these seas in winter. The Lesser Frigate-bird sometimes ranges from the south into these seas and the Dalmatian and Eastern White Pelicans sometimes visit the coast on migration.

244

CHAPTER XIX

~~~~~~

Tropical Seas

~~~~~~

THE BIRDS to be mentioned in this chapter are those specially characteristic of the warm parts of the ocean. Their distribution is considerably influenced by the great ocean currents so that some parts of the ocean outside the actual tropics are included, whilst at least one region within the tropics must be excluded.

In the North Atlantic, as indicated in Chapter XVII, the whole of the Gulf of Mexico, the coasts of Florida and the Bahamas are inhabited in the main by sea-birds of tropical types, otherwise the northern boundary of tropical sea-birds in this ocean agrees approximately with the tropic of Cancer. The southern boundary of their range also agrees fairly well with the tropic of Capricorn.

The Red Sea, Persian Gulf and Mekran coast though lying outside the tropics are characterised by high temperatures, and several tropical birds occur there, so that they will here be included with the tropical Indian Ocean, whose southern boundary may be regarded as formed by the tropic of Capricorn with extensions southward to include the whole of Madagascar, the coast of East Africa down to about Delagoa Bay and the coast of Western Australia to the Houtman's Abrolhos Is.

In the Pacific, as indicated in Chapter XVIII, the

northern boundary must be taken as occurring north of the tropic of Cancer to about 30° N. The coasts of south China, Formosa, the Liu Kiu Is., Bonin Is. and western Hawaiian Is. have a definitely tropical avifauna.

Lower California, which is also here included in the tropical region, presents an interesting mixture doubtless due to the prevalence of high temperatures of the atmosphere and comparatively low sea-temperatures owing to the southward flow of the cool California current. Tropical Boobies, Tropic-birds, Frigate-birds and Terns, birds largely aerial in habits, are here found in the same area as Murrelets and northern Cormorants, which spend most of their time in the cool water.

In the south-western Pacific the boundary of the tropical sea is well to the south of the tropic of Capricorn and includes Lord Howe I., Norfolk I., the Kermadec Is., the southern islets of the Austral and Tuamotu Archipelagoes, Pitcairn I., Ducie I. and Easter I. On reaching the neighbourhood of the South American coast, however, the boundary is deflected sharply to the north owing to the influence of the cold Humboldt Current. The avifauna of the coasts of northern Chile and Peru presents, like that of Lower California, an interesting mixture of forms, for precisely the same reason, but here there is no question that forms of southern type predominate. The birds of the Humboldt current will, therefore, be mentioned in the next chapter. The influence of the cool water is evident in the Galápagos Is., lying on the equator, where a Penguin lives amidst an assemblage of mainly tropical sea-birds. These islands, however, and the coast of Ecuador, are included in the region discussed in this chapter.

In the broad belt of warm water just defined, over half of the 289 species of birds described in this book are regularly to be found at some season of the year, and 123 species breed within their limits. The only family which is entirely unrepresented is that of the Diving-Petrels, but Penguins are represented only by one species in the Galápagos Is. and Auks by two species on the coasts of Lower California. No species of Skua or Phalarope breeds within the tropics, but two of the former and all three of the latter winter in tropical regions.

Albatrosses do not occur in the tropics except in the Pacific, where four species breed on tropical islands. Of these three, as mentioned in the last chapter, range northward from their breeding grounds over the temperate parts of the North Pacific. The fourth species, the Waved Albatross, breeds in the Galápagos group and ranges to the cool waters of the Humboldt current.

The most characteristic tropical sea-birds are the Frigate-birds, Tropic-birds and Skimmers. All the species of these families breed in the tropics, though one Tropic-bird and one Skimmer also breed in temperate latitudes. Out of the 42 species of Terns no less than 30 breed in the tropics, and 6 others occur in winter or on migration, so that this family must be regarded as essentially tropical. On the other hand, only 12 of the 44 species of Gulls breed in the tropics, though about a dozen more visit tropical coasts in winter.

Of the Gannets, Cormorants, Petrels and Storm-Petrels about half of the species breed in the tropics, and others occur in winter or on migration.

The foregoing remarks on the large numbers of species of sea-birds found in the tropics might lead to the supposition that birds were more abundant in tropical seas than in higher latitudes. In reality, however, the opposite is the case. One may travel for days across the tropical oceans and see no birds at all, or only an occasional Booby, Bo'sun-bird, or Man-o'-war Hawk, a few Petrels, or a flock of Terns. Even on many tropical coasts the numbers of sea-birds are small.

On the other hand many small, desolate, sun-baked

islets off the coasts of the continents, and numerous coral islands in mid-ocean, swarm with sea-birds whose cries may be heard for miles across the water and which may appear at a distance like a column of smoke rising from the island. Since many of the species of tropical sea-birds breed erratically at almost any time of year such islands are hardly ever without some nesting birds. Even where the colony of a particular species nesting on an island has a definite breeding season, another colony of the same species on a neighbouring island may breed in a different month, and in exceptional cases birds of the same species may have two distinct breeding seasons in the year on the same island, or the breeding season may differ greatly in different years.

Most of the sea-birds which breed in the tropics do not seem to range very far from their breeding grounds. Probably those which wander furthest are the Frigate-birds, Tropic-birds and Noddies, and a few of the species of Petrels and Terns.

Though the belt of tropical ocean is interrupted by the land masses of America and Africa a number of species are found in all of the three great oceans, and the birds of the tropical Atlantic are not more distinct from those of the Indian or Pacific Oceans, than are those of these two oceans from one another. The isthmus of Panama is obviously no serious barrier to a sea-bird and probably some species have travelled between the Atlantic and Indian Oceans, either round the Cape of Good Hope or via the Mediterranean and Red Seas.

Of species which are found breeding in all three oceans the list is not very large. Petrels are represented by the small Dusky and Audubon's Shearwaters alone, Terns by the Common Noddy, White Tern, Sooty Tern, Brown-winged Tern and Roseate Tern. The Great and Lesser Frigate-birds may also be included, though in the Atlantic they are found only in the south and do not occur in the Caribbean

Sea. The Brown, Blue-faced and Red-footed Boobies are present almost throughout. The Red-billed Tropic-bird is absent from the western Pacific and eastern Indian Ocean and the White-tailed Tropic-bird from the eastern Pacific.

Visitors breeding in the north which winter in all three oceans are the Parasitic and Pomarine Jaegers and the Northern Phalarope, whilst visitors from the south are the White-bellied, Black-bellied and Wilson's Storm-Petrels.

1. *The Tropical Atlantic, Caribbean Sea and Gulf of Mexico.*—Albatrosses, Diving-Petrels, Penguins and Auks are absent from this region or only occur as rare stragglers.

Breeding species of Petrels are the Black-capped and Jamaica Petrels which breed (or bred formerly) in the West Indies, the Mediterranean Shearwater, Soft-plumaged Petrel and Bulwer's Petrel which breed in the Cape Verde Is., the Trinidad Petrel which breeds at South Trinidad I., Audubon's Shearwater which breeds in the Bahamas and West Indies, and the Dusky Shearwater which breeds in the Cape Verde Is. The Sooty and Greater Shearwaters which breed further south pass through the tropical Atlantic on migration and the Manx Shearwater which breeds further north occurs in the tropics in winter.

Breeding species of Storm-Petrels are the Madeiran Storm-Petrel which breeds in the Cape Verde Is. and St. Helena and the White-faced Storm-Petrel which breeds in the Cape Verde Is. The British and Leach's Storm-Petrels are winter visitors from the north, whilst the Black-bellied, White-bellied and Wilson's Storm-Petrels are visitors from the south.

The Laughing Gull which breeds on the coasts and islands of the Gulf of Mexico and Caribbean Sea is the only resident member of its family, but the Ring-billed and Bonaparte's Gulls are found on the American coast in winter, the Lesser Black-backed and

Northern Black-headed Gulls on the African coast in winter and the Grey-headed Gull on both coasts.

Terns are well represented. The Common and White-capped Noddies, and Sooty and Roseate Terns breed on many islands, the Brown-winged, Royal, and Common Terns in the Bahamas and West Indies, the White Tern on Fernando Noronha, South Trinidad and Ascension, and the Swallow-tailed Tern on Ascension and St. Helena. The Caspian, Royal, Sandwich, Gull-billed, Common, Roseate, Little (or Least) and Black Terns are found on the American and African coasts either breeding or as visitors, the Cayenne, South American, Forster's, Large-billed, and Amazon Terns on the American coast, and the Whiskered, White-winged Black and Damara Terns on the African coast, whilst the Arctic Tern passes through the tropics on migration.

The Black Skimmer occurs on the American coast and the African Skimmer on the opposite side. The Parasitic and Pomarine Jaegers are winter visitors from the north.

The commonest Man-o'-War Hawk is the Magnificent Frigate-bird, which breeds in the Gulf of Mexico and Caribbean Sea and on the Cape Verde Is., the Ascension Frigate-bird breeds at Ascension and the Great and Lesser Frigate-birds at South Trinidad.

The Brown Pelican breeds in the West Indies, and this species and the American White Pelican are found on the American coasts, whilst the Pink-backed and Eastern White Pelicans occur on the African coast.

The Brown Booby breeds on many islands throughout the area, the Red-footed Booby in the West Indies and at Ascension and South Trinidad, and the Blue-faced Booby in the West Indies and at Ascension, the Northern Gannet visits the Caribbean Sea in winter and the Cape Gannet ranges northward along the African coast.

The Double-crested (or Florida) and the Bigua

(or Mexican) Cormorants breed in the Bahamas and Cuba and both are found on the American coasts. On the African coast the Common, Cape and Reed Cormorants occur.

The Red-billed Tropic-bird breeds in the Caribbean Sea and at the Cape Verde Is., Fernando Noronha and Ascension, whilst the White-tailed Tropic-bird breeds in the Bahamas and West Indies and at Fernando Noronha and Ascension.

The Red and Northern Phalaropes occur in the tropical Atlantic in winter, and Wilson's Phalarope migrates down the American coast.

2. *The Indian Ocean, Red Sea and Persian Gulf.*— The Indian Ocean differs from the other two great tropical oceans in having land instead of water to the north, so that those migratory sea-birds which breed in the north and keep to the oceans when migrating are rarely or never found there in winter. Albatrosses, Diving-Petrels, Penguins and Auks are absent, or only occasional visitors.

The only visiting member of the Petrel family is the Pale-footed Shearwater, which ranges from the south into the eastern part of the ocean. Breeding representatives of this family are the Wedge-tailed Shearwater which breeds in the Seychelles and Mauritius and on many islands off the Australian coast, Audubon's Shearwater which breeds at the Seychelles and Mauritius, the Dusky Shearwater which breeds at the Houtman's Abrolhos Is., the Persian Shearwater which occurs in the Persian Gulf and Arabian Sea but has not yet been found breeding, and the Reunion Petrel which breeds at Reunion.

The only breeding Storm-Petrel is the White-faced Storm-Petrel which breeds in the Houtman's Abrolhos Is., but the Black-bellied, White-bellied and Wilson's Storm-Petrels range into the tropics from the south.

The Aden, Slender-billed and Red Sea Black-headed Gulls breed on the coasts of the Red Sea,

Persian Gulf and Arabian Sea, whilst the Silver Gull breeds on the coast of Western Australia. Gulls which visit the Asiatic and African coasts in winter are the Lesser Black-backed, Yellow-legged, Great Black-headed, Mew (or Common), Grey-headed, Northern Black-headed and Indian Black-headed Gulls.

Terns are numerous. The Common Noddy and the Crested, Lesser Crested, Roseate, Sooty, Brown-winged and Black-naped Terns breed on islands throughout the ocean, the Lesser Noddy in the Seychelles and Houtman's Abrolhos Is. and the White Tern at Madagascar and the Mascarene, Seychelle and Chagos Is. The Caspian, Crested, Lesser Crested, Whiskered and White-winged Black Terns occur on the coasts of Africa, Asia and Australia, the Sandwich, Common, White-cheeked, Black and Little Terns on the coasts of Africa and Asia, the Gull-billed Tern on the coasts of Asia and Australia, the Indian River and Black-bellied Terns on the Asiatic coast and the Fairy Tern on the coast of Western Australia. Some of these species breed on these coasts and others are migrants from the north.

The African Skimmer occurs on the coast of Africa and the Indian Skimmer on the coasts of India and Burma. The Parasitic and Pomarine Jaegers are winter visitors and perhaps reach this ocean across Asia from the Arctic coasts of Siberia where they breed.

The Great Frigate-bird breeds at the Seychelles, Aldabra and Christmas I., the Christmas Frigate-bird at Christmas I. and the Lesser Frigate-bird at Aldabra and on islands off the coast of north-western Australia.

The Pink-backed Pelican occurs on the African coast, the Dalmatian and Grey Pelicans on the Asiatic coast, the Eastern White Pelican on the coasts of Africa and Asia, and the Australian Pelican on the Australian coast.

The Brown and Red-footed Boobies breed on many islands throughout the ocean, the Blue-faced Booby at Mauritius and Rodriguez and on islands off the coast of Australia, and Abbott's Booby on Assumption and Christmas Is.

The Reed Cormorant occurs on the coasts of Africa and Madagascar, the Socotra Cormorant on Socotra and in the Persian Gulf, the Indian and Javanese Cormorants on the Indian and Burmese coasts, the Little Black and Little Pied Cormorants on the Malayan and Australian coasts, the Pied Cormorant on the Australian coast, and the Common Cormorant on the coasts of Africa, Asia and Australia. In parts of India this species is used by the fishermen.

The Red-billed (or Indian) Tropic-bird breeds on islands in the Persian Gulf, the White-tailed Tropic-bird in the Mascarene, Seychelle and Andaman Is. and at Christmas I. and the Red-tailed Tropic-bird on islands throughout the ocean.

The Northern (or Red-necked) Phalarope winters in great numbers in the Arabian Sea which it reaches overland from its breeding grounds on the northern coasts of Europe and Asia.

3. *The Tropical Western Pacific, China Sea, Malay Archipelago and Coral Sea.*—In this section the birds of the seas and coasts of south-eastern Asia, the Malay Archipelago and north-eastern Australia will be dealt with. The limits of the area on the Pacific side may be considered as formed by the Liu Kiu Is., Formosa, the Philippine Is., Solomon Is., New Hebrides, New Caledonia and Norfolk I.

Diving-Petrels, Penguins and Skimmers are absent from the region, Auks only occasionally reach the Liu Kiu Is. from the north, and Albatrosses are only occasional visitors from the north or south. Petrels are represented by the Wedge-tailed Shearwater which breeds on many islands, the White-faced Shearwater and Bulwer's Petrel which breed on islands in the China Sea, the Bonin Petrel breeding in the Liu Kiu Is., the Collared Petrel breeding in the New

Hebrides, the Tahiti Petrel breeding in New Caledonia, the Pale-footed Shearwater breeding at Norfolk I., Solander's Petrel breeding at Lord Howe I. and the Dusky Shearwater which breeds in the New Hebrides, Norfolk I. and Lord Howe I. The Short-tailed and Sooty Shearwaters and Gould's Petrel, which breed further south, also occur in these seas in winter or on migration.

Breeding Storm-Petrels are Swinhoe's Storm-Petrel on islets near Formosa, the White-throated Storm-Petrel in the New Hebrides and the White-bellied Storm-Petrel at Lord Howe I., whilst the Black-bellied and Wilson's Storm-Petrels are visitors which breed further south.

The only Gull breeding in the area is the Silver Gull which nests on the coasts of Queensland and New Caledonia, the Pacific Gull visits the Australian coast in the southern winter, whilst the Slaty-backed, Herring, Yellow-legged, Japanese, Mew (or Common) Chinese Black-headed and Northern Black-headed Gulls occur in the northern winter on the coasts of the China Sea.

Terns which breed on many islands throughout the area are the Caspian, Crested, Lesser Crested, Roseate, Black-naped, Little, Sooty, Brown-winged and White Terns and the Common and White-capped Noddies. The Fairy Tern breeds in New Caledonia and the Grey Noddy on Lord Howe I. and Norfolk I. The Gull-billed and Whiskered Terns are found on the Asiatic and Australian coasts, the Common and White-winged Black Terns are winter visitors from the north, the White-fronted Tern a visitor from the south and the Spectacled Tern a visitor from Oceania. The Pomarine and Parasitic Jaegers are winter visitors from the north, whilst the Great Skua reaches Australian coasts in the southern winter.

The Great Frigate-bird breeds on islands in the Malay Archipelago and the Lesser Frigate-bird on islands off the Australian coast and at New Caledonia.

The Brown, Blue-faced and Red-footed Boobies breed on islands throughout these seas. The Grey, Dalmatian and Eastern White Pelicans occur on the coasts of the China Sea, and the Australian Pelican on the coasts of Australia and New Guinea.

The Common Cormorant inhabits the Asiatic and Australian coasts, the Javanese Cormorant those of the China Sea and Greater Sunda islands, the Little Black and Little Pied Cormorants those of the Malay Archipelago, Australia and New Caledonia, and the Pied Cormorant the coast of Australia. The Japanese and Red-faced Cormorants also reach the China Sea in winter from the north.

The Red-tailed and White-tailed Tropic-birds breed on islands in the Malay Archipelago, the former also off the coast of Australia and the latter at New Caledonia. In winter the Red and Northern Phalaropes occur in the China Sea and the latter occurs in great numbers in the Malay Archipelago.

4. *Oceania.*—The great area of the Central Pacific is studded with innumerable island groups. From the Bonin and Hawaiian Is. in the north to the Kermadec and Tuamotu Is. in the south and from the Marianne and Caroline Is. in the west to Easter I. in the east the avifauna is comparatively uniform.

Diving-Petrels, Penguins, Auks, Skimmers, and Pelicans are entirely absent, whilst Cormorants and Gulls only occur as occasional stragglers to some of the most northerly groups.

The Short-tailed, Laysan and Black-footed Albatrosses breed in some of the northern groups but are absent from the greater part of the area.

Our knowledge of the Petrels and Storm-Petrels of Oceania is still very incomplete. On the larger, inhabited islands they often breed on mountains densely covered with vegetation and the nocturnal habits make the discovery of their breeding grounds very difficult. Many of the smaller coral islands have never been visited by ornithologists. As far as is known at present the Wedge-tailed and Dusky Shearwaters appear to be the most numerous and breed in nearly every island group. The Christmas Shearwater and Phoenix Petrel breed in most of the eastern groups, Bulwer's Petrel on the northern groups as well as in the Marquesas Is. and the Herald and Kermadec Petrels in many of the southern groups. The White-faced Shearwater breeds in the Bonin Is., the Hawaiian Petrel in the Hawaiian Is. and the Bonin Petrel in both these groups. Gould's Petrel breeds in the Fiji Is., the Tahiti Petrel in the Society Is., Solander's and Murphy's Petrels in the Tuamotu and Austral Is., Cook's Petrel in the Kermadec and Austral Is., and the White-necked Petrel in the Kermadec Is.

The White-throated Storm-Petrel is known to breed in several groups, the Madeiran and Sooty Storm-Petrels in the Hawaiian Is., the White-faced Storm-Petrel in the Kermadec Is. and the White-bellied Storm-Petrel in the Austral Is. The breeding places of the rare Striped and Samoan Storm-Petrels are not known but are probably in the Samoan Is.

Representatives of the Tern family are the Common, White-capped and Grey Noddies and the Sooty, Brown-winged and White Terns which breed on islands throughout Oceania. The Crested, Roseate and Black-naped Terns also occur in some of the western groups.

The Great and Lesser Frigate-birds are found breeding on islands almost throughout Oceania and the former is sometimes used to carry messages from one island to another. The Brown, Red-footed and Blue-faced Boobies are also found breeding on many islands throughout the area, and so are the White-tailed and Red-tailed Tropic-birds. The long red tail-feathers of the latter are pulled out in many islands and used as ornaments by the natives.

5. *The Tropical Eastern Pacific and Gulf of California.*—The eastern portion of the Pacific differs greatly from the western and central portions in having hardly any islands except those close to the American coast. The Galápagos Islands are much the largest and most important, the other oceanic islands within the area being the Revillagigedo, Clipperton, Cocos and St. Ambrose Is. The tropical region south of Ecuador is separated from the American coast by the cold waters of the Humboldt current, so that the coasts of Peru and Chile form part of the southern region. The division between the tropical and temperate avifauna occurs normally about the Gulf of Guayaquil but fluctuates somewhat according to the season and in some exceptional years tropical forms such as Frigate-birds range a long way south on the coast of Peru.

Diving-Petrels are absent from the tropical area. Albatrosses are represented by one species, the Waved Albatross, which breeds in the Galápagos Is., and by stragglers from the north and south. Penguins are represented by the small Galápagos Penguin which is confined to the Galápagos Is.; Auks by Xantus' and Craveri's Murrelets which breed on the coast of Lower California, the latter occurring also in the Gulf of California.

Breeding representatives of the Petrel family are the widely distributed Wedge-tailed Shearwater, the Dusky Shearwater and Hawaiian Petrel, which breed in the Galápagos Is., Townsend's Shearwater breeding in the Revillagigedo Is. and the Black-vented Shearwater breeding on islands off the American coast. Visiting members of this family are the Black, Collared, Cook's, White-necked, Kermadec and Peale's Petrels and the Christmas, Sooty and Pink-footed Shearwaters.

The islets off the coast of Lower California are the breeding-grounds of no less than six species of Storm-Petrels, the Least, Ashy, Swinhoe's, Black,

Leach's and Guadalupe Storm-Petrels. The Galápagos, Elliot's and Madeiran Storm-Petrels breed in the Galápagos Is. and the latter also at Cocos I. The Sooty and Wilson's Storm-Petrels also occur as visitors.

The Dusky and Swallow-tailed Gulls are confined to the Galápagos Is. The Western and Heermann's Gulls breed on the American coast, which is visited in winter or on migration also by the Glaucous-winged, Ring-billed, Laughing, Franklin's, Bonaparte's and Sabine's Gulls.

The Common and White-capped Noddies and the White, Sooty and Brown-winged Terns breed at most of the islands in the area. The Grey Noddy and Trudeau's Tern breed in the St. Ambrose Is. and the Elegant Tern in the Gulf of California. Visitors for the winter or on migration are the Royal, Sandwich, Forster's, Common, Arctic, Large-billed, Black and Little (or Least) Terns, also the Black Skimmer, the Pomarine and Parasitic Jaegers and the three species of Phalaropes.

The Magnificent Frigate-bird breeds on islands off the American coast as well as in the Galápagos Is., where the Great Frigate-bird also breeds. The Brown, Blue-footed and Blue-faced Boobies breed on islands throughout the area, including the Galápagos Is. where the Red-footed Booby is also found breeding. The Red-billed and Red-tailed Tropic-birds breed in the Galápagos Is. and the former also on islands off the American coast.

The remarkable Flightless Cormorant represents this family in the Galápagos Is., whilst the Pelagic, Brandt's, Double-crested and Bigua (or Mexican) Cormorants are found along the American coast. The Brown Pelican breeds on the American coast and in the Galápagos Is., whilst the American White Pelican is a visitor to the coast of the mainland.

CHAPTER XX

~~~~~~~~~~~~~~~~~~~~~~~~~~~~~~~~~~~

The Southern Oceans

~~~~~~~~~~~~~~~~~~~~~~~~~~~~~~~~~~~

THE VAST AREA of the southern hemisphere between
the tropic of Capricorn and the Antarctic continent
is mainly one great ocean and its avifauna shows a
considerable uniformity throughout. As might be
expected this manifests itself especially in those species which range widely over the sea far from their
breeding grounds, since there is no land barrier to
prevent them from passing right round the world.
Whether in fact they range promiscuously over these
southern seas, as was once supposed to be the case,
is now considered doubtful. Such evidence as is
available on the subject has been mentioned in Chapter I when dealing with Albatrosses. It is these birds,
with many of the Petrels and Penguins and some of
the Skuas, Storm-Petrels and Diving-Petrels which
are principally concerned. Some species of all these
families are just as limited in their ranges in southern seas as are similar birds in other parts of the
world.

There is a very marked tendency amongst the
southern sea-birds to keep between definite parallels
of latitude so that the ranges of many species form
circles round the south pole at a greater or less distance from it. This is specially noticeable in the case
of the Diving-Petrels in connection with which it has

been discussed in Chapter IV, but it is also exhibited by many of the Petrels, Albatrosses and Penguins.

As was noted in the last chapter, owing to the influence of the cold Humboldt current on the coasts of Chile and Peru, birds of southern types extend northward along the west coast of South America almost to the equator. The area of the Humboldt current is therefore here regarded as part of the southern ocean.

In the southern oceans, including this northerly extension, Auks are entirely absent, Frigate-birds, Tropic-birds and Skimmers are only found occasionally in a few northern areas, and Gulls are comparatively few. On the other hand all the Diving-Petrels and all but one of the Penguins are confined to the southern oceans; considerably over half the species of Albatrosses, Petrels and Cormorants are found there; and approximately half the species of Terns, Pelicans and Gannets may be found within their limits.

1. *The Open Ocean.*—The special feature of the Southern Oceans is the large number of species of birds which may be seen hundreds of miles from land. In the "roaring forties" on the voyage from the Cape of Good Hope to Australia or on a voyage to or from New Zealand round Cape Horn the ornithologist will probably see daily nearly as many species of sea-birds as he would see land-birds in a country walk at home, and these will range in size from the great Albatrosses to the little Prions and Storm-Petrels. Some will follow the ship, beating to and fro across the stern, and others will circle round it ready to settle down on the water to partake of anything edible thrown overboard. Others, and these more interesting because less known, will be seen flying rapidly over the surface of the water, skimming over the crests and disappearing in the troughs, and only rarely approaching near enough to admit of attempts at identi-

fication. Since where one of a species is present there are usually many others of the same kind, sooner or later one will probably come close enough to allow of a good view and disclose its diagnostic field-marks, but much patience and a good pair of field-glasses are even more essential for these observations than for field ornithology on land, since the observer has no opportunity of following up a bird for a second view and must take opportunities when they come.

Species of Albatross which range widely throughout the whole area are the Wandering, Black-browed, Grey-headed, Sooty and Light-mantled Sooty Albatrosses. The Yellow-nosed Albatross is chiefly found in the South Atlantic and Indian Oceans, the Shy Albatross in the Indian Ocean and South Pacific and the Royal and Buller's Albatrosses in the South Pacific.

Widely distributed Petrels are the Giant, White-chinned, Great-winged, Brown, White-headed, Antarctic, Pintado (or Cape Pigeon), Silver-grey and Blue Petrels and the Broad-billed, Dove and Fairy Prions. The Great and Manx Shearwaters occur in the South Atlantic; the Kerguelen, Soft-plumaged and Schlegel's Petrels, the Mediterranean Shearwater and the Thin-billed Prion occur in the South Atlantic and Indian Oceans; the Wedge-tailed and Pale-footed Shearwaters in the Indian Ocean and South Pacific; the Black, Gould's, Cook's, White-necked and Peale's Petrels, and the Short-tailed, Pink-footed and Grey-backed Shearwaters occur in the South Pacific; whilst the Sooty Shearwater is found in the South Pacific and South Atlantic. The Shearwaters, at least in the southern hemisphere, are generally found nearer the coasts than the other species.

The White-bellied, Black-bellied, Wilson's and Grey-backed Storm-Petrels are generally distributed; whilst the White-faced Storm-Petrel occurs in the South Atlantic and Indian Oceans. The Common Diving-Petrel also occurs widely in the South Atlantic and Indian Oceans but the other Diving-Petrels are generally found near the coasts.

Gulls and Terns are mainly confined to the coasts, but the Arctic Tern occurs in the South Pacific and South Atlantic as a visitor from the north and the Swallow-tailed Tern ranges widely over the South Atlantic and Indian Oceans. The Great Skua has a general range in the southern oceans; whilst the Parasitic Jaeger (or Arctic Skua) is a visitor from the north.

Penguins swim so low in the water and dive so readily that they are not often observed in the open ocean, but the King, Rock-hopper, Macaroni and Gentoo Penguins range widely over the South Atlantic and southern Indian Oceans, whilst the Bearded Penguin may be met with in the South Atlantic.

2. *The Coasts of South Africa and neighbouring Sub-antarctic Islands.*—In this section the birds found on the temperate coasts of South Africa will be mentioned, as well as those of the Tristan da Cunha group and Gough I. in the South Atlantic and those of Kerguelen, the Crozet Is., Prince Edward, Marion, McDonald, Heard, St. Paul and Amsterdam Is. in the southern Indian Ocean. Many of the species mentioned in the previous section as ranging widely in the South Atlantic and Indian Oceans are sometimes met with on the South African coast.

Of the Albatrosses the Wandering and Yellow-nosed Albatrosses breed at some of the islands in both oceans; the Sooty Albatross at the islands in the South Atlantic; and the Black-browed and Light-mantled Sooty Albatrosses at those in the Indian Ocean.

The Giant, Great-winged, Kerguelen, Soft-plumaged, and Brown Petrels and the Broad-billed and Thin-billed Prions breed at some of the subantarctic islands in both oceans; the Dusky and Great Shearwaters at those in the Atlantic; and the White-chinned, White-headed, Pintado and Blue Petrels, the Mediterranean Shearwater and the Dove and Thick-billed Prions at those in the Indian Ocean.

The Black-bellied Storm-Petrel breeds at islands in both oceans; the White-faced Storm Petrel at islands in the Atlantic and the Grey-backed and Wilson's Storm-Petrels at those in the Indian Ocean. The Common Diving-Petrel breeds in the Atlantic islands and the Kerguelen Diving-Petrel at those in the Indian Ocean.

No Albatrosses, Petrels, Storm-Petrels or Diving-Petrels are known to breed on the islands adjacent to the African coast.

The Silver (or Hartlaub's) Gull breeds on the coast of South Africa, to which the Grey-headed Gull is a visitor, whilst the Southern Black-backed Gull is a resident on the mainland coast as well as on the islands in the Indian Ocean.

The Caspian, Crested and Damara Terns breed on the South African coast and the Sandwich, Common, Arctic, Swallow-tailed, Whiskered and White-winged Black Terns occur there as visitors. The Common and White-capped Noddies breed in the Atlantic islands, the Kerguelen Tern on the islands in the Indian Ocean and the Swallow-tailed Tern on islands in both oceans.

The Great Skua breeds on islands in both oceans and the Pomarine and Parasitic Jaegers are visitors to the South African coasts.

The Jackass Penguin breeds only on islands adjacent to the South African coast, the Rock-hopper Penguin on the subantarctic islands of both oceans and the King, Macaroni and Gentoo Penguins on those in the Indian Ocean.

The Cape Gannet breeds on the coasts of South Africa and the Pink-backed Pelican occurs as a visitor. The Common, Bank, Cape and Reed Cormorants are resident on the South African coast, the Kerguelen Cormorant at Kerguelen, the King Cormorant at the Crozet Is. and the Blue-eyed Cormorant at Heard I.

3. *The Coasts of Southern Australia, Tasmania and New Zealand and neighbouring Sub-antarctic Islands.* —On the coasts of these islands many of the species mentioned above as ranging widely in the Indian and South Pacific Oceans occur regularly or casually. The Royal, Wandering, Shy, Buller's, Black-browed and Light-mantled Sooty Albatrosses breed in the sub-antarctic islands of New Zealand and the Shy Albatross also off the Tasmanian coast.

The Wedge-tailed Shearwater and Gould's Petrel breed on islands off the Australian coast; the Pale-footed Shearwater and Great-winged Petrel off the coasts of Australia and New Zealand; the Short-tailed and Dusky Shearwaters and Fairy Prion on Australian islands and the sub-antarctic islands; the Black and Cook's Petrels and the Grey-backed and Fluttering Shearwaters in New Zealand; the Sooty Shearwater and Peale's Petrel breed in New Zealand and the sub-antarctic islands; whilst the Giant, White-chinned, Brown, and White-headed Petrels breed only in the sub-antarctic islands.

The White-faced Storm-Petrel breeds on islands off the coasts of Australia and New Zealand and in the sub-antarctic islands, in which the Black-bellied and Grey-backed Storm-Petrels also breed. The Georgian, Kerguelen and Common Diving Petrels breed in the sub-antarctic islands and the latter also on islands off the coasts of New Zealand and Australia.

The Silver Gull is resident on the coasts of Australia and New Zealand and in some of the sub-antarctic islands; the Pacific Gull is confined to Australian coasts; the Southern Black-backed Gull breeds on the coasts of New Zealand and in the sub-antarctic islands; whilst Buller's Gull is a visitor to New Zealand coasts after breeding inland.

The White-fronted Tern breeds on the coasts of New Zealand and in the sub-antarctic islands; the Caspian and Fairy Terns on the coasts of Australia and New Zealand; and the Crested, Brown-winged, and Little Terns on the coasts of Australia. The Gull-billed and Whiskered Terns are visitors to the Australian coast, the Black-fronted Tern to New Zealand coasts, and the White-winged Black Tern to both countries.

The Great Skua breeds in the sub-antarctic islands and this species and the Parasitic Jaeger (or Arctic Skua) are regular visitors to the coasts of Australia and New Zealand.

The King, Rock-hopper, Victoria, Big-crested, Royal, Grand, Gentoo and Little Penguins breed in the sub-antarctic islands and probably all of them sometimes visit the coasts of New Zealand and Australia; the Grand, Little and White-flippered Penguins breed on New Zealand coasts; whilst the Little Penguin is the only species resident in Australia.

The Australian Pelican occurs on the Australian coast, and the Australian Gannet on the coasts of Australia and New Zealand. The Common Cormorant inhabits Australia, New Zealand and some of the sub-antarctic islands; the Pied, Little Black and Little Pied Cormorants are found in Australia and New Zealand; the White-breasted Cormorant is peculiar to Australia and Tasmania; the Spotted Cormorant to New Zealand and the Chatham Cormorant to the Chatham Is.; whilst the Rough-faced Cormorant is found in New Zealand and the sub-antarctic islands.

4. *The Coasts of Peru and northern Chile and the Humboldt Current.*—This interesting region, though mainly in the tropics, has a sea-bird population largely southern in type, as has been mentioned previously. Until recently it was very little known to ornithologists and some of its characteristic birds were only represented in Museums by a few specimens. Yet the sea-birds of this coast are of greater economic importance than those of any other part of the world, since the guano deposited by them on the almost rainless islands has long been one of the chief fertilizers used by agri-

culturists throughout the world. In recent years the birds have been protected by the Peruvian Government and the guano industry placed on a sound footing under which collection is carefully regulated. As a result the birds are increasing in numbers and the production of guano is also steadily increasing.

A voyage along the west coast of South America is one of the most interesting that can be undertaken by anyone interested in birds, and the intending traveller in this region should not fail first to read Dr. R. C. Murphy's fascinating book about this coast. (*Bird Islands of Peru*, by Robert Cushman Murphy, G. P. Putnam's Sons, New York and London, 1925.)

Here we can only mention the birds which are known to visit the waters of the Humboldt Current and those which breed on the coast and in the Juan Fernandez Islands. It will be noted that the waters of this remarkable current teaming with aquatic life attract visitors which breed in the Arctic and Antarctic regions as well as species from North and South America.

The Waved Albatross is a visitor from the Galápagos Is., whilst the Wandering, Black-browed, Shy, Buller's and Grey-headed Albatrosses are visitors from the southern oceans.

The most abundant Petrels are the Sooty and Pink-footed Shearwaters which occur in immense flocks. The latter is known to breed only at Juan Fernandez whilst the former breeds in the Fuegian Islands and also in the Chilean Andes. The Kermadec, White-necked, Gould's and Cook's Petrels also breed in Juan Fernandez; whilst the Giant, White-chinned, Pintado and Silver-grey Petrels and the Grey-backed Shearwater are visitors from the southern oceans.

The Sooty, Galápagos, Elliot's and Hornby's Storm-Petrels are common on the coast, the first-named being very abundant though it has not been found breeding. The White-bellied Storm-Petrel breeds at Juan Fernandez and the Black-bellied and Wilson's Storm-Petrels are visitors from the south, the latter in great numbers. The Peruvian Diving-Petrel breeds all along the coast.

The resident breeding Gulls are the Southern Black-backed, Grey and Simeon Gulls; the Andean, Grey-headed and Patagonian Black-headed Gulls are visitors which breed inland in South America; Franklin's Gull a very abundant visitor from North America; and Sabine's Gull a visitor from the arctic regions.

Resident breeding Terns are the South American, Chilean and Inca Terns; the Large-billed and Trudeau's Terns are visitors from the inland waters of South America; the Royal, Elegant, Black and Little (or Least) Terns visitors from North America; and the Arctic Tern a visitor from the arctic regions.

The Great Skua is found along the coast but probably breeds further south; the Pomarine and Parasitic Jaegers are visitors from the arctic regions; whilst the Black Skimmer is a visitor to the coast from the rivers of South America.

The Humboldt Penguin which breeds all along the coast is the one representative of its family in this region.

The Magnificent Frigate-bird and Red-billed Tropic-bird range down the northern coast of Peru whenever the warm counter-current replaces the cold Humboldt Current in that region, but they do not breed in this area. The Brown Pelican is also a tropical species which sometimes comes down from the north, whilst the larger Chilean Pelican is one of the important Humboldt guano birds and is confined to this coast.

The Blue-footed Booby is another tropical species which occurs in the northern area, but it breeds in islands in that region and is one of the less important guano producers. The commonest of all birds on the coast and and a very important producer of guano is the Peruvian Booby which is peculiar to the Humboldt current. Most important of all guano birds, and the second species in abundance, is the Guanay Cormorant, which is also peculiar to the region. Other resident Cormorants are the Bigua and Red-legged Cormorants.

Common winter visitors are the Red and Northern Phalaropes from arctic regions, whilst Wilson's Phalarope from North America also occurs.

5. *The coasts of southern South America and neighbouring Sub-antarctic Islands.*—The area included in this section comprises the coasts of southern Brazil, Uruguay, Argentina, Patagonia, southern Chile and Tierra del Fuego with the Falkland Is, and South Georgia. Many of the widely ranging birds mentioned above as occurring in the South Atlantic and South Pacific occur more or less regularly on these coasts. Pelicans and Gannets are absent from this area.

The Black-browed Albatross breeds on islands off the South American coast and at the Falkland Is. and South Georgia; the Grey-headed Albatross on South American islands and at South Georgia; and the Wandering and Light-mantled Sooty Albatrosses at South Georgia.

The Blue Petrel breeds in the Falkland Is; the Giant and White-chinned Petrels at the Falkland Is. and South Georgia; and the Pintado (or Cape Pigeon) and Snow Petrels and the Dove Prion at South Georgia.

Wilson's Storm-Petrel breeds on islands off Tierra del Fuego and in South Georgia; and the Black-bellied and Grey-backed Storm-Petrels at the Falkland Is. and South Georgia.

The Common Diving-Petrel occurs on the South American coast and in the Falkland Is.; the Magellan Diving-Petrel in the Straits of Magellan; and the Georgian Diving-Petrel at South Georgia.

The Simeon, Magellan, Patagonian Black-headed and Southern Black-backed Gulls breed on the South American coasts and at the Falkland Is., and the last-named also at South Georgia. The Grey-headed Gull is a visitor from inland regions to the eastern coasts of South America. The South American Tern breeds on South American coasts and in the Falkland Is. and South Georgia, whilst the Swallow-tailed Tern also breeds at South Georgia. On the mainland coasts the Royal, Cayenne, Sandwich, Gull-billed and Trudeau's Terns occur as visitors.

The Great Skua breeds on the coast of the mainland, in the Falkland Is. and at South Georgia.

The Humboldt Penguin occurs on the South American coast; the Magellan Penguin breeds in South American islands and at the Falkland Is.; the King Penguin on South American islands and at South Georgia; the Gentoo Penguin at the Falkland Is. and South Georgia; the Rock-hopper Penguin at the Falkland Is. and the Macaroni Penguin at South Georgia. The Rock-hopper Penguin also occurs on the South American coast, the Bearded Penguin at the Falkland Is. and South Georgia and the Adelie Penguin at South Georgia but these species are not known to breed in these localities.

The Bigua and Red-legged Cormorants occur on the South American coasts, the Magellan Cormorant on the mainland coasts and in the Falkland Is. and the Blue-eyed Cormorant on the mainland coasts, in the Falkland Is. and at South Georgia.

6. *The Coasts of Antarctica and adjacent Islands.*— We will conclude this account by mentioning the seabirds which are known to breed or to occur south of 60° S. lat. in the region of the Antarctic ice. Apart from the islands close to the Antarctic mainland the most important island groups are the South Shetlands and South Orkneys.

The Grey-headed and Light-mantled Sooty Albatrosses occur in Antarctic seas but are not known to breed. The Giant, Pintado and Snow Petrels breed in the South Orkneys and South Shetlands and on

Antarctic coasts; the Dusky Shearwater and Dove Prion breed in the South Orkneys; and the Antarctic, and Silver-grey Petrels on Antarctic coasts. Other Petrels which occur in Antarctic seas, but are not known to breed there, are the White-chinned, Kerguelen, and White-headed Petrels.

The Black-bellied and Wilson's Storm-Petrels both breed in the South Orkneys and South Shetlands, and the latter also breeds on the coasts of the Antarctic continent. Diving-Petrels do not appear to range so far south.

No Gulls or Terns are known to breed in the Antarctic continent though the Arctic Tern is a visitor to its coasts in summer. The Southern Black-backed Gull and South American Tern breed in the South Orkneys and South Shetlands, and the Swallow-tailed Tern in the South Orkneys, McCormick's Skua breeds on the Antarctic continent and the Great Skua breeds at the South Orkneys and visits Antarctic coasts.

The most completely Antarctic bird is the Emperor Penguin which breeds in winter on the coasts of the continent itself. The Gentoo, Bearded and Adelie Penguins also breed on Antarctic coasts and in the South Orkneys and South Shetlands, whilst the Macaroni Penguin breeds in both groups of islands.

Finally the Blue-eyed Cormorant breeds in the South Shetland group.

Appendix

Systematic List of Birds of the Ocean

Order *Sphenisciformes*

Family *Spheniscidae*

Aptenodytes patagonica, Miller.
  King Penguin

Aptenodytes forsteri, Gray.
  Emperor Penguin

Pygoscelis papua (Forster).
  Gentoo Penguin

Pygoscelis adeliae (Hombron and Jacquinot).
  Adelie Penguin

Pygoscelis antarctica (Forster).
  Bearded Penguin

Eudyptes pachyrhynchus, Gray.
  Victoria Penguin

Eudyptes sclateri, Buller.
  Big-crested Penguin

Eudyptes crestatus (Miller).
  Rock-hopper Penguin

Eudyptes schlegeli, Finsch.
  Royal Penguin

Eudyptes chrysolophus (Brandt).
  Macaroni Penguin

Megadyptes antipodes (Hombron and Jacquinot).
  Grand (or Yellow-eyed) Penguin

Eudyptula minor (Forster).
  Little Penguin

Eudyptula albosignata, Finsch.
White-flippered Penguin

Spheniscus demersus (Linnaeus).
Jackass Penguin

Spheniscus humboldti, Meyer.
Humboldt Penguin

Spheniscus magellanicus (Forster).
Magellan Penguin

Spheniscus mendiculus, Sundevall.
Galápagos Penguin

Order *Procellariiformes*

Family *Diomedeidae*

Diomedea exulans, Linnaeus.
Wandering Albatross

Diomedea epomophora, Lesson.
Royal Albatross

Diomedea irrorata, Salvin.
Waved Albatross

Diomedea albatrus, Pallas.
Short-tailed Albatross

Diomedea nigripes, Audubon.
Black-footed Albatross

Diomedea immutabilis, Rothschild.
Laysan Albatross

Diomedea melanophris, Temminck.
Black-browed Albatross

Diomedea bulleri, Rothschild.
Buller's Albatross

Diomedea cauta, Gould.
Shy Albatross

Diomedea chlororhynchos, Gmelin.
Yellow-nosed Albatross

Diomedea chrysostoma, Forster.
Grey-headed Albatross

Phoebetria fusca (Hilsenberg).
Sooty Albatross

Phoebetria palpebrata (Forster).
Light-mantled Sooty Albatross

Family *Procellariidae*

Macronectes giganteus (Gmelin).
Giant Petrel

Daption capensis (Linnaeus).
Pintado Petrel

Fulmarus glacialis (Linnaeus).
Fulmar

Fulmarus glacialoides (Smith).
Silver-grey Petrel

Halobaena caerulea (Gmelin).
Blue Petrel

Pachyptila vittata (Gmelin).
Broad-billed Prion

Pachyptila salvini (Mathews).
Salvin's Prion

Pachyptila desolata (Gmelin).
Dove Prion

Pachyptila belcheri (Mathews).
Thin-billed Prion

Pachyptila turtur (Kuhl).
Fairy Prion

Pachyptila crassirostris (Mathews).
Thick-billed Prion

Thalassoica antarctica (Gmelin).
Antarctic Petrel

Adamastor cinereus (Gmelin).
Brown Petrel

Procellaria aequinoctialis, Linnaeus.
White-chinned Petrel

Procellaria parkinsoni, Gray.
Black Petrel

Puffinus leucomelas (Temminck).
White-faced Shearwater

Puffinus kuhli (Boie).
Mediterranean Shearwater

Puffinus creatopus, Coues.
Pink-footed Shearwater

Puffinus carneipes, Gould.
Pale-footed Shearwater

Puffinus gravis (O'Reilly).
Greater Shearwater

Puffinus pacificus (Gmelin).
Wedge-tailed Shearwater

Puffinus bulleri, Salvin.
Grey-backed Shearwater

Puffinus griseus (Gmelin).
Sooty Shearwater

Puffinus tenuirostris (Temminck).
Short-tailed Shearwater

Puffinus heinrothi, Reichenow.
Heinroth's Shearwater

Puffinus nativitatis, Streets.
Christmas Shearwater

Puffinus puffinus (Brunnich).
Manx Shearwater

Puffinus gavia (Forster).
Fluttering Shearwater

Puffinus opisthomelas, Coues.
Black-vented Shearwater

Puffinus auricularis, Townsend.
Townsend's Shearwater

Puffinus assimilis, Gould.
Dusky Shearwater

Puffinus lherminieri, Lesson.
Audubon's Shearwater

Puffinus persicus. Hume.
Persian Shearwater

Pterodroma macroptera (Smith).
   Great-winged Petrel

Pterodroma aterrima (Bonaparte).
   Reunion Petrel

Pterodroma lessoni (Garnot).
   White-headed Petrel

Pterodroma hasitata (Kuhl).
   Black-capped Petrel

Pterodroma caribbaea, Carte.
   Jamaica Petrel

Pterodroma cahow (Nichols and Mowbray).
   Bermuda Petrel

Pterodroma incerta (Schlegel).
   Schlegel's Petrel

Pterodroma rostrata (Peale).
   Tahiti Petrel

Pterodroma becki, Murphy.
   Beck's Petrel

Pterodroma alba (Gmelin).
   Phoenix Petrel

Pterodroma inexpectata (Forster).
   Peale's Petrel

Pterodroma solandri (Gould).
   Solander's Petrel

Pterodroma brevirostris (Lesson).
   Kerguelen Petrel

Pterodroma heraldica (Salvin).
   Herald Petrel

Pterodroma ultima, Murphy.
   Murphy's Petrel

Pterodroma phillipii (Gray).
   Kermadec Petrel

Pterodroma arminjoniana (Giglioli and Salvadori).
   Trinidad Petrel

Pterodroma mollis (Gould).
   Soft-plumaged Petrel

Pterodroma phaeopygia (Salvin).
Hawaiian Petrel

Pterodroma externa (Salvin).
White-necked Petrel

Pterodroma cooki (Gray).
Cook's Petrel

Pterodroma leucoptera (Gould).
Gould's Petrel

Pterodroma hypoleuca (Salvin).
Bonin Petrel

Pterodroma brevipes (Peale).
Collared Petrel

Pterodroma longirostris (Stejneger).
Stejneger's Petrel

Pagodroma nivea (Forster).
Snow Petrel

Bulweria bulwerii (Jardine and Selby).
Bulwer's Petrel

Bulweria macgillivrayi (Gray).
Macgillivray's Petrel

Family *Hydrobatidae*

Oceanites oceanicus (Kuhl).
Wilson's Storm-Petrel

Oceanites gracilis (Elliot).
Elliot's Storm-Petrel

Pelagodroma marina (Latham).
White-faced Storm Petrel

Fregetta grallaria (Vieillot).
White-bellied Storm-Petrel

Fregetta lineata (Peale).
Striped Storm-Petrel

Fregetta tropica (Gould).
Black-bellied Storm-Petrel

Nesofregetta albigularis (Finsch).
White-throated Storm-Petrel

276

Nesofregetta moestissima (Salvin).
Samoan Storm-Petrel

Garrodia nereis (Gould).
Grey-backed Storm-Petrel

Hydrobates pelagicus (Linnaeus).
British Storm-Petrel

Oceanodroma tethys (Bonaparte).
Galápagos Storm-Petrel

Oceanodroma castro (Harcourt).
Madeiran Storm-Petrel

Oceanodroma leucorhoa (Vieillot).
Leach's Storm-Petrel

Oceanodroma macrodactyla, Bryant.
Guadalupe Storm-Petrel

Oceanodroma markhami (Salvin).
Sooty Storm-Petrel

Oceanodroma monorhis (Swinhoe).
Swinhoe's Storm-Petrel

Oceanodroma homochroa (Coues).
Ashy Storm-Petrel

Oceanodroma hornbyi (Gray).
Hornby's Storm-Petrel

Oceanodroma furcata (Gmelin).
Fork-tailed Storm-Petrel

Loomelania melania (Bonaparte).
Black Storm-Petrel

Halocyptena microsoma, Coues.
Least Storm-Petrel

Family *Pelecanoididae*

Pelecanoides garnoti (Lesson).
Peruvian Diving-Petrel

Pelecanoides magellani (Mathews).
Magellan Diving-Petrel

Pelecanoides georgicus, Murphy and Harper.
Georgian Diving-Petrel

APPENDIX

Pelecanoides urinatrix (Gmelin).
Common Diving-Petrel

Order *Pelecaniformes*

Family *Phaethontidae*

Phaethon aethereus, Linnaeus.
Red-billed Tropic-bird
Phaethon rubricauda, Boddaert.
Red-tailed Tropic-bird
Phaethon lepturus, Daudin.
White-tailed Tropic-bird

Family *Pelecanidae*

Pelecanus onocrotalus, Linnaeus.
Eastern White Pelican
Pelecanus rufescens, Gmelin.
Pink-backed Pelican
Pelecanus philippensis, Gmelin.
Grey Pelican
Pelecanus crispus, Bruch.
Dalmatian Pelican
Pelecanus conspicillatus, Temminck.
Australian Pelican
Pelecanus erythrorhynchus, Gmelin.
American White Pelican
Pelecanus occidentalis, Linnaeus.
Brown Pelican
Pelecanus thagus, Molina.
Chilean Pelican

Family *Sulidae*

Moris bassanus (Linnaeus).
Northern Gannet
Moris capensis (Lichtenstein).
Cape Gannet

278

Moris serrator (Gray).
  Australian Gannet

Sula nebouxii, Milne-Edwards.
  Blue-footed Booby

Sula variegata (Tschudi).
  Peruvian Booby

Sula abbotti, Ridgway.
  Abbott's Booby

Sula dactylatra, Lesson.
  Blue-faced Booby

Sula sula (Linnaeus).
  Red-footed Booby

Sula leucogaster (Boddaert).
  Brown Booby

Family *Phalacrocoracidae*

Phalacrocorax auritus (Lesson).
  Double-crested Cormorant

Phalacrocorax olivaceus (Humboldt).
  Bigua Cormorant

Phalacrocorax sulcirostris (Brandt).
  Little Black Cormorant

Phalacrocorax carbo (Linnaeus).
  Common Cormorant

Phalacrocorax fuscicollis, Stephens.
  Indian Cormorant

Phalacrocorax capensis (Sparrman).
  Cape Cormorant

Phalacrocorax nigrogularis, Ogilvie-Grant and
    Forbes.
  Socotra Cormorant

Phalacrocorax neglectus (Wahlberg).
  Bank Cormorant

Phalacrocorax capillatus (Temminck and Schlegel).
  Japanese Cormorant

Phalacrocorax penicillatus (Brandt).
Brandt's Cormorant

Phalacrocorax aristotelis (Linnaeus).
Green Cormorant

Phalacrocorax pelagicus, Pallas.
Pelagic Cormorant

Phalacrocorax urile (Gmelin).
Red-faced Cormorant

Phalacrocorax magellanicus (Gmelin).
Magellan Cormorant

Phalacrocorax bougainvillei (Lesson).
Guanay Cormorant

Phalacrocorax featherstoni, Buller.
Chatham Cormorant

Phalacrocorax varius (Gmelin).
Pied Cormorant

Phalacrocorax fuscescens (Vieillot).
White-breasted Cormorant

Phalacrocorax carunculatus (Gmelin).
Rough-faced Cormorant

Phalacrocorax verrucosus (Cabanis).
Kerguelen Cormorant

Phalacrocorax gaimardi (Lesson).
Red-legged Cormorant

Phalacrocorax punctatus (Sparrman).
Spotted Cormorant

Phalacrocorax atriceps, King.
Blue-eyed Cormorant

Phalacrocorax albiventer (Lesson).
King Cormorant

Haliëtor melanoleucus (Vieillot).
Little Pied Cormorant

Haliëtor africanus (Gmelin).
Reed Cormorant

Haliëtor niger (Vieillot).
Javanese Cormorant

Haliëtor pygmaeus (Pallas).
Pigmy Cormorant

Nannopterum harrisi (Rothschild).
Flightless Cormorant

Family *Fregatidae*

Fregata aquila (Linnaeus).
Ascension Frigate-Bird

Fregata andrewsi, Mathews.
Christmas Frigate-Bird

Fregata magnificens, Mathews.
Magnificent Frigate-Bird

Fregata minor (Gmelin).
Great Frigate-Bird

Fregata ariel (Gray).
Lesser Frigate-Bird

Order *Charadriiformes*

Family *Phalaropodidae*

Phalaropus fulicarius (Linnaeus).
Red (or Grey) Phalarope

Steganopus tricolor, Vieillot.
Wilson's Phalarope

Lobipes lobatus (Linnaeus).
Northern (or Red-necked) Phalarope

Family *Stercorariidae*

Catharacta skua, Brunnich.
Great Skua

Catharacta maccormicki (Saunders).
McCormick's Skua

Stercorarius pomarinus (Temminck).
Pomarine Jaeger (or Skua)

Stercorarius parasiticus (Linnaeus).
Parasitic Jaeger (or Arctic Skua)

Stercorarius longicaudus, Vieillot.
Long-tailed Jaeger (or Skua)

Family *Laridae*

Gabianus pacificus (Latham).
Pacific Gull

Gabianus scoresbyi (Traill).
Magellan Gull

Pagophila eburnea (Phipps).
Ivory Gull

Larus fuliginosus, Gould.
Dusky Gull

Larus modestus, Tschudi.
Grey Gull

Larus heermanni, Cassin.
Heermann's Gull

Larus leucophthalmus, Temminck.
Red Sea Black-headed Gull

Larus hemprichi, Bruch.
Aden Gull

Larus belcheri, Vigors.
Siméon Gull

Larus crassirostris, Vieillot.
Japanese Gull

Larus audouini, Payraudeau.
Audouin's Gull

Larus delawarensis, Ord.
Ring-billed Gull

Larus canus, Linnaeus.
Mew Gull

Larus argentatus, Pontoppidan.
Herring Gull

Larus cachinnans, Pallas.
Yellow-legged Gull

Larus fuscus, Linnaeus.
Lesser Black-backed Gull

Larus californicus, Lawrence.
California Gull

Larus occidentalis, Audubon.
Western Gull

Larus dominicanus, Lichtenstein.
Southern Black-backed Gull

Larus schistisagus, Stejneger.
Slaty-backed Gull

Larus marinus, Linnaeus.
Great Black-backed Gull

Larus glaucescens, Naumann.
Glaucous-winged Gull

Larus hyperboreus, Gunnerus.
Glaucous Gull

Larus leucopterus, Vieillot.
Iceland Gull

Larus ichthyaetus, Pallas.
Great Black-headed Gull

Larus atricilla, Linnaeus.
Laughing Gull

Larus brunnicephalus, Jerdon.
Indian Black-headed Gull

Larus cirrocephalus, Vieillot.
Grey-headed Gull

Larus serranus, Tschudi.
Andean Gull

Larus pipixcan, Wagler.
Franklin's Gull

Larus novaehollandiae, Stephens
Silver Gull

Larus melanocephalus, Temminck.
Mediterranean Black-headed Gull

Larus bulleri, Hutton.
Buller's Gull

Larus maculipennis, Lichtenstein.
Patagonian Black-headed Gull

APPENDIX

Larus ridibundus, Linnaeus.
  Northern Black-headed Gull

Larus genei, Brème.
  Slender-billed Gull

Larus philadelphia (Ord).
  Bonaparte's Gull

Larus minutus, Pallas.
  Little Gull

Larus saundersi (Swinhoe).
  Chinese Black-headed Gull

Rhodostethia rosea (Macgillivray).
  Ross's Gull

Rissa tridactyla (Linnaeus).
  Common Kittiwake

Rissa brevirostris (Bruch).
  Red-legged Kittiwake

Creagrus furcatus (Néboux).
  Swallow-tailed Gull

Xema sabini (Sabine).
  Sabine's Gull

Family *Sternidae*

Chlidonias hybrida (Pallas).
  Whiskered Tern

Chlidonias leucoptera (Temminck).
  White-winged Black Tern

Chlidonias nigra (Linnaeus).
  Black Tern

Phaetusa simplex (Gmelin).
  Large-billed Tern

Gelochelidon nilotica (Gmelin).
  Gull-billed Tern

Hydroprogne tschegrava (Lepechin).
  Caspian Tern

Sterna aurantia, Gray.
  Indian River Tern

Sterna hirundinacea, Lesson.
South American Tern

Sterna hirundo, Linnaeus.
Common Tern

Sterna paradisea, Pontoppidan.
Arctic Tern

Sterna vittata, Gmelin.
Swallow-tailed or Wreathed Tern

Sterna virgata, Cabanis.
Kerguelen Tern

Sterna forsteri, Nuttall.
Forster's Tern

Sterna trudeaui, Audubon.
Trudeau's Tern

Sterna dougalli, Montagu.
Roseate Tern

Sterna striata, Gmelin.
White-fronted Tern

Sterna repressa, Hartert.
White-cheeked Tern

Sterna sumatrana, Raffles.
Black-naped Tern

Sterna melanogastra, Temminck.
Black-bellied Tern

Sterna aleutica, Baird.
Aleutian Tern

Sterna lunata, Peale.
Spectacled Tern

Sterna anaethetus, Scopoli.
Brown-winged Tern

Sterna fuscata, Linnaeus.
Sooty Tern

Sterna nereis (Gould).
Fairy Tern

Sterna albistriata (Gray).
Black-fronted Tern

Sterna superciliaris, Vieillot.
Amazon Tern

Sterna balaenarum (Strickland).
Damara Tern

Sterna lorata, Philippi and Landbeck.
Chilean Tern

Sterna albifrons, Pallas.
Little Tern

Thalasseus bergii (Lichtenstein).
Crested Tern

Thalasseus maximus (Boddaert).
Royal Tern

Thalasseus bengalensis (Lesson).
Lesser Crested Tern

Thalasseus zimmermanni (Reichenow).
Chinese Crested Tern

Thalasseus eurygnatha (Saunders).
Cayenne Tern

Thalasseus elegans (Gambel).
Elegant Tern

Thalasseus sandvicensis (Latham).
Sandwich Tern

Larosterna inca (Lesson).
Inca Tern

Procelsterna cerulea (Bennet).
Blue-grey Noddy

Anous stolidus (Linnaeus).
Common Noddy

Anous tenuirostris (Temminck).
Lesser Noddy

Anous minutus, Boie.
White-capped Noddy

Gygis alba (Sparrman).
White Tern

Family *Rynchopidae*

Rynchops nigra, Linnaeus.
Black Skimmer

Rynchops flavirostris, Vieillot.
African Skimmer

Rynchops albicollis, Swainson.
Indian Skimmer

Family *Alcidae*

Plautus alle (Linnaeus).
Dovekie (or Little Auk)

Alca torda, Linnaeus.
Razor-billed Auk

Uria lomvia (Linnaeus).
Brunnich's Murre (or Guillemot)

Uria aalge (Pontoppidan).
Common Murre (or Guillemot)

Cepphus grylle (Linnaeus).
Black Guillemot

Cepphus columba, Pallas.
Pigeon Guillemot

Cepphus carbo, Pallas.
Spectacled Guillemot

Brachyramphus marmoratus (Gmelin).
Marbled Murrelet

Brachyramphus brevirostris (Vigors).
Kittlitz's Murrelet

Brachyramphus hypoleucus, Xantus.
Xantus's Murrelet

Brachyramphus craveri (Salvadori).
Craveri's Murrelet

Synthliboramphus antiquus (Gmelin).
Ancient Murrelet

Synthliboramphus wumizusume (Temminck).
Crested Murrelet

APPENDIX

Ptychoramphus aleuticus (Pallas).
  Cassin's Auklet

Cyclorrhynchus psittacula (Pallas).
  Paroquet Auklet

Aethia cristatella (Pallas).
  Crested Auklet

Aethia pusilla (Pallas).
  Least Auklet

Aethia pygmaea (Gmelin).
  Whiskered Auklet

Cerorhinca monocerata (Pallas).
  Rhinoceros Auklet

Fratercula arctica (Linnaeus).
  Atlantic Puffin

Fratercula corniculata (Naumann).
  Horned Puffin

Lunda cirrhata (Pallas).
  Tufted Puffin

Index

INDEX

INDEX

298

INDEX

INDEX

INDEX